THE DAUGHTER *of* A JUNKIE

A TRUE LOVE STORY

TERRINEE GUNDY

Foreword By M. Kasim Reed
59th Mayor of Atlanta

Copyright © 2023 Terrinee Gundy

ISBN 979-8-9887180-1-7 (hardcover)

ISBN 979-8-9887180-2-4 (eBook)

The Daughter Of A Junkie, LLC

www.thedaughterofajunkie.com

Library of Congress Cataloging-in-Publication Data is available upon request

All rights reserved. No part of this book may be reproduced, stored, or transmitted by any means—whether auditory, graphic, mechanical, or electronic—without written permission of both publisher and author, except in the case of brief excerpts used in critical articles and reviews. Unauthorized reproduction of any part of this work is illegal and is punishable by law.

Printed in the United States of America

Book Design by JM Publishing, LLC

My children, parents, siblings, grandparents, aunts, uncles, cousins, nieces, friends, and Mi Rey know that I love them immensely, so they'll understand why I must dedicate this story to other sons and daughters of a junkie.

CONTENTS

Foreword		*i*
Chapter 1:	"The Man, The Junkie"	1
Chapter 2:	"She's Five Years Old"	15
Chapter 3:	"Love and Embrace Black Men"	37
Chapter 4:	"I Need A Lawyer"	53
Chapter 5:	"Run And Don't Stop"	71
Chapter 6:	"I'm Going To Be A Judge"	87
Chapter 7:	"We're Leaving Tonight"	103
Chapter 8:	"He Gotta Work"	123
Chapter 9:	"Black Man And A White Woman"	135
Chapter 10:	"I'm Not Moving Again"	149
Chapter 11:	"Henderson On Henderson"	161
Chapter 12:	"Mia Michelle Gundy"	179
Chapter 13:	"As Smart As You Are Pretty"	203
Chapter 14:	"You Are The Light"	223
Chapter 15:	"Let's Go Home"	237
Acknowledgements		*255*

Foreword

By
M. Kasim Reed, Fifty-Ninth Mayor Of Atlanta

Today is a very terrific day for me. I have been looking forward to reading *The Daughter of A Junkie: A True Love Story* for some time. When Terrinee Lynette Gundy decided to tell her story and began the incredible journey of writing a book that is as intimate as it is compelling, I was allowed to read the first few chapters. Those first seventy or so pages were breathtaking. There was so much more to this person than I had ever imagined. After reading those first few chapters, the store had closed, and I could not read it again until it was complete. Folks, let me tell you without reservation: this book was worth the wait.

At its essence, this is a story which demonstrates what can happen when you dream and work but always work harder than you dream. It shows the power of Terrinee's dream of becoming a judge at age nine and helping people who looked like her, and many who did not. It served as her north star. Her dream kept her from making "The Big Mistake" as it is so often the case in America's underserved communities. It showed how a dream can protect you from harm and help you develop the grit it takes to come from the ground to the center of Atlanta's loftiest places.

What can a dream do when it is paired with grit, a brilliant mind, and a fearless spirit? I will tell you. It can accomplish the hardest things and it can make your dreams come true. That is the center of this story. It is a leadership story for all people, but especially for Black women in America. It will help you answer that most difficult question that we all must face alone. What do we do when we don't know what to do? That is when your character is revealed. Well, now you have a friend, a guide for moments like that, a woman whose life has been an example of profound womanhood, deep sacrifice and ultimately, joy. I hope you will enjoy taking this journey as much as I have appreciated witnessing part of it.

CHAPTER 1

"The Man, The Junkie"

"I, Terrinee Gundy, do solemnly swear that I will administer justice without respect to persons, and do equal right to the poor and the rich, and that I will faithfully and impartially discharge and perform all of the duties incumbent upon me as a judge of the Municipal Court of..."

Standing proudly, with my right hand raised on that frigid yet bright winter morning in the city of Atlanta, I was sworn in for a third term on the bench while the love of my life, who I affectionately call, Mi Rey (my king), looked on from the third row of the audience.

Traditionally, after anyone in my family achieves greatness, we all celebrate with a good meal and fellowship. While sitting in Breakfast at Barney's, famous for its Mansa Musa tower, with Mi Rey; my honor-roll, teenaged children, Mia Michelle and Kevin; and my cousin, sworn army officer, Dr. Erika McClain, I became overwhelmed while reminiscing about the great distance my life has traveled. Like most, my journey had been filled with many ups and downs, which I proudly view today as more ups than downs, regardless of who may or may not agree. Love and heartbreak, triumph and trauma; it was all fucking worth it to me, especially on days like today: January 3, 2022.

As a young girl, I once saw a PBS special that said, "Growing up in the ghetto is ten times worse than going to war; the ghetto is a war zone every day without reprieve, resources, or any significant ways to protect oneself."

My war zone was Jacksonville, Florida in Duval County, notoriously known once upon a time as "The Bang 'em" for the shootings and murders surrounding drive-thru liquor stores on several street corners throughout the area. While I was growing up, The Bang 'em was known for violent carjackings and having one of the highest per capita murder rates in the country. The rise in carjackings was probably the real reason my daddy saw fit to teach me defensive driving at only nine years old. At one point, Jacksonville could've even been renamed "Murderville!"

By the 1980s, crack cocaine, a.k.a. "That Rock," began to overrun communities throughout America; Duval was no different. Many people didn't become aware of That Rock until it began taking hold of almost every man, woman, and child it encountered. Smoking crack cocaine, or freebasing, as it's commonly called, destroyed so many Black communities. Due to abandonment, the countless number of motherless and fatherless children grew alarmingly as parents became addicted to crack cocaine.

Notably, the rich and famous also didn't escape it. My daddy swears that freebasing didn't become popular until the infamous Richard Pryor fire incident, when the legendary comedian set himself ablaze while smoking crack cocaine. Consequently, Hollywood couldn't resist repeatedly highlighting crack cocaine use with films such as New Jack City starring Wesley Snipes and Chris Rock. That Rock had an undeniable hold on the whole era. So many families were decimated.

So many broken children developed. So many Black communities were left in blight. I wasn't broken, but I'd certainly been battered and gravely impacted time and time again by this epidemic. The havoc in my life would be ancillary, yet equally pernicious.

This story has been told somewhat, likened to Dopefiend and Whoreson by Donald Goins. My story is not only raw, but also for real. I intend to share memories of my life in the ghetto through a lens of happiness, trust, unification, but most importantly, love. Although, I personally cannot give a firsthand account of drug usage. God willing, that will remain true until my last breath. However, I do have a bank of knowledge about the collateral damage of substance abuse, specifically That Rock. I, Terrinee Gundy, am the Daughter of a Junkie.

My daddy has been a great father, but he is also a Junkie, and not just any junkie, the best "Rock Star" (pun intended) to ever do it. Of course, I didn't have to watch any films about the crack epidemic, because I was aware of crack cocaine before most children learned to read. My daddy started smoking That Rock in 1978 and still does to this day. So, let me keep it one hundred. My daddy is a muthafucking rarity; he's a fucking unicorn! My outlook could be seen as unique, and some might even consider me delusional, but I'm not, nor have I ever been, bitter or jaded growing up. My parents taught my sister and me how not to lead with, or wear, our trauma, and always be filled with hope and love—our reoccurring theme.

There isn't a time in my life when my parents weren't present, either in the physically or metaphysical, for my sister or me. We had extremely close relationships with both of our parents, Junkie included, throughout it all. Somehow, someway, my parents managed to be in our lives—raise, inspire, and produce contributing citizens to society while simultaneously being full throttle in a drug-infested world. For the record, my story revolves and relies on the memory, understanding, comprehension, and vantage point of a child who endured way too much, way too soon. Thus, this is how I remember my life experiences, or, what I took from the occurrences and from my developing angle. Others may disagree, but this ain't their fucking story. This is all my fucked-up, yet feel-good story!

Disclaimer, I swear a lot, and I've been swearing as long as I could talk. I have a quote that accurately describes me: I don't drink, smoke, do drugs, eat pork, beef, or chicken. I believe in God and I'm not a whore, but I do swear. For the record, my daddy thinks I swear too much in real life and in this life story. Imagine that, the crackhead reprimanding me for my potty mouth. I politely told him that we all have our vices. I won't be shamed into hiding neither his nor mine. My go-to curse words are various iterations of "fuck" and "muthafuck" with an honorable mention to "whore." So, apologies if my foul, wash-it-out-with-soap mouth is offensive, but then again, it is my muthafucking story.

My parents, Anthony and Linda, met while attending Savannah State College. My mama bragged that my daddy had a lot of women, but she was the only woman to drive his car on campus at Savannah State College (a real honor, I was told). Plus, she was the first to get him to the altar. They left school prematurely while expecting their first child (lost in miscarriage) but not before eloping in my mama's hometown, Tifton Georgia, on the steps of the Tift County courthouse, only after mama's gun-toting father threatened my peace-loving daddy.

"You have until sundown to leave town," he told my daddy.

Refusing to leave without his woman, the bride and groom, along with their two witnesses, her mama, Vera, and his best friend, Larry, were present at the nuptials. Immediately after the ceremony, before nightfall, my parents drove to Jacksonville to move in with my daddy's parents, Marian and Isaac, who would meet my mama for the first time upon their arrival.

My parents were young, sociable, and enterprising. They were the talk of the town. The kind of couple everyone envied because they were unfairly attractive and so in love. It should've been against the law for two people this good-looking to join in matrimony and procreate; but they did. If I do say so myself, they did it quite well with my sister and me. My mama desperately wanted to give my daddy a son, a child to carry on his last name. However, my daddy was ecstatic about having two little girls. From the moment we arrived in this world, he concentrated on us knowing our worth and value beyond societal norms.

My mama, Linda, is four foot eleven, coated in caramel and had a sweet, naïve, yet generous personality. She was a majorette, a talented seamstress and the most beautiful woman in the world to us. She gave us confidence and emphasized the importance of using our God-given beauty but invariably protecting ourselves using God's guidance and grace. My Daddy, Anthony, was a pecan-tanned; silky-haired; quick-witted Jack-of-all-trades; vertically challenged, yet athletic; and a very handsome hard worker with an afro groomed to perfection. He read the newspaper every day. I mean, to this very day the man is a walking encyclopedia. He literally knows more general American and Black history as well as sports statistics than anyone I've ever met.

My daddy was affectionately known in Duval as "Keyball," a nickname he'd earned from his friends "Big Head Bill" and "Sluggo." When he was five, he played football in the projects with a pocket full of keys. The keys scratched the other players, giving him an advantage over the bigger boys. Even though he was small, my daddy was a skilled football, baseball, and basketball player. He also was a competitive pool shark who sunk the balls with precision and confidence. Literally, he was good at almost everything, except for being a faithful husband.

For my sister and me, my daddy was the moon, the sun, the earth, and the eighth wonder of the world. He walked on clear blue waters with the master keys to life. We were the epitome of "daddy's little girl." My daddy taught us everything consequential for a young child: how to spell our names and colors, how to read and write, even how to count bags of money. He taught us Black and American history, how to drive, and about work and the value of money. He prepared us to be as mentally tough as boys while perfectly effeminate as girls. My daddy was going to make damn sure that we were valued for our worth, not our bodies. This was no easy feat in the ghetto; men and women were always trying to manipulate young, pretty girls into using their bodies instead of their brains. He kept us close and protected us by empowering us with self-worth, self-confidence, and business and street knowledge. He was raising self-actualizing and formidable forces, not whores for the streets.

Our lessons on the greater power of brain prowess would serve us well in our lives and educational pursuits. My parents refused to let us make their same mistakes by not completing college. They stressed the significance of education every chance they got. Graduating from college wasn't optional in our household; my parents ran a tight ship with their girls and expected excellence from us. My daddy was adamant that his girls' greatest shot of getting out of the ghetto and becoming successful wasn't going to be through singing, dancing, or acting, but solely through education; especially since we weren't blessed with Tyrese's Coca-Cola voice, Debbie Allen's feet, Viola Davis's chops, or Lil Duval's humor.

Our parents expected and demanded excellence in every way by constantly drilling, "Y'all must get all A's. We will not accept anything less than your best!"

My daddy equally believed in having a balance of work hard and play hard for his girls. Every year he'd take us to the Jacksonville Fair, letting us explore every ride and eat ourselves sick with candy apples, cotton candy, funnel cake, popcorn, and sausage dogs. On Sundays after church, he took his three girls, us and mama, out for "fine dining" at Morrison's or Piccadilly. I can still taste my favorite, green Jell-O with whipped cream. After the meal, we'd take a carefree drive to Jacksonville Beach or Fernandina Beach a.k.a. "the black beach" for curly fries with hot sauce and fun in the glistening sun.

On the Sundays we didn't crush waves, my daddy took us to the movies to see the latest motion picture with movie theatre popcorn and butter. We loved movie popcorn so much; some days, to this day, we go to the movie theatre simply to buy popcorn from concessions. Most times we sat for double features. Present day, I would love it if I could remember movies in full detail; the truth of the matter is that a life of trauma caused me only to hold on to feelings and people I survived with. But, make no mistake, I will never forget feeling wanted, loved, secure, protected, and safe among an ever-evolving, chaotic world.

My daddy's first time freebasing was in 1978, in the back of a corner store at Twenty-Sixth and Canal Street after his childhood friend, Pucci, introduced him to a man named Johnny, who never left his "post" on the stoop. He describes his first hit of crack cocaine as a detrimentally deafening high with bells ringing in his head, along with his heart thumping and racing at one hundred miles per hour all at the same time. Then and there, my daddy knew this drug would devastate and destroy anyone or anything in its path. Unfortunately, it was instantly too late for him. My daddy's been chasing the high of his first hit to this very day.

The year 1978 wasn't all bad. It brought me one of the best gifts of my life when my baby sister, Mia, was born at seven pounds by cesarean section because of her broad shoulders. Mia was the prettiest baby ever, even prettier than me as a baby. At the time, I would've been close to five years old, probably the most mature five-year-old anyone had ever known. In fact, my fifth year of life proved to be such a pivotal year for the development and fiber of my being. Word of advice: Don't underestimate a five-year-old, especially a five-year-old me. Thankfully, Mia wasn't a crack baby; she was conceived before my daddy was introduced to crack cocaine. However, that wasn't the case for my daddy's second son, Anthony, who would later be born with cocaine in his system. His mama and my daddy were freebasing until just before his birth. Despite his parents' addiction, he never touched That Rock; but he did inherit my daddy's love of gambling, especially shooting craps. Nevertheless, all of our lives would be just as rocky.

Mia and I were two little girls who went through so many atrocities. We can remember things vividly no child should've experienced while at the same time scratching entire years from our memory. My sister was very young and really can't remember much of anything before the age of eight, even though she'd been right by my side throughout our journey. Although she can't recall details, her memory does serve in how she felt during those times. Mia can distinctly remember feeling like we could've died or at least felt the presence of an extreme threat to our life, time and time again.

To this day, Mia always says to me, "I know we're not supposed to be here. We're not supposed to be alive!"

The one thing we both know is, for more than forty years, crack cocaine has been a dominating force in our lives. However, do not confuse keen self-awareness with fear. Shockingly or maybe even stupidly, Mia and I had zero environmental fear while living and working in the ghetto: knocking on the doors of dope dealers, facing the police, and dealing with so many people in legal or illegal businesses, simply didn't grant us the luxury of being afraid to persevere through our lives. Where mine and Mia's memories easily collide, is the undeniable, unequivocal lingering smell of crack cocaine. Freebasing is without a doubt one of the most clear-cut, vile, and disgusting odors on the face of the earth. Think of burned eggs mixed with day-old urine, then add fresh feces and that just might come close. For as long as we are alive, we will never forget that indelible stench.

We did, however, manage to escape one of our greatest nightmares by not actually seeing our daddy smoke crack cocaine. For sure, we've gotten a whiff of the aroma and we've certainly seen the aftermath of drug paraphernalia like burned glass pipes and punctured aluminum soda cans. We are grateful for dodging the visual of a crack pipe to his mouth.

We normalized dysfunction to such an extreme extent, it would terrify "normal" people. Truthfully, if being "normal" meant being without my daddy, mama, and Mia, fuck "normal." We grew up fast with adult responsibilities laid at our feet. As a coping mechanism, we made jokes out of every sad or tragic occurrence. Unbelievably, there was no sense of us wearing the trauma in continuance. There was simply no time for resentment; candidly, we were just happy we'd survived every single turn and were alive to laugh about it.

Mia and I have never had a fight in our lives. One of us would submit to the other before allowing a disagreement. Everything in this world that is mine is also hers and vice versa. Everyone, including our own family, continuously commented on our closeness and bond over the years. The bond Mia and I share, our love and our dedication to each other, is the reason, despite it all, that we both believe we're actually alive and not completely batshit crazy. Neither Mia nor I have ever tried drugs growing up, not even a little weed a.k.a. the "gateway drug." To us, it meant the gateway to an inescapable life of hell including but not limited to poverty, whoring, teenage pregnancy, and/or death. In order to succeed, we had to sidestep the seduction of all ghetto trappings and trickery.

When I was eight, Mia and I made a pact to one day name our children after one another, open a law firm titled Gundy & Gundy, and live next door to each other. I kept my promise. My daughter is named Mia Michelle Jr. I also have a son, Kevin III, as well as two additional bonus sons, Kevin Jr. and Devin. Of course, Mia's firstborn daughter, Terrinee Elle, went on to be named after me. Her second daughter, Mia Elle, was named after both my sister and my daughter. Almost all the names in our family have been passed down, so get into it! A life-altering car accident would one day lead Mia down a different path to becoming a rehabilitation counselor in the prosthetics field. She has been an above-the-knee, left-leg amputee since her senior year in high school. However, we're still working on the perpendicular, or vertical, real estate, but there's not much we say we'll do that we don't get done; I expect we'll be neighbors soon enough.

My daddy might have been a Junkie, and my mama certainly had substance abuse demons of her own to deal with, but teaching Mia and me unconditional, undying, unbreakable love was by far a part of their genius for which they deserve all the credit and praise. Believe it or not, being a Junkie instilled quite a few good qualities in my daddy: creativity and resilience. My daddy didn't survive over four decades without rising from the ashes over and over again. Miraculously, he's managed to live a long, productive life while smoking crack cocaine for over forty years.

On January 7, 2022, my daddy turned seventy years old. My sister and I planned to throw him a huge party to celebrate the milestone because he'd never been given a birthday party. Truthfully, we were giving him a party because we couldn't have imagined in our wildest dreams that he'd live to be seventy years old. All my daddy wanted was to celebrate with all of his family and friends—at least those still living because he's outlived so many. Seven out of his eight kids would've celebrated with him: Mia, Mario, Anthony, Nelson Mandela, Quantina Joan, Anthony Jr., Quantina Gloria, and me. Sadly, it wouldn't be possible for Mario to attend the party because he was serving fifteen years in the federal penitentiary as a "three strikes'" convicted felon. By my count, daddy has eight kids, but my daddy's tally would probably be nine. Yep, papa was a rolling stone that hasn't stopped turning. He has had at least one child in each decade over the last fifty years. How does this seventy-year-old crackhead have three children under the age of thirteen? Nevertheless, they're amazing children. But go fucking figure!

There is another kid, Corey, who allegedly belongs to my daddy. His mom showed up on our doorstep when I was about seven or eight years old, claiming that Corey was my daddy's son conceived when they were in high school. The boy was probably ten or eleven then, and no one had ever heard of him, like ever. My daddy never turned away a kid, especially one that could possibly be his own. Soon after, Corey came to live with us for about a year or so. He was an absolute terror, to put it mildly. Speaking of Trauma, the boy clearly came with an endless black hole of preexisting damage and trauma. My daddy, and even my mama, tried hard to love him to no avail. After a time, because he was not willing to abide by their house rules, Corey moved back in with the same family that obviously couldn't control his behavior. For the record, I never thought he was actually my daddy's son. We will probably never know because he's spent most of his adult life in prison.

On Christmas Day 2021, my daddy tested positive for COVID-19, and we had to cancel his seventieth birthday party. Even though we didn't get to celebrate him in the royal fashion we'd anticipated, I privately celebrated his actual birthday all by myself. I cried and cried and cried some more happy tears. Being a part of my family meant never having the luxury of tears, since crying literally lead to death in these tough streets. Fortunately, on this day, through tears, I thanked God for saving my daddy, letting him see the age of seventy, and being eighty-five days clean and sober on his birthday. However, his sobriety wouldn't last much past Valentine's Day. He relapsed and has since been on a nonstop drug binge. But hey, that's the underlying theme of our lives.

He's always gotten high on That Rock as a birthday gift to himself for the last forty-three years! I really didn't care if he was high or not on his birthday, especially after making it to seventy years old. Due to his never-ending drug turbulences, I'm so conditioned to have low expectations about his sobriety. This year was no different, I only cared that my daddy, a Black man, a crack head that had never been to prison, lived long enough to see his seventieth birthday in good physical health. Honestly, I felt grateful for him to have reached this age with no need for daily prescription medications or notable ailments. I must emphasize that, not in our wildest dreams could my sister or I fathom that our crackhead, Black daddy would live to see seventy.

There was a period in my life, when every time the phone rang, I anticipated getting "the call" to tell us that my daddy overdosed or had been killed by a dealer for something drug-related. My daddy was no Rock Star in the common sense of the term, but trust me when I say that he lived a real "Rock 'n Roll" lifestyle for most of his life. In over forty years, his longest period of being clean and sober has been fourteen months, when he moved to Georgia to help take care of me and my two kids, Mia Michelle and Kevin, while pregnant with my son. Thus, Junkie or not, I was happy as hell that he was six feet above ground.

My family and friends, and of course my daddy, are always uncomfortable when I say the words "my daddy is a Junkie." There was so much shame and negativity that came with substance abuse and addiction growing up in the ghetto. Kids and adults alike were cruel, and weaponized the unwarranted shame of drug addiction not only against the Junkie, but against their families. Weaponizing someone's addiction isn't appropriate or cool. So, I want to give other sons and daughters of Junkies the permission to love them despite their flaws and shortcomings. Moreover, I want the Junkie to know that it's never too late to heal old wounds; effort will go a long way, farther than expected because, ultimately, we all just want love. One of my hopes in sharing my journey is that my story will help release the burden of shame and heavy weight other children of Junkies carry on their backs throughout life. It's okay to forgive and love oneself, and the Junkie, despite it all.

Mia and I decided a long time ago that no one was going to make us feel ashamed of ourselves or of our daddy, the Junkie. We were going to control our image and certainly weren't going to let anyone make us feel bad for our daddy's actions. We were children. Why should we pay for his behavior? Therefore, we owned our narrative and started telling everyone, "My daddy is a J." We wanted to beat everyone to the punchline, so no one could use it against us. It worked. It sort of worked, except for the fact that my daddy hated us telling everyone.

One day, my daddy said to me, "Please stop telling my business to everybody."

I responded, "I'm not telling your business. I'm telling mine. This is as much my story as it is yours, and no one, including you, can tell me how to share it."

He's never said anything else about it to me again. He's definitely a prideful man and prefers to be judged for his deeds as a father, businessman and community servant, and not a Junkie. People should be judged on the entirety of their contributions to society, and by any measure, my daddy, despite being a Junkie, was and will always be one hell of a man, and an even greater father. In the purest sense, he was my first forever love. Presently, he fully supports me telling my full truth. Candidly, if I don't tell my truth and share my story, then I'm basically accepting a form of self-hatred and shame.

The number of odds that Black people have had to endure and overcome to succeed and thrive in America can be crippling. My life has felt like walking through a field of landmines, while aptly evading catastrophe. But there is a silver lining—I know how the story ends. I am a mommy of two amazing children, a sister, an aunt, a friend, a lawyer, and a judge; but first and foremost, I am always and proudly The Daughter of a Junkie. This is my story, a true love story complete with the American dream.

CHAPTER 2

"She's Five Years Old"

My mama, Linda, is one of the prettiest, sweetest, and kindest women I have ever known, except when protecting her children. Growing up, we were rarely allowed to stay over with friends or family. She preferred all of our playdates to occur at our house. We were not allowed to go inside anyone's house. To this day, she's fiercely protective of my sister and me. For as long as I can remember, she's instilled in us the know-how to protect ourselves from ever being taken advantage of or violated by anyone. This may sound like a simple notion that shouldn't have to be said out loud, however, in the 1970s and part of the 1980s (especially during the Atlanta child murders), these conversations in my family were foreign and somewhat taboo. But my mama prided herself on two things: one, she would tell us she loved us every day because her mama never said it to her, and two, we would feel safe because she would teach us to protect ourselves. Plus, we were only allowed to be kept by family, never strangers.

My mama did allow me stay with Rose, a non-family member she'd met through her mother in-law. Rose insisted on being my Godmama right after my birth. She loved me like I was her own, and because of my tanned skin and red hair with blonde streaks, she gave me the short-lived nickname, "Dirty Red."

One day, this White woman walked up to our shopping basket in the aisle at Publix as my mama grabbed food off of the shelves.

"Oh my," she said. "Aren't you the prettiest little girl I've ever seen? What's your name, darling?"

Silly four-year-old me eagerly blurted out, "Dirty Red!"

My mortified mama quipped back at me as the woman quietly faded away.

"That isn't your name. Don't you ever let me hear you say that again. If you let people call you anything other than Terrinee, you'll open the door for them to call you all types of inappropriate names. Your name is Terrinee, not no damn 'Dirty Red!' That is all you'll allow people to call you and that's all you'll ever respond to—your name, 'Terrinee.' Do you understand me?"

I've always obeyed and followed her strict instructions related to nicknames because she was so stern and adamant. In hindsight, I realized she never wanted me to be comfortable with anyone calling me outside of my name such as "bitch," "whore," or the "N word" to make sure I instantly knew it was wrong and unacceptable. I always complied with all my parents' rules. I eagerly wanted them to trust and be proud of me, even at an early age. They also forbade me to leave the apartment complex, go inside anyone's home, or come home after dark. It sounds absurd now for a five-year-old, but it was very common in the 1970s for all children to have the freedom of outside with the assurance of community protection.

My mama preached, "No one can protect you, but you."

One of my first tests came when I was around five years old. We lived in Four Seasons Apartments off Arlington Expressway in the "nice" part of town and close to my daddy's job at Publix Supermarket. My parents were determined that we would have a better life than them, so their first thought was that we had to move to a nice neighborhood with good schools. Integration was still a relatively new concept and experiment, but my parents decided to try it out because nice and good meant a white neighborhood where we would have access to better, basic living standards and conditions.

My parents integrated us socially into our new community but didn't assimilate our mentalities from the core of our history or the honor code that we learned from the streets of our hood. Our ethics, honor, and awareness of self was well-established and rooted in our family and heritage as Black people. Thankfully, we never lost our identity as the Core Four: my daddy, mama, Mia and I.

According to my daddy, these white neighborhoods needed a convenient "demand and supply" man. In the 1970s, there was a popular demand for that Mary Jane, and he was going to supply marijuana to paying customers in order to cover our $125 per month rent. This little, illicit side hustle of peddling weed never changed my daddy's drive and intention to work hard and show up daily at Publix; and no one in our extended family was aware of his extracurricular activities of unauthorized pharmaceutical sales.

Despite primarily being one of the only Black families in our complex, I absolutely loved living in Four Seasons. As a toddler, I roamed the property alone like it was my own private compound. I had a German shepherd named Cherry that was very protective of me. I loved Cherry so much. I was obsessed with her. We were inseparable. She was much taller than me, tan and black, and huge like a bear. I never feared that anything would happen to me because Cherry would protect me, and I believe that my parents thought the same despite the history of German shepherds being used to hunt and attack Black people.

I rode Cherry bareback like she was my very own horse, and everyone knew us. We were fan favorites of the complex with Black and white people alike. Of course, we were! Everyone loves cute kids and dogs. They fed us breakfast, lunch, dinner and even sugary snacks from sunup to sundown as we galloped through the day. One of our favorite snacks was homemade Rice Krispies Treats, long before Kellogg's decided to market, package, and sell them. We excitedly devoured every bite.

In the summertime, Cherry and I went to the swimming pool every day, all day. I remember this one particular day like it was yesterday. The swimming pool was crowded and full of people, mainly white people which wasn't unusual. We'd been there most of the day with my teenage cousin, Rodney, having a good time sunbathing and hanging out poolside after having played all morning with my new favorite toy, my baby sister, Mia.

Suddenly, Cherry began to grunt while nudging me toward the pool. I didn't think anything of it, and I don't believe anyone else did either because this would have been nothing outside of our norm. Cherry continued, and to be clear, I thought she was playing with me and still thought nothing of it. Next thing I remember, she pushed me into the pool, jumped in behind me, and began tugging me with her teeth straight to the bottom of the pool. Fortunately, I'd recently taught myself to swim after jumping in the deep end of the pool because I got tired of staying in the shallow end of the pool. It really pissed me off that I was stuck down in the kiddy section. Even though everyone was older than me, I believed that I could do everything they did. Or at least I should be able to, and I was because I willed myself to swim at four years old.

So, when Cherry pulled my small body to the bottom of the pool, I wasn't afraid. Even once we reached the bottom and subsequently got caught in the drain, I still wasn't afraid. I never panicked then or throughout life no matter what was thrown my way. After trying to free my miniature-sized body from the drain, I gazed into Cherry's eyes looking for help. She looked back at me and began to swim to the top. It was my first heartbreak. I knew in that moment that Cherry had planned to harm me or at least that was what I believed.

Despite Cherry's "Cujo" tendencies that day, I remained calm and continued to hold my breath, but I could feel myself beginning to fade as I saw someone finally coming to save me. My tiny little heart gave out on me, as I succumbed to the vast body of water, I found myself trapped by suction and the bad deeds of my dog. The next thing I remembered, was waking up on the side of the pool as my cousin, Rodney, performed mouth-to-mouth resuscitation as a large crowd of terrified people surrounded me.

Much later in life, Rodney told me that this was a defining life moment for him as well. He couldn't believe that he'd been so carelessly standing there that day, numb and paralyzed during the incident. He was adamant that no one, especially my mama and daddy, truly understood how I nearly died that day. He Initially couldn't even bring himself to tell my mama because he felt like he was to blame. However, he'd been entrusted to care for me many times after that and has always been extremely protective of me from that day on. Rodney loved me very much but also carried a strong sense of duty from the marines; after almost losing me at such a young age, he wanted to make damn sure nothing ever happened to me again. Not on his watch!

Later in life, one of my friends argued that dogs, Cherry specifically, couldn't have intended to harm me because she was a dog. To this day, I begrudgingly disagree. Cherry very much had "single white female" energy that day. To me, she decided at the bottom of that pool that if she couldn't have me, no one would, specifically Mia. Cherry had recently grown jealous of all the attention I gave Mia at home.

I would only see Cherry once more after the incident. It was common for animals, including dogs, to be shot and put down for illness and mercy, or if ever the animal became threatening to humans and/or other animals. It was evident that something in Cherry had triggered her to transform from my loving, adorable family dog and best friend (before Mia) to an unhinged, crazed beast. After this evident change, one of my parent's friends, the breeder responsible for Cherry's birth, dispiritedly shot and killed Cherry. In my young mind, the betrayal felt like abandonment. To this day, I cannot come within two feet of dogs. I don't trust them to be close to me.

In many ways, Mia, Cherry, and I had an interesting love triangle of sorts. At any age, the balancing of love can be complex and perplexing and can tip the scales in one direction or another. Obviously, my love juxtaposition undeniably leaned toward Mia standing side by side with Cherry. Even if Mia wasn't in our presence, she remained the keeper of my whole heart. Ironically, Cherry's imbalance of love for me was equal to the imbalance of my love for Mia. But take it from me, if I had to choose between Mia and anyone else in the world, Mia would always and forever be the winner. Sorry, Cherry!

Almost immediately, Mia hypnotized me with her brown eyes beaming at me as I stood hovering over her crib, imagining that she was begging for me to emancipate her from that lonely, stiff place. So, every night, I tiptoed into Mia's crib against the admonishment of my mama and took her out of bondage to sleep freely and soundly in the bed with me. The first couple of nights, my mama was frustrated and continued to harp on me with warnings to stop or I would get a deserving, scathing spanking. I didn't care about her threats or no spanking.

After the third night, I intelligently and slowly explained to my mama, like she was a five-year-old, that it was my job to take care of and protect Mia. I continued telling my mama that Mia needed to sleep with me so she wouldn't feel cold and alone. No baby deserved to feel that way, and certainly not my baby sister. I must've presented one hell of an argument because my mama finally surrendered, from exhaustion, or on the account of my doing such a great job taking care of Mia, or probably both. Needless to say, I won my first case at five years old; clearly, these were early signs that I was destined for a career as an attorney.

I've been taking care of Mia ever since she entered this world. Or shall I say we've been taking care of each other. All I ever wanted in life was a little sister to love and care for. I prayed and prayed for God to send Mia to me. God listened to my prayers. I would've never made it out of the ghetto without my sister. I would've been alone with two drug-abusing parents and no one to understand my plight. Mia literally saved my life in every sense of the meaning.

Yet, on this night when I was five years old, it was my job to save both me and Mia. Can't lie, I missed Cherry the night the police showed up unannounced at our front door while my mama was out at the laundromat. Back then, it was a real gem to have an in-house washer and dryer; and we didn't have one. We had a coin laundromat in our apartment complex. My mama sometimes spent the entire day washing clothes, except for the days when we could use all the washing machines at once. This evening wasn't one of those days. Apparently, everyone in the complex had decided that that day was laundry day. My mama went back and forth to the laundromat all day and night.

Every time my mama left to head back to check on our clothes, either in the washer or dryer, she yelled, "Lock the door and don't let anyone in. I mean no one."

On this day, I heard a loud knock at the front door. I didn't move, and the loud knock came again. Then, I realized my mama was still not back and maybe she was at the door trying to get in. Before I could make it to the front door from my bedroom, the knock got aggressively louder. I immediately checked on Mia, who was asleep in her crib, and proceeded to the window to look outside. There were about three white men dressed in police uniforms at the door.

At this moment, I really needed Cherry because I knew she would've barked loud and viciously to back them up from the door. Instinctively, I ran around the house looking for a weapon of some kind because my mama had been preparing me to protect myself for as long as I can remember. I grabbed a small knife and immediately thought eyes, ears or nose—that was how to stop them. Until my mama returned, I had to protect me and my baby sister. Now, the knocking intensified.

By now, the men realized that someone was in the house and continued pounding the door while screaming, "Open the door!"

I yelled back as loud as my little lungs would let me, "My parents told me not to open the door for anyone! Go away!"

They must've immediately assessed that I was a kid from my shallow voice and began to pipe down. I heard them through the door.

"Hey, this is the police. It's okay. Open the door. Go to the window and I'll show you my badge."

The man was holding what looked like a police officer's badge up to my window, and I stared at him while hiding the knife, to surprise him if he rashly decided to come through the door.

Once he finished trying to manipulate me into opening the front door, I shouted through the window, "My mama said don't open the door for nobody! I don't care if you the police or not. She said nobody and she meant nobody! I ain't opening the door for nobody! Go away and come back when she's here!"

I thought that would've been convincing enough, but he continued pleading with me, "Look at my badge. It's okay for you to open the door, little girl. We're the police."

I looked back dead in his eyes and screamed, "Anybody can have a fake police badge. Leave and come back when my mama is back!"

I started to back up slowly and sat on the couch where I could see both the window and the door, still clinching the knife, while praying for my mama to come home and for Mia not to wake up during this chaos. Thank God Mia slept soundly through the entire ordeal. I saw their shadows still impatiently swarming outside the window.

Suddenly, I overheard my mama yelling at them, "What happened? What's wrong? Are my daughters okay?"

As soon as I saw her walk through the door, I dropped the knife and ran to her with a great deal of relief. I hugged her tightly because I knew she was going to get those men for being at our door while she was away. Trust and believe, Black mamas are a different kind of crazy when it comes to their cubs. My mama was as crazy as Hannibal Lector in Silence of the Lambs about us.

Initially, my mama was alarmed because she didn't know why the police would be at our door. She listened as they explained some case they were investigating. I noticed that her tone changed to quite cordial once they began to explain themselves. She knew nothing of the incident and couldn't help them. As the police officers prepared to leave, the officer that tried to get me to open the door asked my mama if he could speak with her privately. She declined. Anything he had to say, he could say in front of me.

The police officer relayed the facts about my refusal to open the door. He repeatedly complimented my mama about the way she was raising her little girl. He told her that he'd never seen a young kid so smart, and how proud he was for the way I stood up to him. He knew a lot of older kids, and even some grown-ups who weren't as smart as I was at five years old. He continued that he wished more kids listened to their parents the way I did. The police officer then turned to me and said I was right not to open the door and apologized for trying to make me go against my mama's rules. He added that I should keep it up because it would always keep me safe. It always has.

But who rarely apologized—my daddy! He certainly didn't apologize for not leaving his beautiful wife and new baby girl, me. My daddy started working for Publix in 1974. Four days after I was born, he was to be sworn in as an army soldier at 6:00 a.m. on April 15, 1974. He was supposed to leave that morning for basic training at Fort Knox in Kentucky then stationed at Fort Stewart right outside Savannah, Georgia, which would've kept him really close to home. However, his army enlistment date was pushed back in order for him to be with his pregnant wife during my delivery. Technically, I could be called an army brat because the military paid the entire hospital bill for my mama's delivery. Unfortunately, or fortunately, depending on the perspective, my daddy just couldn't go through with it.

He turned to the army officer and said, "Sir, I'm so sorry. I just can't leave my pretty wife and new baby alone. They need me more than the army. I have to stay for my baby."

The officer tried to convince my daddy that he should follow through with his promise, but since he volunteered rather than being drafted, there was nothing more the officer could do except let him leave. My daddy did an about-face, walked out, and hopped on a bus straight to Publix Supermarket. After quitting the army before even starting, he needed a valid explanation for my mama on how exactly he planned to pay the bills. My daddy got off the bus, walked inside Publix and applied for a job. Once he finished and handed in his application, he walked out of the store to catch the next bus to take him home to surprise his wife and new baby with the unexpected change of plans. As he walked to the bus stop, he heard the manager shouting his name in the parking lot. My daddy turned around and started running back toward the guy.

The manager asked, "Hey, man, can you start tomorrow at 5:00 a.m.?"

My daddy replied, "Absolutely!"

"See you in the morning," said the manager. "We will start you off at $5.10 per hour."

My mama was so ecstatic that my daddy quit the army to stay home with us and got a good paying job all in the same damn day. My daddy worked his way up from bag boy to being the best and fastest grocery stock man in the store. My mama took us to visit my daddy at work, and I never wanted to leave. I loved to watch my daddy work. As far as I was concerned, he had one of the most important jobs in the world. I marveled at how fast he moved while working. He took such pride in working and he was extremely competitive about it. As a matter of fact, he was competitive about everything. He definitely passed that trait on to me. I idolized my dad and I wanted to do everything my daddy did—except smoke crack cocaine.

After I begged for months, my daddy finally persuaded his boss to let me come to work with him. He promised that I wouldn't slow him down or get in the way. He had to be at work early, and I was up, dressed, and ready to go, beaming with excitement and joy. I was going to make my daddy proud by doing everything exactly the way I saw him doing it. It was the best day of my life, or so I thought back then. I helped daddy unload the boxes and stock the shelves, ate lunch with him, met all of his coworkers, and even rode a forklift. I also chewed pieces of torn brown paper bag all day pretending to soothe my "adolescent nerves," just like my daddy did when he was working. My daddy believed that we were the pioneers of "bring your kid to work day" at Publix, which is still one of their current policies.

While working at Publix in 1978, he took that experience, along with his work ethic, hustle, and savviness for numbers, to open Pistol Pete's Clothing and Alterations Store. Pistol Pete was my mama's nickname growing up, so my daddy paid homage to his love by naming their business after her. This young, entrepreneurial couple rode around stylishly in their white Plymouth Valiant convertible as they moved on up in the business community of Jacksonville, living the American dream. Since he was a little boy, my daddy had had an entrepreneurial spirit, and was purpose-driven with intent on passing the same to his girls.

Modeling after him, my sister partnered with daddy to open a check cashing business in our neighborhood after she graduated from Clark Atlanta University with a bachelor's degree in biology. At twenty-three years old, my sister owned a business and bought her first home. I decorated it right out of the pages of a home and garden magazine. Mia and my daddy did well until rampant, fraudulent behavior made the business unsustainable. No worries! The Gundy girls are spiritual gymnasts who land on our feet every time. As a result, Mia closed the business and then went on to graduate from the University of North Florida with a master's degree in rehabilitation counseling. For us, education was our go-to and the way out of anywhere, or everywhere.

For my daddy, working hard and grinding was his way out; he had been hustling his entire life. When he was five, he sold glass bottles for a penny. When he was seven, he, sold fruit for Mr. Willie and ran the cash register at Mr. Roberts' convenience store while hiring, firing, and managing the peanut and drink boys for Myrtle Avenue Ball Park during Friday night football games. At ten years old, my daddy could've never guessed at those football games that he would get the chance to be at a Super Bowl game. In 2000, he attended Super Bowl XXXIV held at the Georgia Dome in Atlanta. It was his gift to himself for my graduation from law school. His seat was right behind Halle Berry. Not bad for a Junkie that had been freebasing for over twenty years!

My daddy also saw the legendary Atlanta Braves player, Hank Aaron, play the minor leagues at the Myrtle Avenue Ball Park before heading to the major league and breaking Babe Ruth's home run record by hitting his 715th career home run on April 8, 1974. This was three days before I was born. Greatness was in my cards before I was pushed into the world. In Atlanta, many years later, I had the privilege and honor of meeting Hank Aaron to thank him for his contributions to baseball and especially for contributing to the way the world viewed Black people. We all stand on the shoulders of the great ones that carried the burden before us, not only surviving, but also thriving against all odds.

Speaking of great, another celebrated man to come through Jacksonville during segregation was Jackie Wilson. On Saturday nights, my nine-year-old daddy was personally hired by Jackie Wilson to run errands for him and his friends, Chuck Berry, Sam and Dave, and Gladys Knight and The Pips, when they stayed at the Fiesta Motel on Kings Road and Wilcox Street while on their Chitlin Circuit segregation tour.

Jackie Wilson told my daddy after their initial meeting, "I'll never forget your name because my son's named Anthony too."

Indeed, he was a hard-working man. In 1984, my daddy retired from Publix after working there for ten years making $9.25 per hour—a competitive wage that provided a comfortable lifestyle for us. Frustrated and devastated that Publix refused to promote him to management after a decade, my daddy decided to take his retirement of $10,000 to invest in growing our family business. Years later, after my daddy left Publix, there was a class action discrimination suit filed on behalf of people of color who weren't promoted fairly. My daddy wasn't a part of the suit and still believed he made the right decision by leaving Publix, but he was happy that Black people were finally being judged on their merit and getting rightfully promoted.

Early on, after my daddy's decision to dabble with crack cocaine in 1978, I quickly learned to recognize the signs of when he was getting high: twisted mouth, slurred speech, loss of appetite, and fidgeting. Crack cocaine, without exception, altered his capabilities. My daddy had a pretty, pregnant wife, a young child with a new baby on the way, and worked a full-time, demanding job while managing to take on a new business all in one year. It's possible the pressure of his circumstances lead him to That Rock. But my daddy never allowed me to make any damn excuses, so I won't make any fucking excuses for him now.

No excuses. In 1979, my parents gave me my first paying job at Pistol Pete's where we sold and tailored clothing onsite. I got paid in cash every Friday like all the other employees, making $5.00 per hour; not too long afterward, I began making more than all of his workers due to my superior work performance. I loved having my own money, and to this day I love the feel of cash in my hands.

Everyone said I was too young to work, but my daddy quickly snapped back, "No one is ever too young to learn the importance of hard work, and my daughter is smarter than all of you," he constantly repeated. "Yes, she's a child, and so what! She gets paid more than y'all, not because she's my child, but because she's better than y'all. She's my best employee."

I loved the fact that my parents refused to use the excuse of "she's just a kid." They've always maintained a resolve and steadfast faith and belief in my abilities and intellect above anyone else's, since I was their kid. My daddy never failed to compensate me fairly, despite my young age. As a result, it invoked in me an innate grit for a lifelong relationship with the importance and reward of supply and demand. He knew I was special and knew what he had in me; so, come hell or high water, he was going to develop me into a beast that would hold her own ground with any man, woman, or child.

In our business, my daddy ordered and sold the clothes, my mama managed and handled the alterations with other tailors, and I ran the cash register. Everyone that came into Pistol Pete's thought we were pulling the silliest prank on them with this small kid standing on a milk crate demanding payment from them. After a startled look and a few awkward laughs, the customers changed their tune as they grew amazed and impressed with how quickly I checked them out and with the correct amount.

My daddy schooled me on the importance of accuracy and speed through his example at Publix. I also counted bags of money from his moonlighting gig when he and his skillful on the 1s and 2s friend, Jazzco, threw the best and liveliest after parties to ever come through Duval at the Thunderbird Million Dollar Ballroom. My daddy's first after party was in 1978 for the Florida A&M University versus Howard University football game. He made $15,000 charging three thousand people a cover charge of $5 for entrance into their party. They repeated their magic moneymaking nights with after parties for Rick James in 1979 and Michael Jackson in 1984. After a glorious party night filled with drinking, drugging, and great music, my daddy walked in with brown paper bags of money and dumped them in the middle of our living room.

"Count it for me, baby girl," he told me.

I stayed up all night into the next morning counting bags of money. At first, I took my time to make sure the amount was correct and not to disappoint him with a wrong count. Then, I counted all of the money again to double check myself. The more I counted, the faster I got on the count and the recount. I was never wrong! My daddy even stopped counting after me because he trusted my accuracy and skill more than anyone. I loved counting money and the feeling of cash swiping through my tiny hands. My daddy taught me everything about cash because I needed to be able to spot and feel a counterfeit bill. We were constantly avoiding "the take or cheat." Where we were from, someone was always plotting. So, we had to be knowledgeable about human behavior, our merchandise, and American money.

I loved my job of handling the money and I was great at it, even at five years old. To really excite me, please drop off a bag of (legal) cash. Having my own money instilled confidence in my ability, which defined and even intensified my belief that I was just as qualified, if not better than anyone else. I always knew I was smart. I knew that with my intellect, combined with my work ethic and desire to be obedient to my parents, I was going to get me and my sister out of the ghetto. I continued to work alongside my parents after school, on weekends, and on holidays.

Christmas Eve 1979, Pistol Pete's was booming beyond expectations. We were having one of our best days since opening.

Clothes were flying off the shelves and my parents were restocking merchandise and helping customers while making sure no one was boosting (stealing). We were busy all day and making lots of money, so naturally, we were all jolly and vibrant. Even better, I was due to get off at 6:00 p.m. that evening to leave with my daddy's mama.

My paternal grandma, Marian, hosted an annual Christmas Eve gathering for all her grandkids including my cousins Keyton, Winona, Clifford, Angeal, Tanishia, and Ronald at her house. We drank hot chocolate, ate cake and candy canes, and wrapped gifts with the Temptations on repeat, listening to "Let It Snow," "Silent Night," and "This Christmas" to name a few. It was a good time. My sister, cousins, and I looked forward to this night every year.

My strikingly beautiful grandma was the envy of all, friends, foes, and church members alike, for her beauty, hourglass figure, silky hair, and impeccable style. Her grace in all areas of her life was admirable and unmatched. Grandma Marian was also an entrepreneur and a Black businesswoman ahead of her time. She provided for her family while teaching her kids, and subsequently her grandkids, the importance of hustling to build something of our own despite the odds against us.

When my grandma was eighteen years old, she took a job as a housekeeper for Dr. Thompson and his wife. Grandma Marian faithfully worked for this white family for over ten years until Dr. Thompson's wife confronted her about his adulterous affair. After she instructed Mrs. Thompson that that was a question for her husband, Mrs. Thompson pushed my grandma and threw a cup of heavily spiked lemonade at her, splattering broken glass all over their kitchen.

My grandma didn't want any trouble with this family or the law, so she hurriedly grabbed her things and headed home. Shortly after getting to the Durkeeville Housing Projects and walking through the door, the police were outside to arrest my grandma based on false accusations by Mrs. Thompson. As my innocent, never-been-in-trouble-with-the-law grandma was shoved into the back of a police car, Dr. Thompson frantically pulled up to right his wife's wrongdoing. He privately spoke with the cops explaining that regrettably his wife was an alcoholic and had blatantly lied on my grandma. He demanded for her to be released on the spot.

Dr. Thompson was a good man who emphatically apologized to my grandma for his wife's "mix-up." Knowing my grandma still needed a job to support her four children, Dr. Thompson handed her a card with Mr. Billingsly's contact information to start her new job the next morning at his washing mat. Less than five years later, Grandma Marian would proudly change the trajectory of our family by purchasing that same laundromat after qualifying for a business loan for $85 per month. In the 1960s, this kind of bank approval and financial sophistication for a Black person, let alone a Black woman, was rare. Yet still, she paid off her company's loan with her successful business income earnings.

Grandma Marian took motherhood and family as serious as death because her mama died when she was only thirteen, leaving her to be raised by her daddy, Willie. She decided at a very young age to be the kind of mother who would be dependable, reliable, financially stable, celebrate all holidays with her family and always, absolutely always, keep her family together. She did just that. All of her descendants are all well and alive, and none of her four children—Pat, Barbara, Anthony and Robin—have been in prison.

Like every other year, in 1979, Grandma Marian happily rounded up all of her grandchildren for some holiday joy that Christmas Eve. She had a spacious, roomy grey Lincoln Town Car with burgundy interior gifted from her second husband and the only grandaddy I knew, Isaac. It felt like a stretch limo inside that easily accommodated all of us. The kid-packed, kid-friendly car ride was just as anticipated and fun as the annual Christmas Eve gathering.

We were so busy on Christmas Eve at Pistol Pete's that I hadn't had time to think about my grandma picking me up. All I thought about were Presidents Jackson, Grant, and, of course, Benjamin Franklin. The money was piling up faster than we could empty the register by putting the big bills into the safe. I'd had a great day at work and was excited to see my grandma, Auntie Robin, and cousins pull up. My grandma walked in smiling.

"Let's go, little girl," she said.

Before I could jump off the milk crates, my daddy rushed over and said, "The girl gotta work. She can't go."

Grandma Marian shouted. "What? Are you crazy? She's five years old, and I came to take her to my house for Christmas Eve with all of the other kids. Everyone else is in the car."

As he continued to wait on a customer, I froze on the milk crate and thought, I know after working so good all day that I'm going to be able to leave with my grandma and there is no way she could just leave me.

Finally, my daddy said, "We're too busy. I need her to work the register. Mama, she can't go. I'll drop her off when we close."

My grandma refused to accept defeat and turned to my mama. "Linda, you can't let him do this. She's five years old for Christ's sake. She's worked all day and deserves to come with the other children."

By this time, Auntie Robin had gotten out of the Lincoln Town Car to come inside to see what was taking us so long. "Let's go before all the stores close. Remember, I'm taking her to buy what she wants for Christmas."

Before my grandmother could finish explaining the situation, my Auntie Robin was cursing at my parents to let me go shopping with them while looking deep into my teary eyes.

I was taught way before ever watching The Godfather trilogy to never go against the family. My mama never spoke publicly against my daddy. So no, my sweet, loving mama would be of no help to me.

My mama turned around unbothered and firmly asserted, "Mrs. Nunn, if he said she can't go, she can't go. We all have to work. See you later."

My grandma sucked her teeth and stood flabbergasted. Her five-year-old granddaughter would not be leaving with her on Christmas Eve because she had to work. Auntie Robin continued cursing, and even threatened to call the authorities on them for child abuse and endangerment. My parents weren't the least bit concerned about her idle threats and proceeded to wait on their customers. In silence, while repeatedly shaking their heads, my grandma and auntie went back to the car.

I thought this was the worse Christmas ever. It wasn't the worse Christmas. Not even close. On another Christmas, Auntie Barb's second husband and my absolute favorite, Freddy, bought TVs for all the children. The TV boxes were wrapped so pretty and decorative under my grandma's tree. We were all boiling over with anticipation and excitement only to discover on Christmas that we'd been duped and defrauded with TV boxes filled with center block bricks. So, maybe it wasn't the worst, but a close runner-up.

As my grandma pulled off, I couldn't contain myself anymore. I jumped off that milk crate, darted out of the door, and ran after my grandma's car, screaming and crying. "Please don't leave me. Don't leave me!"

Before I knew it, my daddy grabbed me out of the street and told me to calm down. "You're my daughter. You're stronger and tougher than this. You will never forget what you did tonight. We need you. Pull yourself together and let's go back in here and handle our business. Let's get this money."

Please cue the Marvel music for the superheroes that save the planet, because without thought or hesitation, I stopped wailing, calmed down, walked back in Pistol Pete's, and stepped on that milk crate with an "I'm here to save the day" attitude.

"Who's next?"

Two things were for sure: one, I wasn't going to let my daddy down and two, we were gonna get this money! Fuck Christmas Eve! I was exactly where I was supposed to be, with my daddy, mama, and sister creating a legacy. Mia, my mama, and daddy were my Christmas! As a matter of fact, I can't remember a Christmas Eve or Christmas Day when we weren't working. Except maybe when I was around seven. I have a vague memory of being home with my talking parrot, Bruce Lee, who I proudly taught to say shit.

My daddy was right. I never forgot that night. Later in life, I realized my daddy was giving me more than work ethic. He was providing me with a greater understanding of my worth and value as a person to him and our family. He was building a battle-tested, mentally strong warrior prepared for a cruel, sexist, and racist world. He was arming me with the necessary tools to navigate through it all while changing the trajectory of my life.

We were so serious about the almighty dollar that we convinced ourselves that we were having a better Christmas than everyone else. My daddy gave me an unapologetic love of money. Capitalism is the American way, and it makes the world go round and round. My daddy knew this, and he was going to make damn sure me and my sister did too. He created an environment where love of money wasn't taboo or shunned as it had been in Black communities and churches for generations. By handing me the gift of money and entrepreneurship, my daddy taught me how to break the cycle of poverty by building generational wealth.

"Nothing in America beats hard work and experience," he always said.

In the years to come, unforeseen and unpredictable challenges would come knocking at my door of success, but nothing was going to beat me. I didn't need to play with dolls or toys since getting money was my favorite game!

CHAPTER 3

"Love and Embrace Black Men"

As far back as the first grade, my parents began focusing heavily on my education, thus sacrificed and enrolled me in private school at Victory Christian. My religious private school tenure was enlightening and revealing, yet happily short-lived. I was a model student with perfect books of the Bible recitation. I was smarter than everyone in my class, except for an equally smart set of twins, a Black boy and girl. I hated—that's too strong—I earnestly loathed the fact that I couldn't wear my agreeable, tomboy pants to school because of their stupid and strict "dresses only" rule for girls; additionally, unruly students were beaten with a wooden paddle on their backside. Luckily, time after time, my mama allowed me to stroll into school dressed in corduroy pants, since she also thought it was a stupid ass rule, especially for an institution she paid for.

"What does her pants have to do with learning? Please explain that to me," she'd say.

The last straw came when an administrator struck me with that big, thick paddle for quietly swearing in the hallway. I ended up with a mark on my butt cheek and thighs. My mama acknowledged that I was wrong for cursing in school, but she hadn't given anyone permission to abuse me like a runaway slave for a childish mistake. My teacher secretly agreed with my mama when she told her to withdraw me from the school due to their inhumane practices.

"She doesn't need the focused learning of private school. Terrinee is an exceptional, self-taught student who will learn anywhere," my teacher stated.

My daddy was as happy about not having to pay my hefty tuition anymore as I was about being free to wear pants, rather than silly dresses every day. Moreover, my mama was most joyous and gratified about the message that was sent to those damn people—she will always fight for her kid, so don't fuck with her kid!

Every single person in my family has been raised on "never flight, always fight." Earlier that same year, I came home wailing because this little white boy, Timmy, randomly decided he was no longer going to be my best friend. Instead, he was going to beat me up to drive his point home. To add insult to injury, he told everyone at the playground to call me "Oreo" and "zebra" because I had a Black mother and white father. Despite not being biracial—and Timmy knowing both of my parents looked just like me, Black—I was embarrassed, hurt, and full of unwarranted shame. Timmy's unexpected violence and treachery left me devastated as I arrived home crying to my mama.

Apparently, Timmy's intolerable slurs and antics struck an infuriating and silent chord with my mama. While out grocery shopping, eating out, or just going about her day, my mama endured countless insults or compliments, subjective to the perspective about either being my nanny, babysitter, or having a mixed-race baby with someone other than her husband. I had no idea what the backlash of having a Black child with fair skin could be like. As an infant and growing toddler, I could pass for a little, blue-eyed white girl. Blame that on my Scandinavian DNA. I'm still the only one with funny colored eyes. For the record, my Blackness could never be defined by physical features. Yet, by the third word out of my mouth, it was crystal clear that I was unapologetically Black. My undeniable, ancestral, Mother Africa features certainly became more prominent and dominate as I grew older.

In response to Timmy's actions, my mama sternly commanded, "Stop crying. Right now. First, we are going back to that playground and you're not leaving until you beat that little boy's ass and teach him a lesson to never put his hands on you again. Second, don't you ever come into this house again crying about some bullshit that someone said about you, especially when you know it's not true. You know who your parents are, but more importantly, Terrinee, you know who you are. You will have a lifetime of people attacking you because you are beautiful and smart. People will always be jealous of you, and sometimes they won't even be able to help it. So, here and now, you must learn. You have to be tougher than everyone else, because they will definitely try you. Never let them see you fucking cry. Now, let's go back to this damn playground so you can handle your business."

I stopped crying at once, skipped back to the playground and proceeded to forcibly strike and pound Timmy. An audience of visibly entertained youngsters watched while he received an immensely deserving beatdown from a girl. Going forward, no one followed Timmy's miscalculated example; however, I have been called unflattering, untruthful, and downright disheartening names countless times since that time on the playground. But that was my first and greatest lesson in learning to only care about what the people who love me thought and not those who fed into the lies. Thus, if my family was proud, I wouldn't waste my time on people that meant no damn good or knew nothing about me.

During that summer, my mama took me and my sister to Atlanta to visit with her family, which normally would have been a welcomed change for me to get away from the obligatory summers in my mama's hometown, Tifton, Georgia. For me, spending summers in Tifton was like swallowing distilled white vinegar with a tad bit of sugar; it was supposed to make it better, but it sure did taste awfully nasty sliding down my throat to crash land into a ball of flames in the pit of my stomach. My mama shipped us off to Tifton every dreadful summer. It was excruciatingly painful to be stuck outside in cotton-field heat, day in and day out from June to Labor Day. We also missed going to the beach with our parents, jumping waves while avoiding jellyfish and eating junk food every Sunday at Fernandina Beach. We felt a spiritual connection to Fernandina Beach for many reasons. It was one of the only beaches for Black people before integration. But Tifton, with no beach in sight, was endurable primarily because I loved visiting my granddaddy, Leroy.

Leroy, also known as "Kilroy," was a good man and strict father of ten children. Over half of them have sadly passed away. He was a self-taught, master auto body mechanic and proudly owned his own paint shop in the back of my grandparent's three-bedroom house on Fourth Avenue. In their master bedroom, above their bed, hung five long-armed, ready-to-shoot intruder rifles. When I was eleven, he taught me how to shoot with a sawed-off shotgun. Despite my bruised arm and mama's pleading, he wouldn't let me stop until I discharged the shotgun without it throwing me to the ground.

Both of my grandparents were proud people and set a good example for us by being supremely proud owners of their modest house. It might have been small for a family of twelve, but it was all theirs, and that was all that mattered, especially after learning of the misdeeds and unfair treatment they both endured during sharecropping. To this day, I have no idea how we all fit in that tiny house. We were a family of unicorns that bonded over our differences and challenges. My granddaddy ruled all ten of his children with an iron clinched fist. However, with my sister and I, he was silly putty in our hands. He was the coolest, rugged granddaddy that spoiled us with endless compliments and treats of ice cream, pastries, and candy.

My granddaddy had a glass eye that sat in a cup on the bathroom sink that me and my sister would stand in line to clean. He let us pop it out his eye socket at will, the best and funniest game ever. He was an expert marksman with the one good eye he had left. He smoked a pipe with a tobacco scent that, if I closed my eyes right now, I could still smell to perfection—such a lingering, pleasant remembrance. I loved that he smelled warm, husky, and woodsy like a granddaddy should. My granddaddy's manly, chivalrous presence plus my Grandma Vera's "smack your own mama," down-south, soul food cooking was the only good thing about spending summers in the Sahara Desert of Tifton.

Damn, Grandma Vera sure could cook! She was the best chef in the world to her grandchildren. She was a short, plump and darker skinned woman but a hellacious force to be reckoned with on any day of the week. Notably, she fed anyone, I mean anyone with an appetite, at her modest wood kitchen table. But Grandma Vera wouldn't feed my granddaddy's youngest child, Keith, that he had with another woman who lived one street over from my grandparents. Even though Grandma Vera didn't allow Keith on her street, my granddaddy sneaked me and Mia to visit Keith and his mama.

Nevertheless, Grandma Vera still had a stellar reputation in this small, southern town as a sweet woman that raised ten children. She hand-made all their clothes, worked full-time for thirty years before retiring from C&S Bank, and made three meals every day for her husband and ten children. Grandma Vera was also the lady with the "whooping stick" off the tree in the front yard and would never turn on the window air conditioner, no matter how blazing hot it was outside. She wouldn't let us watch anything we preferred on the one and only television in the whole house.

I got the sense that Grandma Vera didn't like me; however, eventually she was proud of me. She never told my mama, Mia, or I that she loved us. But I'm sure she did. I imagined that being a Black woman in the Deep South during the Great Depression had hardened her in a necessary way, so she didn't have the luxury of surviving and showing emotions. Even though we had a challenging relationship, partially due to the old colorism battle, I respected her strength and steadfastness. Admittedly, there's a little Vera in me, since I too have a revolving door of family, friends, and anyone my kids bring to our house.

In the summer of 1980, a road trip with my mama and sister to Atlanta sounded like a much-needed change from the Tifton summers. Nope! This summer, Atlanta was a terrible idea because preteen and teenaged Black kids were being arbitrarily kidnapped and brutally murdered at alarming rates, coined the Atlanta Child Murders. From 1979 to 1981, approximately twenty-nine Black children and young adults, primarily boys, disappeared or were murdered in Atlanta. Black boys and girls were terrified across America, especially in Atlanta, to go anywhere alone, play outside with friends, or ride their bikes in fear of being taken or worse. Black families and anyone who cared about Black children were on high alert. The spine-chilling topic dominated conversations during our hesitant visit to Atlanta. Naturally, my mama was fretful and fidgety from the moment we arrived. In the midst of everything going on, this trip was still just about me and my family spending time together including all of my mama's siblings in town, except for Uncle Dalee.

One of the most special people in my village was my mama's brother, Dalee, who my granddaddy disowned after coming out to the family that he was gay. I was obsessed with getting to know Uncle Dalee after years of whispers and speculation about his lifestyle. He had a full and fabulous life as a celebrity hairstylist for Rock Hudson, Diana Ross, and Lenny Kravitz, to name a few. Uncle Dalee was so good at his profession that Lenny Kravitz gave him an honorable mention in his memoir. He was even a guest on The Oprah Winfrey Show.

I visited him in Los Angeles while I was attending the University of Georgia School of Law, a few years before he died due to complications from living with the AIDS virus for over a decade. At the time, AIDS was an epidemic that carried a stigma and fear similarly to crack cocaine. As a teenager, I remember giving my daddy condoms and pleading with him to use them because we were worried his drug use and promiscuous ways would lead him to the same fate as Uncle Dalee. I know kids shouldn't be warning and protecting their parents, but welcome to my world. The good news was that Uncle Dalee didn't experience negative backlash within our family related to his medical diagnosis. We'd all suffered enough from his banishment. We showered him with love and supported him until his last breath.

During my Los Angeles visit, Uncle Dalee provided me with a snazzy, adventurous time. He made sure I was exposed to fine dining, Rodeo Drive, the Hollywood sign and Beverly Hills. He even took me to meet Lee Iacocca, the American automobile executive best known for the development of the Ford Mustang, at his jaw-dropping mansion. I won't ever forget that trip for many reasons, but I'll forever remember how I felt to see him full of pride as he bragged and showed me off to all of his friends. I'll also never forget the Hollywood Hills party he took me to with pure heroin, cocaine, and a candy store of pills covering a table as long as the length of a small pool, and me being judged by his friends for not partaking in the festivities. Even for my background, there was a massive, offensive amount of drugs in that place; and considering that I was in law school, my career could've ended before it started.

Once Uncle Dalee finally returned to his house the next day from a long night of partying I asked, "Why in the world would you think that was some place I would want to be, should be, or could be? I'm a second-year law student!"

In his sweet, kind voice he said, "Baby, I'm sorry. I wasn't thinking. These days, all I think about is living my full life the way I want. I'm not dying on my back. I'm going to have fun, do drugs, and party to the end because that's what I want."

I replied, "I love you, Uncle Dalee, and totally understand. But just remember that I choose not to live my life that way. I can't live my life that way. I don't judge you. So, if you need to break out, just send my ass home. And for the love of God, protect me and my career, please."

He said, "Yes, pretty girl! Will Do. And I love you too. I love you so much. I'm so proud of the woman your parents raised. They really did a great job with you and Mia."

His love penetrated regardless of the tomfoolery he engaged in around me. As a matter of fact, I always felt loved with Uncle Dalee, even the first time I met him. I was around seven years old when he came to Jacksonville to style the models' hair for Pistol Pete's big fashion show. Of course, I was the star of the fashion show! The night before my big debut in Pistol Pete's fashion show, my daddy was missing in action on another drug marathon. By this time, my daddy was a full-blown crackhead. We set aside our wrecked nerves and decided the fashion show must still go on whether my daddy was there or not. At a young age, I somehow understood my daddy and how he operated. Absent good logic, I always believed he would show up in time.

Later in life, I found my own way to soothe myself whenever my daddy disappeared. I penalized him by spending his savings that he repeatedly entrusted with me. Basically, my daddy would give me his rainy-day fund when he was doing well. After "ROCK 'n' rolling," he'd return to pay his drug debts and get back on his feet. Well, I quickly became a part of the "two can play that game" school. I decided Mia and I would blow his rainy-day fund on things that we needed before he could give it to the drug man. This Wile E. Coyote game went on for years. My daddy never stopped trusting me with his money. Once, I used $3,000 as a down payment to buy a brand new, black BMW 325. Another time, I used $5,000 as a down payment on the purchase of my first condo.

My daddy loved to say, "Y'all the only people I let rob me without a pistol."

At least I was being productive and had something to show for his money versus him having jack shit after blowing it all on crack cocaine. Plus, he was a proud papa to have helped his daughter with such monumental purchases. See, it all worked out. In hindsight, we could've gotten him killed, but technically he would've gotten himself murdered, since he shouldn't have been smoking crack cocaine in the first place.

Voila! My daddy didn't let me down and figured out how to get back in time for my debut down the runway at my mama's fashion show. He finally appeared off his drug binge to ensure the rental fee of $2,000 was handled with the owner, so my mama's show could go on. My mama planned for this to be her breakout success as a businesswoman insisting on no help from my daddy. She had Uncle Dalee, a superstar hairstylist, the latest threads, and her secret weapon: me. What could go wrong?

Welp, no one showed up. The fashion show flopped due to lack of promotion and advertising. The building had a capacity of fifteen hundred people. There may have been fifty people in attendance. Everyone but me was devastated. I had a magnificent night after Uncle Dalee transformed me into a mini-Hollywood star. I strutted down the runway like only I could with my fabulous hair as graceful as any professional model. It was one of the few times growing up that I remember flaunting my beauty instead of my brains.

Most of my mama's family was at Uncle Fred's apartment off of Campbellton Road to celebrate something that summer in Atlanta. Maybe it was his birthday, which I was happy about because I loved me some Uncle Fred. Despite the necessary watchfulness, we were having a much-needed lively time in Atlanta. My mama's family knew how to throw a get-down, shake-your-booty party with all of the right and wrong accoutrements that, without fail, guaranteed us an entertaining time. I remember dancing, gyrating, and singing to Marvin Gaye, Both Al's (Jarreau and Green), Gloria Gaynor, Donna Summer, and many more, getting down for most of the night while thinking, *This must be what being grown feels like.*

My family constantly asked me to dance because I was look-away terrible with zero-zip-zilch rhythm. I tried so hard with my whole, innocent might. Everyone laughed with me uncontrollably at what an amazingly terrible dancer I was. No one could contain their laughter even after I stopped twirling and dancing around the room. I loved to dance, even if I was "rhythmless" nation. Present-day, Mi Rey, jokes about how hilariously offbeat I can be, and at times unsuccessfully tries to sway me to the beat.

He'd say, "It's unfair for you to be so perfect and good at everything, anyway. This was God's way of reminding the rest of the world that you are in fact human."

I was supposed to be in the bed asleep, but clearly, I never missed a good time, sashaying in my satiny-silk gown or cutting the rug. I stayed up way too late socializing with my family. My family particularly enjoyed my whimsical dancing and attire. It tickled them so much that I became known as Ms. Chancellor from The Young and the Restless. I was famous for donning a Pick 'n Save pink or red, silky—more like polyester or satin—floor-length night gown with matching robe adorned with feathers on the sleeve cuffs paired with clear glass—plastic—slippers for evening family events.

Someone banged on the door and screamed, "Help, they have Dionese!"

Without hesitation, my uncles and cousins grabbed their guns and ran toward the screams. The rest of the party, including my sister and I, followed the mob of terminators to see what in the Sam Hill was going on. As we got closer, I spotted Aunt Dionese who was locked in her car screaming nonstop through a cracked window. Three unknown men surrounded her car in an aggressive manner while shouting threats and banging on the vehicle.

Combined with the Atlanta Child Murders paranoia and our family motto "never flight, always fight," it's easy to imagine the colossal, barbaric violence that ensued shortly after discovering my mama's sister screaming like a pig being slaughtered for bacon that night. Before I could get a closer look at Aunt Dionese's car, everyone began to bum-rush the men, dragging them to the center of the well-lit street. When I arrived at the ferocious core of the beatdown, Uncle Bro aimed his gun at one of the assailants. My granddaddy forthwith ordered no shooting guns allowed because there were too many family members a stray bullet could hit. Uncle Bro had no problem obeying with a swift change of course and brutally pistol whipped that moronic perpetrator.

By this time, everyone, except for Mia, myself and my grandparents, had joined in issuing a feral beating to these presumed predators. Mia, who was around two years old, quiet as a mouse, yet heedfully, sat watching the skull-bashing brawl. My granddaddy stood, armed with a loaded double-barrel shotgun in hand and his .357 magnum strapped to his waist belt, which he proudly wore every single day of my life for as long as I can remember. He was always illustrating his second amendment right to bear arms.

Uncle Jerome respectfully pleaded, "Daddy, can I shoot this muthafucka please?"

Uncle Jerome was the best but all-out crazy as a muthafucka. He brought back a beautifully designed machete from the Vietnam War that Mia and I used to play with regularly in our made-up knife fight game. Nevertheless, he truly unconditionally loved and protected me. I equally loved his unbalanced, out-of-his-mind self so much so I gave my son, Kevin Jerome, his middle name to honor his life after death.

"Daddy, please let me shoot this muthafucka!" Uncle Jerome shouted again.

"I said no damn shooting, and that's what I mean," said my granddaddy.

Apparently, this gruesome course of action did not quench my mama's thirst for street justice, because she walked over to a heavily tree populated area and began pulling a small, but well-rooted bush from the ground. I fixated on her yanking this baby tree from the earth to defend my aunt's virtue, while thinking, No fucking way can she pull that fucking bush out of the solid hard ground. No fucking way!

I was in awe with my mouth wide-open at the shear might of this Smurfette-sized woman. My mama hammered into the assailant with the freed-from-the-earth tree, with sprouted roots dangling from the bottom and dirt flinging as she made barbarous contact with his limp, bludgeoned body while accidentally slashing Uncle Mike in the process. I couldn't take my eyes off my mama! This is the moment when I truly knew my mama was touched, and I would never try her! Moments later, my grandma demanded for the bloodbath to cease and for everyone to get in the house before the police arrived.

Not sure whether her meager voice was heard or not, my granddaddy firmly said, "Vera said stop and go inside. Now!"

There was blood splattered on everybody with the exception of me, my sister, and grandparents. While my unbothered, composed granddaddy did a head count, Uncle Jerome stood with two large, black trash bags and hot face towels. He told everyone to strip down to their underwear, put their soiled, bloodied clothes and shoes in the trash bags, and wipe every bit of blood off their dirty face and hands.

Uncle Jerome sent Uncle Fred to get clothes for all the naked men, women, and teens before the police arrived. Next, Uncle Jerome twisted the top and grabbed both large black trash bags, swiftly headed behind the apartment building—still wrapped only in a flimsy towel around his athletic waist—to set all the incriminating evidence on fire in an old, rusty tin barrel. Lastly, he packed up all the weapons in their possession and hid them outside, fully expecting and preparing for the apartment and vehicles to be searched by the authorities. As Uncle

Jerome briskly walked back into the apartment, we heard police sirens closely approaching. Uncle Jerome quickly threw on an old T-shirt and some loose-fitting jogging pants. Everyone else had already changed.

No one moved an inch, and no one spoke a single word. There was no hasty discussion about what to say or what to do when the police eventually arrived. Our family had more than a few encounters with the law and knew the universal protocol of shut the fuck up whenever talking to lawmen. If one of them got arrested, there was a pool of required funds for bail and an attorney. But under all muthafucking circumstances, shut the fuck up.

The doorbell was sounding off approximately a half-hour later; but, still no one moved or spoke, "Ding-dong, ding-dong."

The doorbell rang again, and my cool breeze granddaddy strolled to open the front door. He welcomed the police inside, without hesitation, with his semi-automatic, loaded .357 magnum at his hip. Some Black men are justifiably afraid of encounters with law enforcement, but my assured granddaddy never displayed fear when interacting with the police. He approached life with a "them or me" attitude, prepared to see his maker every single day, but found solace in knowing that he was going to give it as good as he took it. The two police officers proceeded to explain that they were onsite to investigate the assault of three pulverized Black men that had been badly beaten and rushed to the hospital.

One of the officers turned to the center of the filled room to ask, "Do any of you know anything?"

Only a few people meekly said no, and the rest of us either had the "no" look on our bewildered faces or shook our heads.

The police officers stayed the course and their fact-finding mission got dicey fast once they questioned the ownership of my family's expensive, gold necklaces, watches and diamond rings found outside at the scene of the incident while inquiring. They brandished the jewelry in front of us. All of them were devastated as they realized that all their precious, fine jewelry had been involuntarily relinquished. No one could or would implicate themselves by claiming that fancy shit. Finally, the police acquiesced without more hard, damning evidence, credited to the handy work of Uncle Jerome, and left without consequential incident or resulting arrests.

The authorities never returned or followed up after that night. However, unidentified men returned the next evening and shot up Uncle Fred's empty apartment like a slice of Swiss cheese. By the grace of God, the drive-by shooting didn't yield any injuries or fatalities. Consequently, with the insistence of Uncle Mike, Uncle Fred backed up an orange U-Haul truck and packed his entire apartment up that very same day, scurrying off to a new, safer dwelling.

I love this family of mine through and through, even with their imperfections. I sincerely and truly love something different about each one of my mama's siblings: Auntie Royce's grace and elegance, Uncle Bro's impeccable baking skills and humor, Uncle Dalee's loving spirit and free will, Auntie Carolyn's stubbornness, Uncle Jerome's everything, Auntie Brenda, my mama's twin, for her mental toughness and fortitude, Uncle Mike's smile and handsomeness, Auntie Dionese's optimism and creativity, and Uncle Fred's kindness and humanity.

My daddy, along with all of them, made damn sure I knew how to love a Black man through and through. My family taught me the importance of not looking for perfection, but rather identify and focus on the good that lies at the core of a Black man. All Black men deserve praise and love. I was born for the fulfillment, gratification, and pleasure of a Black man. I was destined to love an imperfect Black man who was absolutely perfect for me with my entire heart and fiber of my being. Undoubtedly, the man I was going to fully and faithfully love was going to be an extraordinary human, a unicorn on his own accord with strong elements that equated to him being a purple squirrel. And until I found that man, I chose to focus on myself and my goals, leaving boys to take a back seat. At the right time, I would be inspired to unabashedly and unconditionally love that man just as I did with my daddy, granddaddy, uncles, and cousins. Mi Rey, El Uno was that perfect man for me. He's my king, the one and my never-ending love.

Mi Rey constantly says, "We're perfect for each other because we're the same kind of fucked-up in the most endearing ways. We wholeheartedly understand one another."

I was positive that when a Black man was cared for and loved unconditionally, he would run through a brick wall to provide and protect for his own. I've moved through life with not just an understanding, but a defense of all Black men regardless of their flaws because Anthony, Issac, Jack, Leroy, James, Jerome, Dalee, Mike, Fred, Keith, Linwood, Bill, Rodney, Keyton, Ronald, Clifford, Xaver, Baraka, Rashid, Aloyshus, Brian, Greg, and James Jr. gave me the gift of loving imperfect Black men at an early age. I fully love and embrace Black men in whatever form they decide to show up. I wholeheartedly believe in their greatness, intellect, superiority, and love. I also loved that if anyone dared to fuck with any one of us, best believe the whole entire fucking clan showed up to respond accordingly and in-kind! There was more of us; hence, pick somebody else's muthafucking family! This sense of safety and security arose out of an abundance of love and tribalism fostered within both sides of my family for which I will be forever grateful.

CHAPTER 4

"I Need A Lawyer"

My favorite auntie, Robin, was getting married to Joey and I was set to be the flower girl in the wedding. Auntie Robin and Joey were unquestionably the best dressed, except for my parents, and the most fun couple I'd met in my young, adventurous life. Auntie Robin was gorgeous, tall, and slim with a milk chocolate complexion and luxurious long black hair like a real-life, Foxy Brown. To top it off, auntie had a larger-than-life personality paired with a gigantic heart that loved to a fault. Even more, she was a selfless giver that happened to be fiercely intelligent. Oh, and I cannot forget, anally organized.

A critical detail about Auntie Robin: she was the master of all things related to cursing. Yes, I am supremely impressed with master cursing, and maintain it should be a competitive sport in the Olympics. Auntie Robin would take the gold medal without any close competitors because no one, and I do mean no one, could curse better than her. I would take the silver medal, since I relentlessly practiced and ill-advisedly mimicked my own cursing after her until I could curse better than everyone except Auntie Robin. Both of my great granddaddies, Big Bubba, who was dark as night and Leroy Sr., who was light as day, would tie for the bronze medal. To me, cursing effortlessly and eloquently was one of the superlative attributes and a superpower justifying my fanatical love for Auntie Robin.

Imprudent as the concept to praise and applaud master cursing, the art form of swearing in the ghetto should be likened to an all-purpose, MacGyver Swiss Army knife. Providing limitless opportunities to express oneself passionately and exhaustively, master cursing can help one avoid an upcoming ass whooping, robbery, or a murder when executed perfectly with precision and skill. It will back a muthafucka the fuck up with quickness without ever having to use bodily harm. The key paramount factors of master cursing were to be wholly authentic and downright believable. It had to come from the pit of the gut with a tidbit roaring from the chest and lungs, and a fear of the shit coming out of the mouth to be undeniable. Solemnly, off the top of my head, I can think of at least twenty-six different ways to constructively use fuck and muthafucka.

Auntie Robin and her man were such an amusing, shit-talking kind of couple. Granted, the mixture of an exorbitant amount of recreational drinking and drugging further contributed to their slap-the-knee Richard Pryor type of humor. Like my daddy, That Rock had gotten a tight hold on Auntie Robin. I'm not exactly sure when Auntie Robin started freebasing. It was for sure several topsy-turvy, colorful years in the 1980s. Although her drug abuse came after my daddy's insatiable craving for crack cocaine, they never freebased together.

My grandma's heart and resources were being pulled in two opposing but equally destructive directions as she unequivocally fought to save her only beloved son and her youngest, cherished daughter from the addictive enslavement of crack cocaine. Full disclosure: the adults, except for my super-healthy, athletic Auntie Pat, including most of the kids, but certainly not me, have done some form of illegal, illicit drugs in their lifetime. No judgment, just the hard, honest truth about life for poor, urban families that lack proper and adequate resources, like housing, food, education, and upward mobility.

Since March 31, 1989, Auntie Robin has been faithfully clean and sober. Before that proud day, my grandma and I habitually visited Auntie Robin weekly at the rehabilitation center where I eagerly played checkers, backgammon, and bid whist with auntie and the other residents. It almost felt like we were at an extended, adult summer camp. Our routine visits were entertaining, especially since I got to hang out and do fun activities with Auntie Robin. Once, she reminded me of how deadly serious her predicament was after relapsing only a single time.

"Mama told that me if I don't get it together, my home is going to be under the stars, so she hopes I really like moonlit, dark nights with fading, blurry stars."

I was utterly lost. "Huh?"

Auntie Robin continued, "I'm going to be homeless with nowhere to go. I'm going to be a motherless child. Do you understand now?"

I just sat there staring into her sunken eyes thinking inside my developing, young brain. Damn, that's really fucked-up.

Then, I finally responded. "Auntie, I believe in you, and I love you. I will come play with you anytime you need me."

She just burst out with a deep belly laugh. "Little girl, you are something else. I love you too, but my grown ass don't need no damn playmate. But I know what you mean and appreciate you trying to help me."

After years of sobriety, Auntie Robin enlightened me on how my visits during that less-than-desirable stretch of drug treatment meant so much to her. She didn't know how to ask or receive help, and quite possibly, thought she didn't need help. Despite her pride, Auntie Robin needed me, and I proudly stepped up to the plate to be there. All the same, God in heaven knew she'd invariably been there for me one hundred percent, without fail or question throughout my life. Coincidentally, she was also there for my mama when it mattered most during my birth.

After leaving college, my daddy and mama reluctantly moved in with my grandma, her second husband, Isaac, and a teenage Auntie Robin in their three-bedroom house. In 1968, Isaac moved my grandma and her kids out of the Durkeeville Housing Projects into a better, more prestigious home he'd purchased for $11,000, paying a mortgage of $78 per month. Isaac was a godsend for rescuing my grandma from her hopeless marriage to a man like Mister from The Color Purple. Upon my mama's initial meeting with Grandma Marian, my daddy presented her as his impregnated wife, leading to a rocky relationship since my daddy was engaged to another woman when he eloped with my good and pregnant mama. Regardless of their pent-up tensions and, especially after having miscarried their first pregnancy, my grandma wanted her son's firstborn child, yours truly, safely delivered.

My mama would have two more miscarriages after Mia: twins and an ectopic pregnancy. Even though my mama was devastated over the loss of her twins, the ectopic pregnancy was imminently about to kill her. The doctor told us that seconds after he removed the baby from her fallopian tube, it exploded in his hands. If the unborn baby had burst inside my mama, we would've been motherless children. Praise God for his grace in saving my mama.

Now, who was going to save my daddy from my mama? I previously bragged and gloated about my daddy being skilled and gifted at the whole kit and caboodle. He was naturally a damn good gambler, a card shark and pro at shooting craps. He'd been playing poker all night when he should've had his narrow ass at home driving my mama to the hospital to deliver his new baby. Yes, I'm biased and even now slightly in my feelings since I was the about-to-be-born baby. Certainly, he shouldn't have been out gambling while my mama was nine months pregnant under any circumstances. He thought he'd multitask. Of course, he absolutely wanted to be there for the delivery of his first child, yet sorely needed to blow off escalating steam before halfheartedly leaving to enlist in the US Army. For the record, this was four years before his dance with the devil of crack cocaine.

Thank goodness my mama was living with my daddy's family, or she would've been alone going into labor. This was before cell phones, so she had no idea how to contact my daddy. Her water broke while she was in the tub and my hairy head pierced from between her open legs. Despite their rocky, rambunctious relationship, my mama painstakingly decided to bellow out for help to my grandma. Without hesitation, my grandma ordered Auntie Robin to carefully drive my mama to the hospital while she waited at home on edge to inform my daddy that his baby was on the way.

My mama was wildly panicking and stark raving mad all at the same time. She was at the hospital hollering and suffering through labor with still no sight of my absent daddy. While Auntie Robin patiently awaited my entrance to this whole new world, she perused a magazine left behind by a previous patient and stumbled upon the name, "Terrinee."

Instantly enthralled by the name, she enthusiastically made the suggestion. "Linda, if it's a girl, you should name the baby Terrinee."

My weakened, uninterested mama snapped back, "Terrinee it is! If he wanted it to be Kimberly, his ass should've been here."

Once deciding on a proper, befitting name, I was vaginally pushed out shortly afterward, coming in at seven pounds with stark baby blue eyes, extremely pale skin and light, sandy blonde hair; I'm the only one in my family to have such features. Back then, the sex of the unborn baby was not revealed until birth. My mama wanted a healthy boy, and my daddy wanted a healthy girl. As usual, his wish was granted. My weary mama yearned to meet her healthy baby girl and for her husband to walk through the door to caress and comfort her.

The nurse cleaned, weighed, and meticulously swaddled me to suitably hand me over. She attempted to gently hand me over when my mama snatched her hands back in an uproar and refused to touch me. My mama immediately began screaming uncontrollably and yelling for the nurse to leave right away to locate her rightful Black baby.

"That's a white baby! Go find my baby—my Black baby! Y'all switched my baby with a white baby! Jesus, how do I tell my husband that I lost our baby?"

Beyond perplexed and confused about how to manage this unhinged woman, the nurse stood back nervously while awkwardly holding the sweet, unclaimed baby girl. She explained that the darling, denied baby never left the room. Therefore, the soundless, but very much alive, baby was definitely the baby she'd pushed out between her legs. My mama unceremoniously proceeded to curse and call the nurse every unflattering word: bitch, whore, cunt, muthafucker, and everything else but the child of God for nefariously switching her Black baby with this white baby before her eyes. By now, the obstetrician burst into the room to find out what in the Sam Hill was going on since my mama's outrageous antics were heard throughout the hospital floor. The nurse quickly updated the doctor.

The doctor began emphatically explaining to my mama that the lovable, adorable baby was in fact the newborn baby he pulled from her vagina. In the midst of all the noticeable chaos and commotion, my daddy walked in, oblivious, and right up to the doctor, grabbed his irresistible newborn baby, and threw me into the air. He proudly professed to everyone that I looked just like him and that he had the most beautiful baby in the world. My daddy's on-the-spot affirmation of my birthright immediately placated and soothed my mama.

Taking her opportunity while he was mesmerized with me, my mama slyly looked up to inform him, "Since you weren't here, me and Robin changed her name from Kimberly to Terrinee."

My daddy blushed and said, "A beautiful name for my beautiful baby. I don't know if I'm going to be able to go to the army and leave my baby."

Now, it was time for the not-so-little-anymore, perfect baby named by Auntie Robin to shop and pick out the perfect little flower girl dress. At seven years old, I couldn't think of anything I wanted more than to be in Auntie Robin's wedding. All week, I'd been daydreaming about how good-looking I was going to be in my flower girl dress. Auntie Barb, a licensed cosmetologist, would surely give her loyal employee Shirley Temple candy curls to finish my look. Auntie Barb hired me as her assistant in her very own beauty salon, Hot Chocolate, aptly named to describe her own dark and smooth skin tone. Like my grandma Marian, Auntie Barb had fine, long, silky, jet-black, hair. Make no mistake about it: beauty ran in my family.

On the day of my dress appointment, I was sweeping up hair when Auntie Robin busted through the front door of Hot Chocolate with a disturbed look on her face. My first scatterbrained thought was that the wedding of my young life had been called off and I wasn't going to be the flower girl. Thankfully, I was half-wrong. Most regrettably, I was half-right.

"Anthony just called to tell me that Terrinee can't be the flower girl in my wedding. I'm so devastated. I begged him not to do this. But he just told me to stop all my hysterics because she ain't going to be in it and that's final."

My daddy and auntie's fiancée, Joey, had a huge argument over high-dollar, hot goods that one of Joey's friends sold to Pistol Pete's. Certainly, it was not Joey's fault, unbeknownst to him, his friend sold stolen merchandise to my daddy. My daddy didn't see it that way. Street code was, once Joey vouched for this man, he was extending his good name, trust, and reputation that he was an honorable, stand-up person. My daddy trusted this guy because Joey trusted him. Joey disagreed and thought it was ludicrous and illogical for him to be held accountable for another man's actions and that my daddy only had his own business acumen to blame.

To boot, my daddy felt forced to sell the ill-received clothing, Jordache jeans and Members Only jackets, because he simply couldn't afford not to recoup the money he'd paid Joey's friend for the pricey, high-demand merchandise. Either way, the quarrel caused a huge family disagreement with my mama standing with her man and Auntie Robin caught between her brother and husband-to-be, leaving me totally fucked. Just that quickly, I lost my beloved dream role as Auntie Robin's flower girl.

My parents yanked me out of the wedding before anyone could say, "You may kiss your bride." No one consulted me about my ill-feelings and great disappointment regarding this situation. I was totally devastated, as was Auntie Robin. Especially since a strange young girl, who she didn't even know, stood in for me at the wedding. I felt, as a child, I should've been excluded from this absurd adult spat and allowed to have my memorable day in Auntie Robin's wedding.

Secretly, I thought and prayed that my parents would eventually come to their senses before the big day. They never wavered.

As fate would have it, many years later, I finally got to be in Auntie Robin's wedding when she married her second husband, Uncle Dennis. I love Uncle Dennis because he loves him some Robin. He loves her the way Mi Rey loves me. Clearly, I was too old to be a flower girl, but I had an even more significant role this go around, and the best part was that no one could abruptly snatch it from me. I had the distinct and illustrious privilege of being Auntie Robin's maid of honor alongside her two lovely and most-fitting bridesmaids, Auntie Barb and Auntie Pat. Moreover, the super-duper cherry on top was that I gave the wedding reception toast.

Fate would also prove that my daddy was not wrong about Joey's friend who sold him stolen merchandise. This guy was arrested for shoplifting and decided to save his own ass by turning state's evidence against all of the people he duped into buying stolen goods, including my daddy. This thief never briefed the authorities on the fact that my daddy had no idea that the goods were stolen when they were initially acquired.

By this time, Pistol Pete's had two thriving locations: Cesery Boulevard and another on Myrtle Avenue. In their businesses, my parents strategically implemented divide and conquer. My daddy operated the Myrtle Avenue location simply because he was more street-savvy, apt, and capable of handling himself smack dead in the heart of the ghetto. My mama oversaw the Cesery Boulevard location in a nicer part of town. She wasn't alone. Joseph and Pierre, their Haitian, expert tailors, handled the bulk of the alterations for clothes purchased from either location.

On this particular day, I'd been with my daddy at the Myrtle Avenue location while my toddler sister and my mama were alone at

Cesery Boulevard. My daddy was reminiscing with me and my cousin, Keyton, about Pistol Pete's youth basketball team he coached that went undefeated in a citywide league led by Otis Smith, a professional basketball player and starter for the inaugural Orlando Magic team. Naturally, I was the team mascot and cheerleader. I suppose this was where my deep affection for basketball began, like an endless love affair.

In the middle of my daddy's anecdote, one of his friends stopped by the store to chit-chat with him about local police raids looking to recover stolen merchandise: Jordache jeans and Members Only jackets. The police swooped in and raided his next-door neighbor's house earlier that day. Quietly, my daddy's mind began racing with worry about the police targeting our stores next. Without delay or discussion, he quickly ushered his friend out the door using the excuse the store would be closing early today for an unforeseen emergency, but not before sending Keyton home to his sister, Pat.

After he slammed shut and locked the door, my daddy went straight into damage control. He started ordering clueless, little me to go and grab large, black trash bags from the back of the store. I scrambled to grab and toss the bags to him as he frantically began yanking all the Jordache jeans and Members Only jackets down off each hanger and shelf, filling the plastic bags to capacity. Just as we were walking toward the back door to exit, my daddy abruptly dropped the heavily loaded, black trash bags mid-step and dashed back to call our Cesery Boulevard store to give my mama a succinct, cautionary run down. Not a moment sooner than wrapping up his short and sweet recap, the police zoomed in on two wheels skidding outside my mama's location.

She cut my daddy off mid-sentence to whisper right before hanging up the phone. "Keyball, they're here. Don't y'all come here!"

Recall, our Cesery Boulevard location primarily completed alterations and did not carry merchandise for sale. Nonetheless, my mama was completing alterations on two pairs of the Jordache jeans purchased from the Myrtle Avenue store. She needed to hightail and find those stolen jeans and remove the original, incriminating merchandise tags before the police busted inside the store. But it was too late. The police stormed inside, waving and shaking a warrant to search the premises for stolen goods.

At the same damn time, my mama spotted both pairs of Jordache jeans hanging off the sewing machine table, out of their line of sight and behind the checkout counter. Mia quietly sat on the floor unaware of the calamity while playing with her Black baby doll. As a distraction to the police, my mama snatched up Mia while sliding to slyly pop off the price tags from the Jordache jeans ever so discreetly. Instantly, an officer ordered my mama to wait outside until the lawful search warrant had been fully executed. No evidence of stolen goods or any other illegal activities was found during the police's roughshod search of Pistol Pete's.

All of the cops came outside barking at my mama. "Where are the stolen goods?" one of them shouted. We know you have them! Where is your husband? Did he take the stolen goods? If you don't tell us something, you're going to jail today!"

My mama was bullishly non-responsive to the police officer and just continued to stare him down. The universal familia protocol of shut the fuck up.

The most callous, cold-hearted police officer yelled at my mama. "Bitch, do you hear me?"

In a flash, she scowled back to send a crystal clear message that she wasn't afraid of him. "Fuck you, Pig!"

By this time, my mama had effortlessly chewed up and swallowed those two merchandise tags. There was not a single, solitary shred of evidence to implicate my parents in the theft. Additionally, the police dreadfully knew they'd messed up royally after realizing that there were two Pistol Pete's locations. The original search warrant was only for Cesery Boulevard. The same disrespectful cop firmly instructed one of his brothers in blue to handcuff my mama and put her and three-year-old Mia in the back of the car because they would be held until a new, different warrant was legally obtained and properly executed on the other location. In the back of the police car, Mia was hysterically crying in front of the nasty, unpleasant cop until my mama snapped.

"Stop crying. Wipe those tears from your face and don't you dare shed another tear in front of this pig. He's not worth our tears because he's a disgrace. We are going to be just fine, and we'll be home by dinner with your daddy. Do you hear me, Mia?"

Like a programmed clone, Mia instantly stopped crying.

I suppose there weren't any formal child protective services back then since my three-year-old sister was cruelly put into a hair-raising jail cell. However, knowing Mia almost better than I know myself, she preferred under all circumstances to be right beside her mama, even in a jail cell. Thankfully, my daddy and I, by the grace of God, didn't have a face-to-face encounter with the police that night.

On our drive back to our beautiful home, my daddy covertly pulled behind a dumpster and threw the trash bags into it. He didn't set them into a blaze like Uncle Jerome, probably because he planned to return for his merchandise at the appropriate time. On our way home, we stopped by Mickey D's for two cheeseburger happy meals and two quarter pounders with cheese. Once we arrived, I completed my homework and then proceeded to chomp down on my yummy happy meal. I stashed Mia's happy meal in the oven to keep it fresh and warm. My daddy was constantly on and off the phone, working diligently to get my mama and sister home. While my daddy and I waited anxiously, we goofed off, watched TV, and played tonk until he found out the status of my mama and sister.

My daddy taught me how to skillfully play so many card games: go fish, speed, I declare war, gin rummy, spades, bid whist (with and without the kitty), and poker. Playing cards taught me life skills such as analytical and logical competency, how to keep the cheat off me, and how to read people. My daddy wanted Mia and I to be prepared for these streets, so he made merciless monsters and beasts all in one by making us fierce card sharks. He stayed up all night playing and beating me and Mia at card games until we finally whooped him. Also, it homed in on our competitive nature. My daddy never let us beat him. When we won, it was because we'd earned it. The best was that he was proud when we finally beat him.

At that age, I didn't understand the significant difference between owning or renting a house. I only knew we went from renting a modest $125 per month apartment to now living in a "moving on up" $600 per month house off Fort Caroline Road. We were now living in a dreamy, capacious four-bedroom house with an oversized kitchen complete with a washer and dryer as well as a two-car garage sitting on a half-acre of land. Mia and I each had our very own bedrooms. Although we never slept in separate beds, it was still gratifying to have the bona fide, real option. Akin to the Jeffersons, we were grabbing our fair shot of prosperity which made all the sense in the world to me, since my daddy naturally walked just like George Jefferson.

I was inordinately conscious of being the lone Black family in our neighborhood; however, our neighbors were quite friendly. One of our white neighbors had a pool in their backyard and extended an open invitation to swim anytime. The wife stayed home to tend to their house and kids instead of working outside the home. Good googly moogly! She made the most delicious fried bologna sandwiches with yellow mustard on toasted white bread. The edges were trimmed off with precision. It was such a scrumptious and satisfying snack after a strenuous day of swimming. Unlike Mia, who later proved to be wise beyond her years, I hadn't astutely elevated from not eating pork quite yet.

My parents gave the most epic house parties too. My daddy had every pop and soul album that electrified all of their gatherings. Mia and I hid out of sight and marveled at the joy and happiness of these young, beautiful Black people. During the New Year's Eve Party that year, Mia stole a Heineken when no one was watching during our Dom Pérignon champagne toast, hiding in my daddy's tan 1978 Grand Prix in the garage. By the time we found her, she was as drunk as Cooter Brown, caressing the steering wheel and pretending to drive my daddy's car. My parents along with me and the rest of the party laughed our britches off for at least an hour.

Our lives in our new spacious house was simply magnificent and good times except when my mama annoyingly woke us up before daybreak to pack her electric blue, white-top Volkswagen convertible to the brim with our basic belongings. She was pretending to divorce my daddy, yet again, for staying out all night and not coming home for days at a time. She invariably presumed he was either out playing poker, at the dog racetrack, or committing adultery. However, a third possibility of him out smoking crack cocaine categorically should have been contemplated since he was chronically known to go "missing" on a drug marathon when he was getting high. Mia and I downright loathed when my mama resorted to these childish, pointless charades for my daddy's undivided attention. We repeatedly prayed for these boy who cried wolf, senseless tantrums to cease. She wasn't leaving the man she loved madly for nothing.

After eating dinner, doing my homework, and playing games with my daddy, that day was beginning to feel just like any other day before the police showed up at our front door. The doorbell rang and scared the shit out of me and my daddy. Neither of us moved or spoke. We were frozen for about ten drawn out seconds, which felt like an eternity, pondering about who was at our front door. The doorbell rang again, and my daddy walked slow-paced to the front door with me daintily scurrying behind him. Someone on the other side of the door shouted and banged a billy club on our front door.

"It's the police. Open up," an officer yelled.

"Do you have a warrant?" said my daddy. "If so, let me see it. If not, please get off my property because without a warrant I'm not opening my door."

"Sir, we will be back with one. Guaranteed."

As we walked back to the sofa, my inquisitive, growing mind questioned him about not opening the door for the police. I wondered if he was in trouble for not doing so. Thinking back on the police coming to Uncle Fred's apartment in Atlanta, my granddaddy freely and willingly opened the door without asking about a warrant. My street-certified lawyer daddy didn't.

My daddy explained, "Without a warrant, they can't come in our house without my permission, and I'm not letting them come in without a warrant. But I need a lawyer to fix this and keep them from coming back."

After I was safe and secure with Auntie Pat, he turned himself in to the police for the release of my mama and sister later that evening. The police had absolutely no case against my parents or Pistol Pete's.

After a thorough investigation, they dropped all charges. Turned out, my parents were the only people not prosecuted from the Jordache jean and Members Only raids. A short while ago my biggest dream was to be a flower girl in Auntie Robin's wedding. Here and now, I had a new and improved, life-altering dream all because a dumbass criminal decided to lie, steal, and cheat my parents.

"Daddy, when I grow up, I'm going to be a lawyer so I can fix things for you," I said, blushing.

My daddy quickly responded, "You picked a great career because with a law degree you can have any job you want, except be a doctor. You will write your own ticket."

Ironically, about twenty years later, Joey would need a lawyer too. After divorcing Auntie Robin, he married another woman. Just like when he was married to Auntie Robin, Joey had a very tumultuous, unhealthy relationship with substance abuse. From my understanding, after a night of arguing while high on drugs, Joey killed his wife. On December 3, 2003, Joey was sentenced to life in prison without parole. Another life, another family—two families—destroyed by the direct or collateral damage of drugs.

I affirmed at a young age that drugs would not destroy my life. Drugs would not destroy my sister's life. Drugs would not destroy my unborn children's lives. I would not accept that fate. I was hell-bent on breaking my family's generational curses and achieving my far-fetched dream of a better life for me and Mia. The distance I was going from the distance I started seemed impossible, even insurmountable at times. The journey wasn't fair, fast, or without obstacles at every turn. However, I always envisioned myself across the finish line.

My unmatched discipline, God-given intellect, unbreakable faith, unconditional love, with an undying desire to protect my baby sister would get me to my irrefutable dream and take both of us away from this ghetto's godforsaken hell and inescapable traps. From the night the police unlawfully showed up at my house without a warrant, I valiantly, boldly, chartered my fate forward to becoming a lawyer.

I audaciously told anyone who would listen. "When I grow up, I'm going to be a lawyer!"

In those days, girls were pressured to be teachers, nurses, and bank tellers.

Yet, not once did I believe becoming a lawyer was impossible for me. Neither did the Core Four, Grandma Marian, Auntie Robin, or Auntie Barb.

Whenever I was continuously told or impolitely suggested to choose a more suiting profession such as teaching or nursing, my progressive daddy quipped back lightning fast, "Don't tell my daughter that nonsense. She's going to be a lawyer!"

CHAPTER 5

"Run And Don't Stop"

My parents were both working doggedly in our businesses, which meant that Mia and I automatically became responsible for the household duties. Most times, we cooked, cleaned, shopped for groceries, did the laundry, and made sure we completed our daily schoolwork. In my childish mind, the welcomed dysfunction was magical, creative, and tribal—we were arrogantly the Core Four.

My parents were self-actualizing and were surprisingly transparent about everything, which emboldened us to become the best versions our ourselves, even at eight and four years old. Academically, my daddy taught me all of the material I would be covering in school well in advance: how to count, color, read, write and solve math problems. By the first grade, I knew my times table through the twelves, which wasn't taught in the school's curriculum until the third grade.

"It's my responsibility to teach my children. Teachers should just reinforce. I will teach you at home first and then school will be just for practice and repetition," Daddy told me.

Since they trained us early, my parents trusted us without doubt to complete our schoolwork. Once, my mama mistakenly signed my weekly graded work sent home. The teacher called to say the signature didn't match the usual signature from previous weeks. My mama chuckled inside and replied that her husband signed her name but assured the teacher that she'd reviewed every assignment. She was tickled because she was well-aware that I always signed her name for both Mia and me. Mama made the mistake of signing her own name when she knew good and gotdamn well that was my job. Going forward, she continued to let me sign all paperwork from school. Since Mia and I were both honor roll students, my parents never gave a second thought about us doing our work. They coached us well, and I had a master plan. I knew for sure that I was getting out of the ghetto, and I knew doubly that my brain was my only ticket out.

My mama wasn't happy to be called in for a parent-teacher conference to discuss concerns about Mia skipping recess daily to complete her homework for the following day. The teacher claimed she thought Mia could've been experiencing physical abuse at home. Why would that white lady say that to my half-crazy, sensitive Black mama? Unapologetically, my mama proceeded to curse the teacher out for calling her to the school for such bullshit.

"My child is not being abused at home. She's very loved. It's apparent that you don't understand smart, disciplined Black kids. Who in the hell calls a parent to school because their child did their schoolwork in school? Who? Does that make any damn sense?"

Mia simply was a great taskmaster at a young age. She concluded that if she skipped recess to complete her homework for the day, she would have significantly more playtime in the evening at home; if nothing else, Mia and I were practical and logical. Of course, the teacher never bothered Mia or my mama again. I was always obsessed with school, making sure Mia and I did well at every turn. We were avid readers, constantly looking up unknown words in the dictionary to increase our literacy and reading comprehension.

Believe it or not, I founded a high-demand school in my den for the neighborhood kids. In class, I made all the kids call me, "Ms. Gundy." Everyone complied without complaint. I collected old copies of worksheets from teachers during the school year to prepare a well-organized, deliberate lesson and gathered adequate school supplies. Our daily schedule consisted of hard start and stop times which included lunch; I made fried bologna sandwiches just like our neighbor. Our recess was kickball in my backyard. I didn't allow late students in my class. Everyone busted their asses to be on time for school. Their parents loved my school because of the structure it provided, and it kept us safely out of the streets. Moreover, it was free, quality education, if I do say so myself.

In the summertime, my school was at full capacity, I conducted a rigorous interview process to determine who was serious about learning. In my school, Mia held the only guaranteed spot at four years old. How could I deny my baby sister access to my school? I could never do that, especially since I was her full-time caregiver. Where I went, she went. Auntie Robin's only child, Ronald, also attended, but I required him to interview like the rest of the bunch to avoid the appearance of nepotism.

Truthfully, I tyrannized him to earn his spot to harden him for those Duval streets. His spot was also guaranteed, just unannounced. Being raised more as our brother than a cousin made him a shoo-in. We were triple trouble. Ronald was known as the fire-starter of our family. No matter how many times Auntie Robin whopped him, he set things in our homes on fire. Ironically, he never burned any houses down, yet I innocently set two apartments a blaze myself. Although Ronald was a typical boy, mainly there for recess and free food, he worked hard not to disappoint me. He loved me so very much. To tell the truth, Mia only cared about PE and free lunch too, but that didn't keep me from being tough on both of them. My other students needed to know that if my sister and cousin were pushed hard, I expected as much or a lot more from them.

I used to take offense at being told I should become a teacher, because I was already a teacher at seven years old. If I hadn't decided to become a lawyer to help my daddy, I would've been a professional math teacher. Teaching my sister, cousins, and neighborhood kids turned out to be quite fulfilling. Not only did I look forward to teaching, but I also equally looked forward to learning every day. The more I taught my students, the more I learned myself. I especially enjoyed the summer reading that I assigned for my class. I even extended the readings year-round for me and Mia. We read books religiously at lightning speed, which I'm sure contributed to our high comprehension in various school subjects. More importantly, we traveled an illuminating world through our reading, so we never felt trapped in the ghetto. We always knew there was a great big world waiting. Duval wasn't ever able to trick us into believing we had a ceiling over our heads.

My neighborhood school came to a quick, unexpected halt once we moved out of our spacious, luxurious house. Now we were back with the renters for $300 per month a second time at the Four Seasons Apartments. My daddy was no longer selling enough weed to maintain our ritzy lifestyle and his crack cocaine habit simultaneously. These apartments seemed less classy this time around and looked more like a dump, especially after living in first-rate houses with spacious backyards. To add insult to injury, our bills were constantly paid late or not at all, resulting in the lights and telephone being disconnected and having multiple cars repossessed. With nothing but excuses and false promises, my daddy went on to rub salt in the wound when he moved his "daddy," Tody, into our modest three-bedroom apartment. He gave him Mia's room for a couple of months. Tody was having hard times after going blind. How in the hell can we help someone having hard times when we were having hard times ourselves? That summed up my parents—having a heart of gold and giving to the needy the best way they knew how.

Be that as it may, this was Mia and I's first time meeting our "grandfather," since we'd always been told Isaac was our amazing, wonderful granddaddy. Maybe we didn't care for Tody because he wasn't Isaac or maybe because he was a rude, smelly chain-smoker. Him calling us "little cockroaches" had plenty to do with our disdain. Seriously, how did someone move in our house and call us names? Later in life, Grandma Marian randomly told us a vile story that would explain and justify why we intuitively never liked Tody.

The Core Four still managed to have a good laugh in tough times. Mia and I were jumping up and down on our parents' bedroom mattress and left a huge hole in their wall. Our beating came from lying about rearranging the furniture to hide our bad behavior. As always, I volunteered to take the twenty licks in my hand before Mia; she was deathly afraid of spankings. My daddy never spanked us because he didn't want his girls to be comfortable with a man's strike, and my mama only beat us with a belt in our hand for fear of leaving noticeable lashes or bruises on our fair-skinned bodies. The method never mattered to Mia; she just didn't want no whooping. When it was her turn to take her twenty licks, she took off running back and forth around their bed despite my mama shouting for her to stop. My daddy and I just watched. Finally, my mama caught Mia, but she screamed and kicked her way loose again.

"Keyball, you're going to have grab her and sit on her!"

"No. Just leave her alone."

My mama was determined to show Mia who was boss that night and didn't succumb until my daddy was holding Mia over his lap with my mama attempting to spank her. My daddy and I laughed so hard at this ridiculous scene; he couldn't hold Mia for long either. Finally, my mama gave in and joined the laughter. Mia had escaped punishment once again.

Daily, our lives grew more and more unpredictable. My daddy still held his job at Publix while running two businesses, but he was also doing drugs a lot more. This pressure took him from selling marijuana as a petty dealer to a pure cocaine drug dealer to maintain the overwhelming number of monthly bills. The Core Four and the other big-time drug dealers in my family were the only ones aware of my daddy selling drugs—well, except for when he was selling Viagra pills for $20 a pop when I was a teenager. Everybody and their mama knew about him selling those little blue pills, but no one had a clue about the cocaine.

My daddy would also make a run or two down from Miami to the Florida-Georgia line to pick up eighteen to twenty ounces of cocaine for my mama's brother who was moving weight in South Georgia. He refused to cross the state line into Georgia with drugs from fear that the state patrol would automatically stop him with his Florida tag. My uncle would have to send someone to meet us right before the state line. Stupidly or intelligently, he took me along as to look more family oriented and less narco-runnerish. It worked. We got pulled over once with almost $20,000. That amount of cash would warrant an explanation. Thankfully, the state trooper saw me in the back reading my book and let him go with a warning without searching the vehicle.

My daddy could've maintained this facade while selling cocaine for much longer if he hadn't become a Junkie. Everyone knows the number one rule is to never get high on your own supply! In his defense, my daddy made a gallant effort, because by any stretch of the imagination, all of this was still quite impressive for a Junkie. Seriously, how in the world did my daddy escape without a criminal drug history? To the rest of the world, he was merely a hard-working family man with a full-time job who managed two successful family businesses along with his pretty little wife.

Pretty as my mama was, it didn't stop her and my daddy from having serious marital issues, even after surviving the birth of his first son, Mario, with another woman in 1981. Of course, there was the initial shock, pain, and embarrassment for my mama when Mario was born, but she never considered leaving her adulterous husband. After laying eyes on Mario, she couldn't help but love his cute yet familiar face.

She always said, "Babies are innocent and shouldn't be punished for the sins of adults."

My mama loved Mario, welcomed him into our home, and helped raise him with my daddy. Mario even calls her "mama" to this day. On the other hand, her relationship with Mario's mother was antagonistic for many years. Mario's mama sliced my mama's leg wide-open, leaving a permanent scar during a fight between them over my daddy. My mama never got over being assaulted—but who would? Many people thought my mama was a saint for loving my brother, and she had saint-like characteristics.

Years later, my mama's circumstance with Mario served as an example in my own failed marriage. My former husband also had a son, Devin, who is a month older than my own biological son, with another woman while married to me. Just the same, I love Devin. We have a great relationship and I continually work hard for my kids to have a close relationship with him. As far as I'm concerned, he's also my family. While I wouldn't claim to be a saint, I'm proud to say my mama taught me well.

The day would come when my mama was so fed up with my daddy's bottomless, endless adultery that she felt compelled to have a romantic relationship with another man—one of my daddy's friends. Too much, too little, too late was where my mama remorsefully drifted, leading to her own unfaithfulness. Out of guilt or spite, or both, she confessed her misdeeds to my daddy. I was startled out of sunken sleep by my daddy's thunderous shouting and my mama's reverberating cries. I heard him packing to leave her for a single indiscretion. Every dog has its day, and some have two. It was downright laughable for him to believe he had the luxury of tearing our family apart because my mama cheated after suffering years of his embarrassing track record. Muthafucka, please!

As an attorney in training, my disgruntled parents presented me with my first divisive case at the tender age of eight years old that unforgettable night. After calming my daddy down, I sat both of my parents across from each other at our dark oakwood dining room table with me seated at the head. I allowed my daddy to speak first, expressing his deep pain for her betrayal and unfaithfulness. Then, I allowed my mama to express her feelings of bitterness and remorse for hurting him. The two of them carried on back and forth for over an hour and half with me refereeing, still from the head of the table. I intervened to end this mediation, once each party was given ample opportunity to express themselves. Besides, I was tired and tired of their foolishness—even at eight years old.

I probably should've cared more about my mama's infidelity, but my daddy's habitual indiscretions made me numb and lacking in compassion. I told my daddy he had it coming due to his prior history of cheating, especially after my mama suffered the embarrassment of an extramarital affair resulting in a whole entire human and permanent physical scaring! I further proceeded to state that my mama was never to be seen with that man again, and that my daddy was going to forgive her as she had done for him too many times to count. But under no circumstance was he leaving my mama for one little-big indiscretion. Even further, I—we—wouldn't and couldn't let that sorry ass man rip our family apart, so it was time for both of them to grow up. My daddy was so impressed with my handling of the situation, mediating them, and my comprehension of the issues, that he easily acquiesced with my demands.

He said, "One thing is for sure. My baby girl damn sure gonna be a lawyer. Absolutely!" All three of us burst out laughing while group hugging as my daddy turned to kiss and hug my mama, telling her he loved her and that they would get through it.

Of course, my daddy didn't change his Tony the Tiger stripes. For everyone but my mama, my daddy's perpetual and habitual infidelity was predictable. Time and time again, after violently attacking him or firing her gun at him, sometimes shooting our TV, she continuously forgave him and took him back with open arms. Yet, still, he continued his terrible habit of not coming home for days. My mama's first inclination was that he was either gambling money we didn't have or with another woman. I would bet my last dollar my daddy wasn't gambling or cheating again, but instead freebasing. Nevertheless, he hadn't been home in two days and my mama was losing her shit. I was sure her own addiction, snorting lines of powder cocaine during this tirade, added to the chaos. To my knowledge, my mama has never smoked cracked cocaine. My daddy has never introduced crack cocaine to anyone, especially my mama.

I would've never guessed what happened next when Mia and I saved my mama's life one scary night. My sister and I loved my mama so very much. Per usual, we tried to console her to no avail. It was clear to us that my mama battled chronic, manic depression because she'd made several failed attempts to harm herself in the past. Shortly after I was born, my mama slit both of her wrists in a suicide attempt.

She regularly told my sister and I, "No one loves me and I'm going to jump from the ledge of our balcony to end it all."

We pleaded with her not to jump but we were simultaneously vexed at her for disregarding our love. We were right there with her—always right there! We were there caring for and loving her every minute of every day, so our feelings were hurt when she spoke such foolishness. Back then, mental healthcare was nonexistent, especially for Black folks. My mama was young, naive, inexperienced, and dealt with a lot of emotions. She didn't know how to cope, which led to her suicidal tendencies. My mama should've never felt ashamed about her mental health state or how she survived. She was above judgment in my opinion. She was thrusted into a fast-paced, unhealthy lifestyle with a loving yet cheating husband whom she adored and worshipped while attempting to stay on solid ground. It was a lot for a young wife and mother to balance. She was simply unprepared to navigate it all.

We were all prone to having dark thoughts due to our tumultuous life experiences, especially considering the events we'd already survived. However, I am grateful I've never had thoughts of suicide once in my life. But bad things happen to good people all the time, especially good people like us—the Core Four.

My mama almost died that night. Actually, I'm sure she died, but me and Mia revived her after she overdosed off of my daddy's supply. We all knew where my daddy hid his coke stash—at the bottom of the dirty clothes hamper in our bathroom. My mama locked herself in the bathroom. I'm not sure how long she'd been there. Once we realized she'd been non-responsive in the bathroom for an extended period, we decided it was time to pick the door lock. We were really good at picking locks with a wire hanger, since doors were often inadvertently locked in our homes, or maybe they locked us out. Either way, we got in.

We found her passed out on the floor with an ounce of cocaine busted open with about half of it missing. We were certain it was up her nose. Hear me and hear me clearly—we were not ever fucking going to DFACS—not today and not ever! We were going to keep our family together no matter what happened. My parents always told us the number one rule in chaos and danger was never to panic, and to always use your brain to think of a way out. Our lives also led me to become a very organized person with my thoughts and things; it was the only way to reasonably control and prepare for chaos.

First things first, we had to get my mama up off that floor because her body was ice-cold, but she was still breathing. Thank God! We picked her tiny, but heavy, body up and placed her in Mia's bed. We avoided her bedroom at all costs after getting a whooping for putting a hole in the wall. We put my incoherent mama in Mia's bed, covered her with blankets, and grabbed a warm rag to put on her cold forehead. I told Mia to hold the warm compress there until I returned. My mama was not going to die—not on my watch! But I had to prepare for all possible outcomes, which meant I needed to get that drug-infested bathroom cleaned up. I wrapped a scarf around my mouth and nose, then put on my mama's yellow dishwashing gloves, because I certainly didn't want to inhale any amount of cocaine.

I mocked my parents' example and heeded their words: "Never touch the cocaine, Terrinee. Never!"

I gathered the opened ounce of cocaine, along with the other two ounces in the dirty clothes hamper and flushed all the dope down the toilet. Next, I vacuumed the bathroom floor to get all the residue left behind from my mama's mess. Finally, I emptied the bag from the vacuum cleaner, changed out of the clothes I cleaned up in, and took it all to the dumpster to ensure that there was no evidence of drugs in our house. It was enough that my mama was sick or worse, but my parents couldn't go to jail or lose their kids.

When I finished, I went into Mia's bedroom to check on my mama who was sweating profusely but still unconscious. I told Mia we had to make sure she was breathing and sent her to grab a mirror out of the bathroom while I went to get a cold towel to cool her body down. I had no idea what time it was, but it was the middle of the night. I slid the mirror under her nose, and it fogged up. Perfect, she was still alive! Note, my daddy still wasn't home. So, we still couldn't call the ambulance. If we did, as soon as they discovered she'd overdosed, in the system we'd go, realizing our worst nightmare. I know it was a lot for eight- and four-year-old children to have this level of deductive, critical thinking, but we did. In hindsight, we should've called a family member for help. But we couldn't have them judging our parents or taking us from them either. Our parents needed us. We wouldn't leave our parents for anyone.

Still, no sight of my daddy. Mia and I continued the lifesaving system I created, alternating hot and cold towels on mama's forehead every thirty minutes. Being from a churchgoing family, we knelt and prayed for her to wake as we'd been taught. We didn't sleep a wink that night. We operated like well-oiled machines, changing every half hour from hot compress to cold, checked her breathing with the mirror, prayed, held hands, and repeated. Our adrenaline soared as we focused on caring for our mama. We were focused on surviving—even if it was just for the night until my daddy got home. Finally, my mama woke up!

We jumped up and down and screamed, "Thank you, Jesus! Thank you, Jesus!" while bear hugging my mama.

She had no idea what was going on or no memory of what happened. Just then, my daddy walked in, and we explained every detail. I thought my daddy was going to be furious with me for flushing his dope down the toilet.

He sweetly said, "I don't care about no drugs. I just care that all my girls are okay. I'm so proud of y'all for taking such good care of your mama. Next time, call 911. Don't worry about us. We can handle whatever, but I can't handle losing any of you. I can't live without y'all. You understand? Daddy loves y'all so much. I'm so sorry I wasn't here."

None of us stayed mad at him no matter how much he disappointed us. He had all of us wrapped around his finger. I don't think my mama even asked where he'd been, which was very unusual for her. We all just moved on like the night before never happened. It was possible that she felt guilty for her overdose and was primarily focused on pulling herself together. Although it would take years for my mama to finally kick her drug habit, she did it once my daughter, Mia Michelle, was born. She re-dedicated her life to the Lord and was determined that she'd be a better example for her grandchild. And that she is. My mama has been clean and sober for over sixteen years with an amazing relationship with all her grandchildren: Mia Michelle, Kevin, Terrinee Elle, and Mia Elle.

Every time we'd avert a catastrophe, my daddy made a valiant attempt to fly straight for a period. Give him credit for trying, but it never lasted long. Not long after my mama's overdose episode, my daddy left his eight- and four-year-old daughters stranded alone in the middle of the night. Regularly, my daddy left cash on the kitchen counter for Mia and me to do the grocery shopping. Normally, we rode our bikes to grab the groceries. On this day, we needed a car ride to be home before nightfall.

"Daddy, it's grocery shopping day. I have made the grocery list already and I need you to take us to Publix," I said.

My daddy replied, "No problem. I'm headed out now. Are y'all ready to go?"

We hopped in our only car, my mama's convertible blue Volkswagen with the white top, and headed out. Five to six minutes later, our daddy pulled to the front of the store, let us out, and said he would be back in thirty minutes. We perfectly timed ourselves to be done in twenty-five minutes and sat out front on a bench waiting for him with our filled cart of groceries. Our parents were habitually late, so we were not alarmed when he hadn't returned in exactly thirty minutes. While we waited, we searched through our grocery bags and found snacks to munch on. We carried on entertaining ourselves with That's My Car, one of our made-up games where we picked out and pretended we owned luxury vehicles.

We were so consumed with our childhood game that we didn't realize that our daddy was over an hour late until a white woman walked by and asked, "Are you all okay? Where are your parents?"

Without hesitation, I covered for him. "They're in the store. We're good. Thank you," I said.

Mind your own fucking business, lady.

We had to move from the front door as not to draw attention to unsupervised Black kids. We decided on a remote area in the parking lot where no one would notice us except for our late-ass daddy. We sat behind our cart of groceries for hours until Publix closed with no sight of our daddy. It was pitch black in the parking lot since the store had turned off the outside lampposts. The temperature dropped leaving us so chilly that we resorted to putting our arms inside our T-shirts.

Mia and I had an insanely, unhealthy amount of faith in our parents. Against our instincts and better judgment, we still believed, while shivering behind that grocery cart, that either one or both would arrive soon. We couldn't fathom the possibility of being completely abandoned. Even further, due to our reoccurring fear of being permanently taken from our parents by the authorities, we also couldn't ask for help. We would risk child protective services being contacted, or worse, a perverted stranger could violate us. What a fucking conundrum! So, we sat and waited and waited, then waited some more. No daddy! No mama! No one came to get us. It was now well past midnight.

We asked ourselves many questions: "Where the hell do our parents think we are? Why haven't they come looking for us? There was no way they would have just left us…"

We opined in the middle of the night, our minds racing with thoughts of the most unpleasant acts, including the possibility of being hit by a car, kidnapped, raped, or worse: killed. After my mama almost died, we were prone to imagine the worse waiting in that cold, empty, and dark parking lot into the wee-wee hours of the morning. No one, not even our parents, was coming to save us.

It was time for us to move from that parking lot and get home safely to find out what happened to our parents. We concluded that something terrible had happened for neither of them to have come. The distance between Publix and our front apartment door was less than a mile. We walked and rode our bikes on that path more times than we could count in broad daylight. But this time we had a full cart of groceries that we'd paid good money for, and we weren't leaving our food behind. I explained to Mia that we had no choice but to get ourselves home, so we had to foot it. I made sure she understood to run as fast as she could in front of the buggy, where I could always see her.

I told her, "Run and don't stop for nothing."

As many times before, it was up to two little girls to figure out how to survive another fucked-up situation. Mia obeyed, and we ran home faster than Usain Bolt ran the hundred-meter relay with our hearts pounding and beating against our chests. Fortunately, we made it safe and sound with no incident except for racing hearts. We walked in and our mama asked us where our daddy was because she thought we were with him. When he finally did make it home later that night, he blamed her, claiming she was responsible for picking us up. They spent an hour blaming each other for abandoning us.

Mia and I knew he was to blame because he had our only vehicle, but we really didn't care. We were honestly just happy that nothing bad had happened to them and that we were all home together, safe and sound. Blame it on his head and crack cocaine, not his heart. They were both shoulders back, head held high proud of us for doing exactly what they had prepared us to do—stick together and survive no matter what. There were no victims or villains in the Core Four. We had ups and downs, highs and lows, light and dark, but we never dwelled on anything. We were simply happy to be alive and together. Love, not crack cocaine, is the most powerful drug on Earth. We had an abundance of love in my family. The Core Four were high on each other!

CHAPTER 6

"I'm Going To Be A Judge"

At the tender age of three, I accidentally set our home on fire, for the first time, in our initial Four Season's Apartment before Mia was born—and then a second time at nine years old. The fire was drug-related, but not crack cocaine in this instance. It was that Mary Jane a.k.a. marijuana. It was very common for young folks to smoke marijuana. Much hasn't changed since the 1970s. Both of my parents smoked a lot of weed, which was seen as harmless except they would allow me to roam around the house finding humor in whatever mischievous thing I got into as a toddler.

My first adventure of navigating the wilds of our apartment, was during one of my daddy's card parties. My parents were young, in love, and enjoyed entertaining their friends. Even more than entertaining, my daddy loved having his kid around in true "daddy's little girl" fashion. I followed his every step. I even sat outside the bathroom door waiting for him to finish doing his business. My daddy and I had an unbreakable bond that could've easily led to envy or jealousy from my mama.

The dichotomy of mother and daughter relationships can be difficult or tricky, especially in my case. But I must give my mama credit. She was happy and supportive of my daddy and I's close relationship. She still wanted a second baby because it felt like my daddy had robbed her of true motherhood, considering I was his shadow. She wanted some of that obsession for herself. And who could blame her? For a while, her wish came true. Eventually, my daddy had two babies and my mama just threw her hands up at the fact that we were both "daddy's little girls."

She'd repeatedly say, "Terrinee is her daddy's baby, and then I finally got a baby too. Mia was all mine until he stole both of my babies."

As a baby, I sat calmly in my daddy's lap at the card table while he held me with one hand and covered his cards with the other. The card game often got intense with a lot of playful shouting and talking trash. After a while, I would climb down, sit at my daddy's feet and play with my toys. I never went too far from his presence. I wasn't walking yet, but I crawled like a racehorse and pulled up on everything in sight. The story goes, that as the card playing grew more intense, I apparently pulled up on the table and grabbed a beer can, flopped back on the floor at my daddy's feet and began drinking from the beer can with absolutely no one paying attention to me. Suddenly, I stood up on my feet without any help and took off walking back and forth through our living room, beer can still in hand.

My mama screamed, "Terrinee is walking! She's walking!"

Daddy met her excitement. "Look at my baby go!"

Now, captivating the attention of everyone in the room, I stopped and took another sip out of the beer can in my hand. This time everyone noticed!

"Keyball, I'm going to kill you. You gave my baby a Colt 45."

He laughed hysterically and replied, "Woman, you got to be cold crazy and out of your mind. I wouldn't give my baby no beer. The girl reached up there and got it herself. You have to admit that that Colt 45 got her walking real good. Only my child would start walking drunk."

Everyone got a roaring laugh out of my daddy's joke. Considering my childhood track record, it was no surprise when I set my room on fire the first time. My daddy was smoking a joint while he lay on the sofa, then put the joint in the ashtray while watching TV. My busybody self picked up the joint, unbeknownst to my daddy, to play with the flare of orange, yellow, and reddish colors with which I was enthralled. I walked to my bedroom with the lit joint.

As toddler behavior goes, I got distracted with my toys and laid the joint on a coloring book. I sat on my floor quietly entertaining myself with my Black baby doll. There was no alarm to signal the fire in our apartment. Like smoke can do, it filled the house as its own alarm, alerting my daddy to the danger. He immediately came looking for me. I never made a sound while he called my name, and the panic in his voice intensified as he approached my room where the fire started.

"Thank you, Jesus," he said when he saw me unharmed.

He grabbed me from the floor and darted toward the front door as I continued to clutch my baby doll. "Come on, baby. Let's get the hell out of this gotdamn place," he said.

He must've really been scared, and the situation was serious because my daddy rarely curses. We ran down the stairs, backed away from the apartment building, and stood watching as the smoke escaped our apartment.

My daddy continued holding me and just kept kissing my face until I blurted out, "Cigarette."

I didn't know what a cigarette was, I just repeated what I heard the adults saying about the rolled paper with fire at the end.

"Cigarette? Girl, you did that?" my daddy questioned while smiling and laughing.

In that moment, he concluded what happened. He wasn't mad at me though. He always made me feel as if he thought I was perfect, even when I wasn't, which gave me an extreme amount of confidence and self-assuredness throughout my life.

Right before I burned down our other apartment in a second fire at Four Seasons, Mia's first major accident happened. It was an average, sunny day when Mia and I were doing what we did best—horsing around and enjoying the fresh air. Earlier that day, we'd been racing each other to the top of a tree. I won, of course. I always won. I was a great climber. I discovered I was also good at rock climbing the first time I tried. I'd been climbing trees my whole life; rock climbing was like climbing trees. So, I was a climber, and Mia thought she could fly.

At Four Seasons, we always lived in the second-floor apartments. My daddy adamantly believed that living on the first floor was a security risk, inviting burglars and/or violators into our home. Mia was a miniature daredevil, always looking for a thrill, even at five years old. She regularly trotted her little compact, muscular body to the top of the outdoor stairs and slid all the way down the dull, metal banister to the very bottom while ferociously giggling. My mama, my daddy, and I all repeatedly chastised her about such supremely dangerous behavior. Unfazed by our daunting warnings, Mia continued to drop down the rail at her pleasure.

Mia would laugh and scream. "I can fly. I can fly. See, I'm flying," she'd say.

My mama persistently forewarned. "You're not going to be happy until you fall and bust your head to the white meat."

Mia was attempting her normal slide when she hurdled over to the right, lost her balance, and plunged down the flight of stairs smack-dab on her face. Lying there stretched-out, facedown, I didn't know if she was breathing, paralyzed, or dead. I had never been so petrified in my entire life. I, Terrinee Lynette Gundy, would not, could not, live without Mia Michelle Gundy.

I rushed to my baby sister, who was sprawled over the cement below and wailed. "Mia! God, please let her be alive. God, please let her be okay."

Seconds later, Mia squealed with agony, and I knew she was alive. Our downstairs neighbor came out and tried to aid us.

I hollered at the neighbor as I gently raised Mia to carry her up the stairs to our home. "Get back. Don't touch my sister. I got her!"

The nosy-ass neighbor asked, "Where's your mother?"

With my piercing, green eyes, I said, "Taking a nap. I can wake her up to help with my sister if you back up and leave me alone."

Finally, and thankfully, she retreated to her apartment because my mama and daddy weren't home. Furthermore, our fucking telephone service had been disconnected once again, so there was no way to notify either of them of the emergency. I was very nervous as I climbed those stairs with Mia in my arms, trying to shield us both from the threat of being taken away. I hadn't even had the chance to assess her injuries before we got inside the house.

I gently placed Mia on the sofa to examine her for blood, broken bones, sprains, scratches, or bruises. I looked for anything that would force me to involve the authorities and break up our family; the only thing worse than losing our family would be Mia dying. Look at God.

There was nothing life-threatening. Mia escaped the fall with no fever, with merely a busted chin that healed without leaving a scar. I didn't need to be a physician to know that this was something I could handle. From the daytime stories, I knew that she couldn't go to sleep, in case of a concussion. I wrapped her in a blanket, gave her half of a Tylenol to prevent a fever, and badgered her all day to keep the tired sleepyhead awake. It worked.

When my mama got home, we rushed Mia to the emergency room where the doctor gave the same instructions I'd been implementing all day. He told our mama that if Mia ran a fever or began slurring words, bring her back. I normally would've been worried about getting in trouble, but not this time. I saved Mia's life, so I knew I was in the clear. To celebrate, my mama rewarded Mia and I with our favorite McDonald's hot fudge ice cream sundae with nuts.

Unfortunately, ice cream wouldn't fix when I burned down our other place in a second fire at Four Seasons Apartments! This day was not unusual from any other school day when Mia and I would come home to fix dinner, do our homework, do the rest of our chores, and get ready for bed. We were the definition of latchkey kids. By this time, we'd seen our parents smoking joints or snorting powder cocaine and became fully aware of their drug addiction. They'd leave drug paraphernalia around the house like the feather "roach" tweezers, dusty plates or mirrors, and miniature weight scales. There was also the stain of seeing crack paraphernalia—glass pipes or used soda cans with holes in them—just casually laying around our home. However, I cannot reiterate this enough: I give special thanks to baby Jesus for never letting us see our daddy in the undesirable act of smoking crack cocaine with a pipe to his mouth.

Mia and I thought this day was no different until we attempted to switch on the lights, and they weren't working. We tried calling our parents to tell them the lights were off again, but the phone was off too. Thanks, crack cocaine! Onward and upward—we proceeded with doing homework until our parents came home to hopefully rectify the matter. We lit candles throughout the house, including the kitchen, living room, bathroom and our bedrooms. We were prepared with plenty of candles because this happened regularly now that our daddy was a full-blown Junkie.

The Four Seasons Apartment finally grew on me this second go round after accepting that we wouldn't be living in a large, beautiful house. Through my nine-year-old sentimental spirit, I grew to adore my bedroom. I had two Michael Jackson posters on the wall: one with him wearing a red leather jacket with one glitter glove and the other with him in a yellow sweater, which was my absolute favorite. I also had a matching desk with a bookcase hutch complete with books, including a dictionary and a pristine, full set of encyclopedias to accompany my full-size bed.

I sat at my desk and started my homework by candlelight. Mia came to tell me she'd finished her homework and was now hungry, just as I completed my homework. We went to the kitchen, and I made two sandwiches, because without electricity, I couldn't use the stove to cook. We sat at the kitchen table eating our sandwiches, chitchatting about the day and pondering when our parents would get home.

"Shh, do you hear that?" I said to Mia.

She was non-responsive but acutely aware of the noises. We both believed that someone was in the house, possibly for my daddy's dwindling drug stash hidden in the dirty clothes hamper. I slowly got up from the chair. Mia followed directly behind me as I approached the coat closet to grab the machete that Uncle Jerome brought back from Vietnam. Holding the machete with a tight two-hand grasp, I tiptoed around the corner near the back of the house toward the noise.

The noises increased to crackling and popping sounds as we rounded the corner just past Mia's bedroom. I pushed Mia farther behind me and grasped the machete even tighter, preparing myself to attack whatever uninvited guest was in our home. We arrived at my bedroom door, where the noises were clearly coming from, only to be frozen in time. We stood and stared at my desk hutch engulfed in flames from floor to ceiling. And yet again, no fire alarm went off.

I dropped the machete on the ground and instructed Mia to run to my friend's house to call 911. I recalled a PBS after-school special (we watched a lot of PBS growing up) saying that water spreads fire and it was better to smother the blaze. I grabbed the blanket off my bed and started waving at the fire. Seconds later, I knew I had to get out of that apartment, or I would die in it. The blaze had grown entirely too fast and massive. I decided to make a run for it, and just before reaching the front door, I remembered my daddy's drug stash.

The police and fire department were most certainly coming to our apartment with this ongoing fire; there was no way I could leave without getting rid of the drugs. I diverted from the front door, grabbed a dish towel from the kitchen to cover my mouth and nose to avoid smoke inhalation (PBS again), and then dashed to the back of the apartment, past the engulfed bedroom, and got the drugs. The stash was low, and that was good because one flush down the toilet got rid of it all. Again, I realize this was a lot for a nine-year-old child to have the presence of mind for this level of deductive, critical thinking, but I did. By this age, my life experiences along with Linda and Anthony's teachings had prepared me for exactly that level of intense problem solving.

I then sprinted to my friend's house so fast that Mia and I got to their front door at the exact same time. I was so scared my parents were going to be livid with me for burning up the apartment and losing everything including my daddy's moneymaking stash. He needed his drug stash to hustle, so we could replace everything that was currently in our apartment burning to ashes. The truth was he was doing more drugs than selling at that time. My position was, and is, that the side effect of crack cocaine caused that fire, not me and Mia! The firefighters, police, and ambulance showed up before my parents and kept asking us a bunch of questions. We absolutely knew what to do—shut the fuck up. We didn't say one word. Mia never spoke anyway; I always spoke on her behalf.

My daddy always said, "You've always been Mia's lawyer. You do all the talking and negotiating for the both of you."

When my parents finally pulled up, we both dove into their arms.

"Daddy, I'm sorry," I said. "I'm so sorry I burned the house up! We lost everything, and I had to throw it [the drugs] away! I had no choice—I had to! I'm so sorry, Daddy. Please don't be mad at me."

My daddy picked me up off the ground and pulled me into his arms and looked me dead in my blue-green eyes. "I don't care about none of that stuff. It's all material stuff that I can get back ten times over. But I could never get another Terrinee. I could never get another Mia. How could I be mad at you for saving you and your sister? Naw, baby girl. Daddy can't be mad at you. I'm proud of you. You are my hero. You saved you and your sister. You're my hero. Daddy loves you and your sister so much. I'm so proud of my girls. Y'all my heroes!"

Later that year I visited one of my own heroes: Auntie Barb. She and her girls, Tanishia, Angeal, and Winona, lived in River Oaks Apartments on Harts Road. I loved spending time with my three older female cousins, especially Tanishia who was four years older than me. She had an illustrious Barbie doll collection to be envied. I was more interested in toy race cars, trucks, trains, riding dirt bikes and ATVs, or shooting BB guns. But I was most interested in making cash money.

However, I did believe I should've had a similar menagerie of Barbie dolls as Tanishia. The closest I came was with the release of the Black Judge Barbie doll on September 16, 2019. It was such a serendipitous day since it was also my grandma's birthday. The Black Judge Barbie with the short bob haircut looks just like me. I bought my daughter, Mia Michelle, and my nieces, Terrinee Elle and Mia Elle, as well as my youngest sisters, Joan and Glo, Judge Barbie for Christmas that year to subtly encourage them to become judges as well. My daughter, nieces, and little sisters may not become judges, but I have a strong hand already in ensuring that they at least get law degrees.

Auntie Barb worked hard to make sure I became a lawyer. She was so super cool, and a Bad Mama Jama. My daddy said that she was the best swing dancer Fernandina Beach saw during their weekend parties. She was especially sweet as good ole American apple pie to us. Mia was her favorite and I was a real close second. Besides, I still had Auntie Robin. But when it mattered the most, Auntie Barb was always there for me. She sacrificed for us like we were her own daughters, just like my grandma and Auntie Robin—a debt I could never adequately repay!

Before dedicating her life to Christ, Auntie Barb was a real badass and didn't tolerate any harm aimed toward her family. Auntie Barb was as strong and tough as any man in our neighborhood. She had a reputation among friends and family of sometimes "being mean as hell." Auntie Barb was such a badass that she once carved the letter B into a woman's face to put her in her place. I fully respected the hell out of her and her power. I admired her ability to be petite, Black, and a woman, yet still feared. That was no easy feat for a Black woman, especially in Duval.

When she was a young girl in the Durkeeville Housing Projects, Auntie Barb was known as the "Equalizer" way before Denzel

Washington and Queen Latifah. Her reputation proceeded her, even as an adult; no one ever dared to bother Auntie Barb nor her family in her apartment complex. I would wander the property fearlessly certain that I was under her protection. This unspoken protection caused me to foolishly let my guard down one day and make it difficult to protect myself in the way my mama taught me.

I was a classic tomboy, and so was Mia. We wore pants all the time, climbed trees, bowled, roller skated in the rink or streets, wrestled kids, played kickball, tug of war, and built forts. I was always the last one in the house right before dark. The opposite was true for Mia, the rule follower, who routinely was the first to head home from the playground at the hint of nightfall.

Per usual, Mia walked back to the apartment ahead of nightfall while I continued to play on the swing set. Relenting to the fact that it was time to go home before night caught me outside, I saw two unfamiliar teenaged boys as I slowed down the swing. Initially, they paid me no mind and I didn't pay much attention to them. Failing to anticipate trouble was against my mama's indoctrination. My little ass should've spotted these strange boys, instantly realized that I was alone, intuitively found a makeshift weapon, and sprinted directly to Auntie Barb's apartment. I mistakenly felt safe while alone on that playground under the guise of my auntie's protection.

My mama always said, "No one can protect you, but you!"

My training subconsciously or consciously kicked in the moment one of the boys asked, "What's your name?"

Fuck me. I must get the fuck out of here right now.

I didn't respond. I hastily got up and started to briskly walk away when I could hear them discussing my curvaceous body. At nine years old, my lower body was developed, having my mama's shapely hips and small waistline. Growing up, I received unwarranted backlash about my God-given DNA; for a long time, I was ashamed of my body because I wasn't straight up and down like the rest of the young girls. Once realizing my own daughter also inherited our family shape of small on the top but thick on the bottom, I swore to make sure she loved her body free of shame or others' judgment.

By now, the boys caught up and one stood directly in front of me while the other stood behind, bantering with each other about wanting to hang out with me. Suddenly, the boy from behind wrapped one of his arms around my upper body while simultaneously using his other arm to put his hand over my mouth to prevent my screams from being heard. The other one grabbed my feet, lifting my entire body in the air, and together carried me behind a secluded apartment building. I scuffled, wiggled, gyrated, and screamed the whole time but couldn't get loose even an inch.

As we approached the secluded area, I heard my mama's voice in my head, "No one can save you, but you! Think, Terrinee!"

I stopped screaming and got still as if I was ready to acquiesce and comply, which made my attackers become less aggressive. I scanned the ground for some kind of weapon but didn't see anything in sight. My head, hands, and feet would have to suffice. I internally repeated while still thinking of my mama's teachings: eyes, ears, or nose. Eyes, ears, or nose. The assailants smoothly placed my body on the ground as one of them held my tiny wrists while the other one released my feet and began to unzip my pants. Thank God I had on pants; they bought me the extra seconds I needed!

Eyes, ears, or nose.

The boy reached for my zipper, and I gently slid one of my legs out and side kicked him as hard as I could in his ear. At the same time, I head-butted the other one. Ask Cousin Ronald. I had a killer head-butt! With my hands now freed, I filled them with as much dirt as I could grab and thrusted a separate hand toward each of them, throwing dirt in their eyes. All of this happened in seconds, allowing just enough time for me to free myself and run like hell all the way to Auntie Barb's front door. I had no idea if the boys chased me or followed me because I never once looked back! It was eyes forward, straight ahead, and with all my might get to Auntie Barb, who would kill them for touching me!

I quickly made it to Auntie Barb's door, and before I could even finish the story about what happened to me, she had her shoes on. She gathered all my cousins, who were also skilled street fighters, and was out the door to look for the predators. We searched for hours to no avail. Finally, one of her neighbors said the boys were there as visitors of a friend but she didn't know their names. My Auntie Barb called the police and gave them all the information gathered from the neighbor along with my details of the incident and a description of my attackers. Nothing resulted from the police report, and everyone seemed to just move on because I was "okay" and there wasn't penetration during the incident. But was I really "okay?"

I realized at nine years old that being violated came in so many different tangible and intangible forms. Being defiled wasn't only being raped or beaten. It was also being made to feel unsafe, vulnerable, and insecure in my own surroundings. All my family, especially my mama, were very proud of me for "fighting back and getting away," but I didn't feel proud. I should've never been in that position in the first place. I knew better and I was taught better. After that, I became even more cognizant of my surroundings and protecting myself.

My mama's fear of us being molested or violated was even heightened after my snatch-and-grab incident. She became even more cautious about my sister and I being around boys, especially older boys. But I had a neighbor and male friend who was developmentally disabled who I felt compelled to protect. I don't remember his name or exact age, but I think he was around eighteen or nineteen years old. I do, however, vividly remember what happened to his life. Although he was older than me, he was very childlike due to his disability. We spent hours playing silly games and carelessly laughing together. He had a very sweet, whimsical personality and was delighted to be my friend. I never sensed any concern from my mama about me playing with this much older teenager. Her assessment, like mine, was that this boy was nonthreatening and safe to be around her little girl.

So, of course, nine-year-old me was floored to learn my mentally disabled friend had been charged with some heinous crimes. He was harmless and incapable of hurting anyone. I truly believed he was not guilty. Stunned and confused about why the police would take away my gentle and kind friend, my daddy told me that he was being arrested for killing a woman as well as doing unthinkable, vile things to her body. I was angry about losing my friend. I needed some understanding of what was going on. Why was this happening? In my adolescent opinion, my disabled friend was not guilty of killing or hurting anyone. He was a Black boy guilty of being poor, uneducated, and having a disability.

I described this focal life experience during my investiture speech after being sworn in as a municipal court judge on June 18, 2013. I wish I had the words to properly describe the look of joy, pride, and love on my daddy's face when I was sworn in that day. It was as if he'd flashback to that day all those years ago when his nine-year-old little girl proclaimed her future. The true blessing was that her Junkie daddy was there to bask in it by the grace of God. He never doubted that I would become a judge. I decided to become a lawyer to help my daddy, and now a judge to help my community.

Months later after my friend hadn't returned home, I asked, "When is he coming home to his mom?"

My daddy replied, "He's never coming home." He continued explaining that my friend was found guilty of the charges and would spend the rest of his life in prison.

I questioned with a puzzled look, "Why? He didn't do anything!"

My daddy sadly responded, "Why? Because the judge doesn't look like us, so the boy never had a fair chance."

I firmly stated, "Guess, I'm going to be a judge too so people around here can have a fair chance."

My daddy proudly responded, "I like the sound of that. Yes, you will, Judge Gundy."

CHAPTER 7

"We're Leaving Tonight"

With the second fire, my entire room burned to the ground and my family lost everything. We moved back to the Northside, the poverty-stricken side of Jacksonville, and into a shack on Fourth Street and Wilcox Street. For most of my life we were considered poor or working class, even when I thought we weren't. Either way, we were always fighting to get ahead. This time was different. For the first time, I felt poor. This place was a real dump for the low price of $200 per month. Four Seasons, which I missed immensely, seemed like paradise compared to this hellhole. This cold, dark, and grungy one-bedroom house had oversized, disease-infested rats that cried out at night like they were in labor. A single stray bullet could easily hit any one of us. There was one bathroom and two doorless rooms. One had a shabby, inoperable fireplace which my daddy constantly mentioned as a stupid selling point to us. Even worse, we all slept in one room in our only bed.

It also was the first time I'd come to realize that my daddy had lost compete control of our lives—the major pitfall of being a bona fide Junkie. My daddy had always been an optimist, even at rock bottom.

With no money, failing businesses, and a disgruntled wife, my daddy began diligently looking for a way to right his wrongs quickly and get us out of this shit hole. He was forced to take a job at Cub Foods supermarket to make ends meet. At first, we thought the move to the rat motel would be short-lived. Wrong. It seemed to be the beginning of a long, excruciating nightmare that never ended.

Shortly after moving to the pits of hell, I was robbed at the tender age of ten. Regardless of our plight in life, we were always thinking of ways to make money; all of us had entrepreneurial, hustling spirits that began with my grandma and continued with my parents. I had a costume jewelry business that I started with seed money from Grandma Marian. Every weekend, she drove me to the Pecan Park Flea Market to set up and sell my jewelry. One weekend, I made the mistake of turning my back and taking my eyes off my money before securing the cash box while I was getting replacement inventory. When I turned back around, I noticed my cash box was gone. I searched and searched until I had to face the fact that my money was gone. I was devastated, but more wrecked about my careless mistake.

My grandma was heartbroken for me. "Terrinee, let's just pack up your stuff. Leave this place and never come back."

That was exactly what we did. My grandma always showed up for me, but later that year she would break my heart about a family secret. I wasn't really heartbroken, but it was how my adolescent brain processed the situation. We had the biggest blow up about whether "Tiny" not Tody was my daddy's biological father. It was our only argument about anything, and despite my justified anger, my grandma didn't deserve to be ridiculed by me. Months later, I apologized profusely and expressed that I missed her terribly. We never spoke of my disrespect again.

However, there was a point when I begged Grandma Marian to tell my daddy the truth. I grew sick and tired of him using "not knowing his father" as a bullshit excuse to smoke crack cocaine. My grandma vowed she would do anything to get her son off drugs, except agree that Tiny was his father. She maintains that he isn't. Candidly, I'd resolved that I'm forever riding with my grandma on this one no matter what. We never spoke of it again. Case closed. Fuck Tiny! However, it was not that simple for my daddy.

Growing up, my daddy had a great relationship with his presumed-to-be father, Tody. However, there was always a pull inside of him that he could never quite figure out. Eventually, the time came for him to get the answers he'd been looking for all his life. After a random conversation with an old man claiming that Tiny was his father, my daddy immediately dialed 411 hoping to find Tiny's phone number. Without hesitation, the operator gave him a Vero Beach, Florida number and he immediately placed the call.

When Tiny answered on the first ring, my daddy got straight to it. "This is Anthony Gundy, and I heard you're my daddy."

Tiny, without any pause said, "It's true. I'm your daddy."

My daddy didn't waste a moment. The very next day, the four of us went to meet Tiny for what would be the first and last time for all my daddy's thirty-two years of living. We weren't allowed to meet Tiny at his home, where he lived with his wife with whom he had four other children. He and my grandma were both married to other people when my daddy was conceived. As soon as we walked into Tiny's friend's house, my daddy had always looked just like his mama until my eyes saw Tiny. My daddy was a carbon copy of Tiny, bearing the same height, skin tone, shoe size, walk, and the same swag. My daddy became enamored with Tiny: his stories, explanations, and excuses. I was unimpressed and disinterested in everything coming out of Tiny's lying mouth.

In a couple of hours, we learned that Tiny was a skilled saxophone player who traveled with the likes of Ray Charles. Musicians were known for a partying lifestyle, such as philandering and partaking in heavy drugs or, more accurately, shooting heroin. Tiny followed suit. It was no surprise that Tiny had also served six years in prison for selling marijuana. Incarceration skipped a generation. By the grace of God, my daddy never went to prison for selling drugs or anything else for that matter. Unfortunately, Corey and his adult sons, Mario and Anthony, would all one day be convicted felons.

Mario remains incarcerated today and consistently reminisces in his cell, "If only I'd stayed in Athens with you while you were in law school, my life would be so different. I know for sure I wouldn't be here. Life was so good with you, and I was doing so well in high school. But I couldn't help but chase a bunch of nothing and nobodies in Jacksonville. If I had listened to you, Big Sis, I know things would've turned out so much better for me."

My brother, Anthony, proclaimed that I'd always been like a mama to all my siblings, and they were fearful of disappointing me more than anyone else. Whether that was true or not, I wanted to be a big sister that set the right and most responsible example for my siblings—and parents. Based on our environment, Mia and I could've just as easily had the same fate as our brothers. But we were fortunate enough to make better decisions whenever faced with bad choices that escaped none of us. I wanted all of us to make it with every fiber in my being, but I couldn't want it for them more than they wanted it for themselves. My brothers had a hard time listening to my daddy, and an even harder time separating the man from the Junkie. Mia and I listened to my daddy faithfully. We never wavered and it aided us in escaping the trappings of the ghetto and rising together from a life of poverty and disparity.

Yet, we couldn't escape the hard times, bad news, and unfortunate accidents of that year we lived in that Northside hellhole with faulty basic life essentials. Valentine's Day in the fifth grade was the only good memory I have from that year. My daddy gave all three of his girls Valentine's gifts every year. As children, my sister and I primarily got heart candy, red carnations, and money. This year, I got the most beautiful white dress to wear to school on cupid day. It was sheer perfection. My daddy gushed over how beautiful his big baby girl was in that white dress. I felt so pretty and poised all day. Yep, undoubtedly, that's the only good memory I have from that entire year.

That pick-me-up came at the perfect time; I hadn't felt pretty since chipping my front tooth, resulting in a hole left in the middle of my tongue. The Jacksonville Coliseum gave out toys as well as new clothes and shoes to less fortunate kids every Christmas. With my daddy getting high more and more, and our bills behind, we knew the toy giveaway was our only hope of receiving Christmas gifts. It was freezing cold that morning when Grandma Marian packed Cousin Ronald, Mia, and I up to head for the toy giveaway. When we arrived, the line was already around the coliseum, but we didn't care. We were just so happy to be there and excited to see what toys we'd get.

As we stood in that cold, long line, we began horsing around as children often do in boredom. It was so damn cold that I came up with the bright, dumbass idea to put my arms inside my jacket. What a very bad decision! Out of nowhere, Ronald ran behind me and pushed me down onto the concrete. I fell face-forward, and since my arms were pinned inside my jacket, I couldn't use them to break my fall. Instead, I broke my face. Even worse, I fell with my mouth wide-open, chipping my tooth and puncturing a gaping hole in my tongue. There was blood everywhere. The worst part was that there were no toys for me, my sister, or Ronald after I got hurt because my grandma made us leave immediately for the emergency room.

The good news was that the doctor said my tongue would heal naturally over time and that I could only eat soup and ice cream. I took full advantage of eating ice cream for months. The other good news was that there wasn't any nerve damage, but I would need to see a dentist to fix my cracked front tooth. My parents never took me to see a dentist growing up. It was so embarrassing and unattractive to walk around with a chipped front tooth. I walked around covering my teeth as if I had no front teeth from the age of nine till about twelve or thirteen years old when it was finally repaired. My tooth debacle was the main reason I immediately rushed my nine-year-old son to see Dr. Heavenly to immediately fix his chipped front tooth. Kevin fell slipping and sliding like little boys do. I refused to have my Black son shamefully walking around hiding his smile, looking like he'd been in a bad bar fight.

Sadly, while living in that ugly ass, old ass dump on Wilcox Street, it was an accident prone, life-altering year for the Gundy family. Mia was just as Evel Knievel–spirited when we moved to the Northside as she'd been at Four Seasons Apartments. Per usual, she was the first one to volunteer for the more dangerous antics that sooner or later would lead to injury. This time, at six years old, Mia's second accident was much more severe and earth-shattering.

Corey, my daddy's alleged oldest son, was sadly back. Thankfully, he wasn't living with us this time, but, unfortunately, he started coming around again since we lived on the Northside, closer to his grandma's house. Corey would speed around on his bike like a Tasmanian devil through the neighborhood terrorizing us and anyone he encountered. It was rumored that he'd been riding around on his bike snatching purses from nice old ladies and robbing good folks. I have no idea what the truth was, but I do know for certain that he caused my sister's second major accident, giving her a Freddy Kruger face.

Corey, the menace, pretended to offer us a joyride on his bicycle. I declined because there wasn't enough room for both of us, and because my instincts said he couldn't be trusted. He insisted that we would all fit. One of us would ride on the back of the bicycle while he stood up to pedal, and the other would sit on the handlebars. Naturally, Mia volunteered for the more hair-raising position on the front handlebars, and I reluctantly agreed to ride on the back. He started off peddling slowly, finding his balance on the bike with our bodies weighing down the front and rear. Initially, I relaxed and began enjoying the ride while thinking to myself, this isn't such a bad idea after all. That misguided thought lasted two minutes before Corey began terrifyingly speeding, weaving through cars and popping curbs.

Enjoying what she perceived as playful danger, she mistakenly egged him on. "Go! Go! Go!"

As the only sane person present in that moment, I hopelessly begged Corey to slow down and let us off before someone got hurt or possibly killed. Unsurprisingly, the more I desperately pleaded for him to slow down, the more he accelerated. He had a demonic energy that found pleasure and entertainment in my fear. He reached a speed of what felt like fifteen miles per hour, maybe more. At that point, even Ms. Daredevil screamed for him to slow down as we approached our raggedy, shotgun house. We scarily cautioned him that there was a tricky turn up ahead. Corey ignored all of our warnings and pulled up to the front door of our house in true madman fashion. He hit the brake so hard that the bicycle tires left skid marks on the sidewalk. I frantically jumped off the rear of the bike just in time to woefully watch my sister's frail body fly midair. She crash-landed, thumping down in the middle of the road, face down on the hard pavement.

Mia bellowed so loud that her excruciating cries resounded down to the end of the block and back, causing several distressed people to run out of their houses to check out the bloody scene. This included our distraught parents who fortunately were home to aid with their pain-stricken, mutilated daughter. That Rock kept my daddy occupied and often away, but thank God he was home on this dreadful night. I lay in the middle of the roadway holding and rocking Mia, hoping to soothe her agonizing pain and deafening cries. As soon as our mama laid eyes on Mia, she hollered and cried out at the unbelievable sight of her baby girl's disfigured, shattered face. Mia's face looked like it had been mauled and busted by a raging pit bull or great white shark. Our enraged and exasperated mama was instantly provoked to rightfully and violently attack Corey.

She pounded, punched, pummeled and kicked him nonstop while he repeated "I'm so sorry. I'm so sorry. I didn't mean it."

My mama didn't believe his lying, demented ass, and neither did I! But none of that mattered in that moment. My sister was gorily laying on her back with half of her face disfigured and covered in gaping blood with smashed-to-smithereens, exposed facial tissue. Our daddy gently picked her up and carefully placed a busted, battered Mia in the back of our old, rusty blue station wagon, covering her with a Pepto Bismol–pink wool blanket. With a venomous look that could kill on her face from the front passenger seat, my mama rolled the window down and threatened to murder Corey if her daughter wasn't going to be okay. Our daddy speedily but carefully backed out of the driveway, and we rushed to the emergency room full of freight. We prayed the entire car ride for my sister to survive and have a full recovery.

The attending physician told us that there was nothing we could do but be optimistic that her wounds would heal while carefully keeping her exposed, blue-veined and ripped face clean as well as the blood-pus-soaked bandages changed to prevent an infection. The doctor informed us Mia would likely have permanent, deforming scars on her gorgeous face. I deeply hated Corey for this and other harmful things he'd done to me, and I would never forgive him for hurting me or robbing my sister of her God-given beauty. From the first moment I held Mia, I thought she was the most beautiful baby in the world. She should've been the "Gerber" baby for all of America to see. Every feature on her little body was divinely perfect to me.

After getting the devastating news that Mia's face may be permanently disfigured, the hospital made an obligatory call to the police and Child Protective Services. From the looks of it, she was a strong candidate to be viewed as an abused kid. Out of all the incidences that would've landed us in the system, who in the hell would've thought it would be this bullshit. Our parents did everything right this time. They were present and responsive. Even in her severe medical condition, a pain-stricken Mia was coherent enough to make sure our parents didn't go down for Corey's bad deed.

When the police was aggressively interrogating my mama, Mia abruptly interrupted and said, "My mama would never hurt me. I fell off a bike. Leave her alone!"

Without delay or hesitation, the cops took the word of a six-year-old. The officers stopped with the questions, turned around, and simply left as easily as they came. As they were leaving, Mia asked our mama for a mirror, but she didn't have the heart to give her one. Our daddy reluctantly passed the mirror to Mia.

Mia screamed at the sight of her shredded face. "I'm ugly. I'm so ugly. I hate myself."

Trying to make light of the situation, I interjected, "At least you have all of your teeth."

Our daddy leaned in to hug Mia and reassured her that she was alive and "still his beautiful, baby girl".

"I'm never going to school," Mia said. "I'm going to wear a Halloween mask to hide my face."

Our mama swore to Mia that she wasn't going to have to wear a mask. She promised her that she'd be back to normal in no time despite the doctor's prediction of permanent damage. We all pitched in to care for Mia, but it was our mama who was determined to will her child back to perfection. The attending nurse instructed our mama on the best care plan to heal Mia. She told her the first couple of nights were the most imperative and that someone needed to stay up throughout the night to clean Mia's face with peroxide, because her wounds would leak and sweat. Our mama followed the instructions to a T and didn't sleep for days while watching over Mia while caring for her and cleaning her face. After about two weeks, when the leaking was minimal, our mama created a regimen where she applied ointment from an aloe vera plant and natural cocoa butter to Mia's face three times daily. Mia stopped wearing the bandages and her skin started to naturally graft back to the original state.

My sister's face was restored to its natural state, completely free of blemish, after months of this daily regimen. It was nothing short of a miracle. The doctors couldn't believe that Mia's face had healed without a single scar, thanks to our mama. Mia's skin was so clear and smooth that no one could even tell she'd ever been mangled. My sister's mishap and recovery tamed our daddy for a short time. It was incredible how he managed to always be there for us when it mattered the most. As soon as the emergency had been diverted, he was back to his shenanigans as if he'd never missed a beat. That Rock was howling his name, silencing the rest of our needs, which he continually neglected.

In the early days, my daddy only went missing on the weekends and returned by Sunday to report to work on Monday. These days, he was craving That Rock so badly that he began missing a substantial number of days from Cub Foods. Eventually, they gave my daddy an ultimatum: go to rehab or lose your job. He chose rehab, not because he wanted to get clean and sober, but only to buy enough time to figure out his next high. The detrimental impact and catastrophic damage of crack cocaine was evident to me even at ten years old. I learned that sobriety was a personal, intimate choice that can only be made by the Junkie. Until the Junkie decides, all other commitments, opinions, or determinations mean absolutely nothing.

Rehab was good for one thing. It allowed my daddy to be clean and sober long enough to pursue an amazing business opportunity that could save Pistol Pete's from ruin. My daddy loved to "Keyball" people into submission. He easily persuaded an aging businessman to cosign $80,000 worth of dry-cleaning equipment despite the fact both Pistol Pete's locations had failing financials, yet another effect of crack cocaine. So, we were back in business with the possibility of future prosperity and upward mobility. We opened Pistol Pete's Dry Cleaners off Kings Road in a building my daddy built from the ground up. We inherited the long-term customers of his large financial investor. The business was doing well. My daddy also started a new business: T&M Night Club, named after Mia and I, in an extension of the dry-cleaning building. We were hired to prepare the club during the day and reset the workstation of the bartenders and waitresses before they arrived at night.

On this particular day, we'd finished setting up the club and proceeded out front to play around and goof off with one another. While playing, Mia accidentally punched my right breast, giving me a sharp, persistent pain without relief for hours. After it continued long enough, my parents took me to the emergency room where a painful lump was found. The attending physician informed my parents that he needed to operate immediately by cutting open my underdeveloped breast to ascertain whether it was a malignant tumor. Furthermore, because of my age, he'd have to do so without any anesthesia. Against my complete and absolute dismissal of the terrifying suggestion of cutting my tender breast open like filleting a piece of meat, my mama resolved that immediate surgery was necessary to get a proper medical diagnosis.

The doctor uttered, "Possible cancer," and my opinion or objections no longer mattered.

He got right to work, numbing the intended breast area for the incision. I was petrified at the thought of being cut, but I was trying to make my parents proud by being brave as the doctor attempted to stick a pointy, long-ass needle through my tender right breast. All bravery went out the window as soon as I laid eyes on that razor-sharp knife. I lost it! It took the nurse, my mama, and my daddy to restrain me. Mia watched from the corner of the room, begging them to let me go as the doctor proceeded to slit and extract breast tissue. It was by far the most excruciating physical pain I'd ever experienced. I left the hospital with a gaping hole the size of a nickel in my breast. It was filled with gauze that was changed twice a day. Thankfully, after finding out my tumor was benign, my breast did go on to heal, leaving only a raised scar behind. My sister affectionately called it "a piece of penny bubblegum."

I survived my breast massacre and thought things were moving in a better direction before the IRS bombarded our lives without advance notice, warning, or empathy. They padlocked the doors of the dry cleaners and night club. A former disgruntled Haitian employee reported my daddy to the IRS for unemployment wages, and they took immediate action for unpaid taxes. We just couldn't catch a damn break! My daddy swore this action, not crack cocaine, was the beginning of the end of his marriage.

After the IRS padlocked the front doors of Pistol Pete's Dry Cleaners, a burglar broke in and stole all our customers' belongings while under the seizure of the IRS. The customers went berserk and complained to the IRS about losing their clothes in the burglary. Based on their nonstop protests, the IRS agent decided to return possession back to my daddy to calm the grievances of the community. One day, right before my daddy was allowed back into the building, I was riding by Pistol Pete's on my bike when I saw a tall, skinny, dark-skinned man peering through a broken window.

"Hey, what are you doing in our building?" I called out. "Are you trying to rob us? Call the police! This man is robbing us again."

The thief turned around to see me yelling for help, climbed out of the broken hole in the window, jumped on his bike—yeah, he was also riding a bike like me—empty-handed and peddled as fast as he could to get away. Bravely, I mean stupidly, superiorly stupid, I decided to follow him. I followed him down Kings Road, passing the liquor store before I lost him. However, he was apprehended right away because I was able to give such an accurate description of the intruder to the police. My parents were moved beyond words by my courage and fearlessness after I shared the details of my hot pursuit. However, my daddy was adamant about me never repeating such dangerous behavior again.

"Terrinee, your only job is to make sure you and your sister get home safe every day. Just make it home and we'll do the rest."

I was the only eyewitness to the break-in at Pistol Pete's. My parents were hesitant about letting me testify in the criminal trial against the defendant, but I was so resolute about stopping him from doing this to anyone else. I needed to make sure he was punished as an example to the neighborhood that no one could rob us and get away with it. Reluctantly, they agreed to let me testify and I turned out to be a breakout star witness.

Everyone had underestimated this poor, little Black girl my entire life. The defense attorney learned how terrible a mistake that was on that day. Since I was a child and a witness for the State, the prosecutor gave me softball questions which hoodwinked the public defender into mistakenly believing that cross-examining me would be like "taking candy from a baby." I clobbered this seasoned lawyer's case with a specific detailed accounting of the incident, identifying the accused down to his exact clothing as described in the police report. The prosecutor knew there would be a conviction once I corrected the public defender on facts about the case. The burglar was found guilty on all charges. Besides being pleased with myself, I was ecstatic about my $35 witness fee.

My contentment was short-lived. It would only be a matter of weeks before my life was forever altered. My mama had emphatically reached her limits with my daddy and his antics. The extended wear and tear crack cocaine had on their marriage and our family became dire. It was payday and my mama was fiery mad, shouting at my daddy.

"Where is the fucking paycheck, Keyball? Our rent is three months behind. We have no food, the phone has been off for weeks, and the gas has been cut off again. Where the fuck is your paycheck?"

At first, my daddy was non-responsive with his mouth twisted like he had a stroke, slurring his words and fidgeting with his eyes rolled to the back of his head: a telltale sign that he'd been getting high. He started spewing absurd excuses about why he didn't have a dime in his pocket after being paid earlier that morning. Frustrated and entirely fed up with my daddy's preposterous lies, as well as his surging addiction to crack cocaine, my mama stormed out of the house without explanation or even a simple goodbye. He followed suit an hour or so later, not because he was worried or searching for my furious mama, but because he was breaking out to chase That Rock. Mia and I both knew that once he left that day, he would be missing for days.

Unbothered with the ordinary chaos of our lives, my sister and I bundled up under warm blankets again since there was no heat. Thank goodness we had electricity to watch TV. After a couple of hours, we heard a loud banging at the front door; surely that wasn't my daddy returning. For only a second, I was hopeful that he was going to choose us over crack cocaine today, but my optimism dissipated as fast as it appeared. Maybe in her hasty departure, my mama forgot her keys. I got up and walked toward the front door where I saw Grandma Marian standing on the front porch. Fuck me!

I knew my grandma was there because she'd been calling over and over and couldn't get in touch with us because the phone was off. The last thing I needed was to be interrogated by my grandma about the negligence of my parents—or to be more exact—her crackhead son. He was still my daddy who I loved and protected at all costs. My parents were crystal clear that we weren't to open the door when they weren't home for anyone, including my grandma. Today was the worse day because along with the telephone, the heat was also off, and there was no food in the house. Surely my grandma would storm through the house and take full account of our deplorable living conditions.

When she spotted me through the window, Grandma Marian said, "Open the door, Terrinee."

I yelled through the front door. "Grandma, I can't. My mama and daddy aren't home. My parents said we can't let no one in the house or we'll get in trouble."

My grandma pleaded. "Terrinee, please open the door. They meant don't open it for strangers. Come on, open this door. Now!"

Hesitant about my next move, I wanted to let my grandma in the house, or even better, leave with her and get away from this tragedy of a dwelling. Habitually, I chose to obey my parents though.

"Grandma, I can't. I'm sorry. Please don't be mad at me, but I have to obey my parents. They'll be here later. Come back then."

"I'm leaving groceries out here for y'all," said grandma. "Please make sure you get them once I leave. Tell your mama and daddy I need to hear from them."

Though it pained me to reject my grandma, I believed I had no choice but to heed my parents' rules. I also felt compelled to protect them by keeping my grandma in the dark about our worsening conditions. We were grateful and overjoyed about the food she brought. We were starving. Literally!

The day quickly spiraled from a bad day to the worst day of my life! Our mama returned later that evening, tearing through our front door.

"Start packing now," she shouted. "Pack only what you must because we're leaving tonight!"

Our mama spoke as if we were going into witness protection that night. My sister and I were non-responsive and slightly dismissive of her because she had a history of packing up our house to leave my daddy only to come right back. Neither of us were in the mood for this tonight. It was just too fucking cold outside. It was an unusually cold, bitter night.

"Get up, now, I said. We're leaving tonight. We're moving to Atlanta tonight. If you don't pack anything, you won't have anything. I got three bus tickets and we're leaving tonight. I'm divorcing your daddy. Hurry up! We must leave before he gets home, so get up and pack right now!"

I wasn't packing nothing because I wasn't leaving my daddy for her, Jesus, or nobody else. She was out of her entire mind. Mia, on the other hand, was up carefully, almost delightfully, selecting the items to pack.

She aided my mama in leaving my daddy, stating as she continued gathering her things, "Mama, you're doing the right thing. You need to leave him. He hasn't been treating you right. It's time for us to move out of this ugly house."

I ignored them both and kept watching TV, because I, nor anyone else, was leaving my daddy, tonight or ever. My mama left the front door open while she loaded several black plastic trash bags (these black plastic trash bags were always a bad sign) into a dingy yellow taxicab. I sat in the middle of our house staring straight into the back seat of the taxi where Mia sat with her backpack and teddy bear with such an "eager to leave" look so sweetly painted across her face.

Startling my gaze, my mama stood directly over me. "It's time to go, Terrinee. We have to leave before we miss our bus. It leaves at midnight."

I grabbed the chair clutching myself up to my elbows and around the arms of the chair. "I told you I'm not leaving my daddy. I won't have him come home to this cold house and be alone. You want to leave, then go. But I'm not coming. I'm not leaving my daddy. I'm not sneaking out on him in the middle of the night. And you're going to leave without even saying goodbye."

"Terrinee Lynette Gundy! You are coming with me now. You have one of two choices: get your ass up and into the cab or I will drag you into that cab. But, make no mistake, we are leaving, and you are coming with me."

Before I could get another word out, my mama yanked me out of the chair.

"No, I'm…"

I continued screaming and hollering in protest while being dragged against my will to the taxi. I cried, slobbered, sniffled, heaved, and wheezed all the way to the Greyhound bus station. The Greyhound bus would become a staple in our adolescent lives. Together or separately, Mia and I would have more frequent rider miles than anyone should at our age, burning the roads back and forth between Florida and Georgia, religiously sitting directly behind the bus driver.

We pulled up and Mia rubbed my back trying to console me.

"Terrinee, it's okay. I packed some things for you too. I grabbed the things I know you love and would want."

I howled even louder while looking for my daddy to appear at any moment to save me, but her words made the nightmare unbearably real. We never actually believed our mama was leaving him when she packed up our house in the middle of the night. This time our mama was sincere, and more importantly, she was right about getting her pretty, smart little girls out of that hellhole. Her decision would fundamentally and forever change the trajectory of our lives. Her decision was a promissory note to a better, brighter future with the opportunities and possibilities we deserved—the life we would have regardless of the life we'd just left behind.

Oddly enough, it was my seven-year-old sister who knew the jig was finally up. Even more impressive was her young discernment telling her to be kind enough to pack my things for me when I couldn't accept change. Thank God Mia took care of me so I wouldn't wake up in a new city, in a new home, with a new life and absolutely nothing from my old life, including my daddy who I loved so dearly despite all the bruises and bumps.

Come to think of it, Mia would always take care of me, and I would take care of her. It was always us, no matter what. I have absolutely no idea how I would've survived my many roller-coaster glitches in life without her. I, without question, needed Mia to even the playing field against my all-loving, totally druggy parents. Mia saved my life more times than I could count—sometimes with just her presence.

"Always take care of each other. Love each other, even more than you love us."

This was just another time Mia saved me and did exactly what our parents taught us. With Mia, I would be alongside my hero. My other hero—my daddy, the Junkie—followed right behind us to Atlanta.

CHAPTER 8

"He Gotta Work"

After arriving in Atlanta, my mama immediately enrolled us in school; she wanted to establish some sense of normalcy as quickly as possible. My first day, in the middle of sixth grade at Camp Creek Middle School, was an eye-opening experience. All my classmates and most of my teachers were Black. They weren't just Black, but well-spoken, well-to-do Black folks. I hadn't seen so many middle-class Black people, who felt more like upper-class to me, before moving to Atlanta. At eleven years old, I knew that I had, finally, culturally, landed in the right place. Moreover, for the first time in my life, I felt like I belonged in this unexpectedly prosperous place with such beautifully excelling Black people. The only thing missing was my daddy!

Back in Duval, I was teased and taunted by the neighborhood kids for not being "Black enough" because I was intelligent and spoke proper English. Looking back, I'm surprised I wasn't mocked about my unseasonable wardrobe in Atlanta. Mia and I were definitely stuck in a time capsule because we wore our summer gear, only shorts and never pants, the entire winter in Atlanta. Florida girls to our bones.

In Atlanta, I was normal, and I was grateful for like-minded peers. My first true friend was Toi. She was a taller, slender version of me with hazel eyes instead of blue-green, extraordinary confidence, and humor that came from a good home. Toi's parents, Rosemary and Charles, were educated entrepreneurs who extended their good graces by treating me like one of their own. Toi was one of the first to remind me that my beauty was still exceptional despite my chipped front tooth. She and I became instant best friends when she asked me about a school rumor in the middle of dressing for gym class in the girls' locker room.

"Do you go with Richard? Is he your boyfriend? I have to know because there's no way he has a girlfriend as pretty as you. No way!"

"No, I don't have a boyfriend," I said. "But I think he's a nice guy. He's been very sweet to me."

She made me pinky swear right there in the locker room that I would never be his girlfriend. I had no interest in Richard. Besides, my daddy would've never approved of me having a boyfriend, but I did appreciate Richard's kindness toward the new girl with no friends. Well, now I had one friend, Toi, thanks to that misunderstanding about a friendly guy.

We initially moved in with my mom's sister, Carolyn, along with her husband, Linwood and their autistic son, Brian in Atlanta. Their house was unlike the homes I'd seen in Jacksonville, especially homes owned by Black people. It was a beautiful, fully furnished, three-story, three-bedroom house with a living room, dining room, and oversized kitchen stocked with a plethora of food. There was a finished basement which included a den, fireplace, full bar, as well as Brian's playroom, all sitting on a half-acre of land. None of the windows had burglar bars. In fact, all their windows had either custom drapery or blinds. Their home was in a predominately Black, affluent neighborhood located off

Herschel Road in College Park, Georgia filled with lawyers, doctors, politicians, and entrepreneurs.

Aunt Carolyn was a homemaker with a first-rate life and family. I just wasn't sure where we fit in; I thought we too had the perfect life with my daddy back in Jacksonville. My mama stayed in the plush guest bedroom upstairs while Mia and I were relegated to sleeping on the floor in the basement's den. The floor in a nice house is still the damn floor. To be fair, nothing would've been good enough without my daddy. I liked Atlanta a lot, but I still missed my daddy immensely. To add insult to injury, this would be my first year not seeing him on my birthday.

On the flip, living with a real-life lawyer helped me connect the dots relating to my future that might have taken me years to obtain. Uncle Linwood was an attorney and partner at Thomas Kennedy Sampson & Tompkins, now the oldest Black law firm in the state of Georgia. He immediately took a strong interest in preparing me for a legal career. In a short amount of time, he provided me with a straightforward, clear roadmap to obtain my goals. He thoroughly and carefully explained the necessary steps to become a lawyer: graduate high school with high marks, participate in extracurricular activities, and have a good SAT score; complete a four-year degree with honors from a university and score well on the LSAT to be competitive for admissions into law school; obtain a JD after finishing a three-year law school program; and pass the Character and Fitness Test and Bar Examination to become a licensed lawyer.

His influence, guidance, and direction had to be divine. With his treasure map, this was going to be light work. The easiest part of my life was being disciplined about my schoolwork. The rest of my life was a chaotic jungle. The good thing was, I was the lion and king of the jungle ready to roar at all times in my wilderness.

My mama was busy navigating her own wilderness. It appeared to me that our newfound situation was equally hard on her. She never made a fuss because she was singularly focused on us having a place to call our own; however, she most certainly struggled with the emotional and financial weight of it all. My mama was now working two low-paying jobs at Wendy's and Red Lobster on Old National Highway. We once rode through the Wendy's drive-thru to surprise her. I was heartbroken to see my mama slaving and killing herself only to barely make ends meet. After working her ass off for months, she finally got her ducks in a row to secure our own place at Helmwood Apartments on Herschel Road.

Our new community was across the street from her sister's subdivision and full of multi-kid, working-class families, which meant that most of us were latchkey kids, freely roaming the property. The kids there were hell-bent on bullying me and Mia. There was nothing we despised more than bullies, so we were forced to stand up and defend ourselves. As the new girls on the block, Mia and I attracted "we must be suckers" kind of energy because of our fair skin, light eyes, and inherited good looks. Please don't let our pretty faces and petite frames fool anyone into believing we were soft, weak, or anyone's sucker. Actually, it was the very opposite! We were from Duval— "The Bang 'em." We totally walked through the world with I wish a muthafucka would energy and spent most of our initial days at Helmwood Apartments proving just that with our Muhammad Ali hands.

I sorely wish I could remember the kid's name that was tormenting my sister, but I don't—blame it on my traumatic life experiences. But I will never forget how he made my sister cry and tried to shame me. Mia was a tough little cookie in her own right. She didn't talk much except to me and my parents, or unless something needed to be said.

She didn't bother anyone unless she was bothered first but was a stealthy assassin against those who attempted to tease or threaten her. If Mia was crying, there was someone that needed to be dealt with swiftly. I didn't need to know what, when, or where. I only needed to know who. Without thought or explanation after seeing Mia's tears, I went looking for the bully who hurt my sister.

As I walked up the hill toward his apartment, a crowd gathered behind me, ready to see a savage fight. Much like a boxer, I blocked out the boisterous crowd to singularly focus on beating the kid who had fucked with my little sister. I had him clearly in my sight when my furiously focused eyes locked with his, momentarily stopping me in my tracks and bringing the crowd to a halt. I charged him like a raging bull as if he was dressed in all red from head to toe. He was totally caught off guard and unprepared for my fury. I rammed him, threw him to the ground, and punched his face and chest while the surrounding crowd snickered and laughed. His visible embarrassment led to his only line of defense: exposing my body. He ripped my shirt off, revealing my bare, nonexistent chest. I wasn't fazed! Actually, I was even more motivated to kick his ass. He brought my Viking genetic roots front and center. Valhalla muthafucka! No one, and I mean no one, was going to harm my sister.

After the epic, topless beatdown, no one dared so much as to look at Mia the wrong way, let alone have the courage to taunt or bully her. As proud and brave as I felt for defending my sister, I omitted this incident while recapping every detail of our lives to my daddy during summer break in Jacksonville. Without having his family as guardrails in Jacksonville, my daddy was still struggling and completely out of control smoking crack. Sadly, he was waiting days on end, which turned into months, for my mama to come back home. He was in the middle of a full-fledged binge, still freebasing more than working.

Yet, I couldn't wait to tell my daddy all about my Atlanta experiences, especially about the prosperity of Black people. Conveniently, I left out the part about my mama "partying," and still doing a lot of drugs. I suppose she was masking her own pain from our crumbling family.

Initially, our daddy appeared to be running on all cylinders. For a couple of days, he attempted to continue this facade of being happy, healthy, and sober because we were home. When he wasn't working, he was spoiling us with trips to the beach, movies, candy stores, and to eat out at our favorite restaurants. We were convinced that our lives were going back to our version of the Partridge Family soon enough. After smoking crack cocaine for over forty years, my daddy is still capable of readily recalling facts and circumstances better than 99 percent of people. Astonishingly, he doesn't remember much during what he called the "black hole" era of his fragmented life. He told me that losing his wife and kids was the darkest and lowest point in his life. His memories are mostly blurred patches due to his bleak sorrow combined with continual freebasing. This sentiment we agree on because I recall even less than usual about that summer after we moved to Atlanta. I do have one memory that I'll never forget!

After several days of pretending to be clean and sober, my daddy busted out like a can of biscuits to get that crack cocaine monkey off his back. We sat for days crying our eyes out because he was getting high even after losing his family. Even worse, he disappeared and was missing just as we'd come home. We were panicked with thoughts of him laying out in the open air, alone, in jail, cold, dead from OD'ing or a fatal drug altercation with a dealer and/or user. So many bad things ran through our heads since we were prone for bad shit to happen. No matter the reason for his vanishing act, my sister and I had bloodshot eyes and hoarse voices from bawling, heaving, and agonizing over him. Enough of this crying! It was only causing me to break the cardinal rule: don't ever panic. Crying didn't help a thing; it only hampered my ability to think rationally and strategically.

It was time for me to find Waldo the Junkie and for him to come out of la-la land so that he could get back to making the doughnuts before he was fired. The repeated, blatant lies to his employer had run thin. So, I borrowed Cousin Ronald's bicycle to conduct a block-by-block search party. After about forty-five minutes of looking for a needle in a haystack, I rolled up and noticed our "oldie but goodie" blue station wagon parked in the yard of an apparent trap drug house with three young corner boys, presumably armed, standing outside and serving their customers. Although That Rock had turned many women and children into junkies, I couldn't help but notice their minds racing in disbelief that I was there to cop drugs.

I screamed while still standing across the bicycle. "Ya'll seen the man driving this car?"

No response, I laid down my bike and stepped closer. "Hey, y'all seen my daddy? That's our blue station wagon. We've been looking for him for days. I just want to make sure he's alive."

The tallest, who I assumed was in charge, spoke. "That man owe me money. We keeping that car until we get our money. He owes us $300."

I was as nervous as a whore after working on her back all Saturday night sitting in church Sunday morning. I stood there wondering if the drug debt would cause him to kill my daddy. Don't panic, Terrinee. Stay focused and get the information you need. I selected my next words carefully to avoid making any statements accusing them of illegal, illicit activity. I didn't want us at a grand double funeral with matching RIP T-shirts and tombstones.

"No problem, we want to pay you all of your money. I just need to find him so I can get him to work and make sure you get the $300 owed."

Still clueless about my daddy's whereabouts, I had to bait the drug dealer into a conversation to reveal whether my daddy was still among the living.

"Listen, little girl," he said. "That J ain't going nowhere until I get my money. So, you need to run on home and tell your mama to bring my money. Then, I'll let him go. Until then, I'm keeping him inside that house and the keys to that clunker."

All I needed was for this small-time, barely older-than-me drug dealer to let my daddy drive home in his car. My daddy was being held against his will (debatable) in a drug dealer's boarded-up shack with no electricity, running water, or furniture. It reeked with the stench of sixteen skulls and horse manure combined with halitosis from eight rotten teeth. I had to get us, including my daddy, safely away from there while not showing weakness or fear to these gun-toting corner boys.

These young men seemed reasonable versus the drug dealers we encountered in Little Haiti while visiting my mama's distant relatives in Miami. Apparently, our family in Miami expected drive-by shootings regularly. Our first instruction was to sleep on the floor. Normal people would've probably exited stage left. Not us—we just complied. Drug dealers came to chat with our second or third cousin for a bit then later returned, riddling the house with holes like Swiss cheese. Stupidly or crazily, Mia and I weren't afraid as we lay on the floor waiting for the fireworks to stop. We left the next morning like it never happened, but we were smart enough not to ever visit them again.

Stupidly or crazily again, I wasn't afraid to carefully negotiate with this drug corner boy. "Respectfully, you seem like a smart businessman. You want your money and I want my daddy. Both of us need him to go to work. He needs to pay you and our bills. None of that happens without you releasing him and our raggedy car so he can get to work. I know you would be taking a risk doing either or both, but tax him for the inconvenience. Make him pay you an extra $100, so he'll owe you $400. And I'm going to make sure he pays you first as soon as he gets his paycheck. But he gotta work to pay you."

"On the strength, I'm going to let him leave with you, but now you're responsible. Whatever happens is on you," said the drug dealer. "Just remember, a dead junkie don't pay no bills, but if y'all don't bring my money back, that's exactly what y'all gonna have. You got one week with the extra C-note you promised."

Between Grandma Marian and Aunt Barb (his enablers), they absolutely would do whatever it took to pay the $400 drug debt to keep my daddy alive, so I wasn't the least bit moved by the drug dealer's warning—threat. On the contrary, I stood there dusting my shoulders off while patting myself on the back for zealously negotiating my daddy's freedom. I was going to be one hell of a lawyer! Deeper into my short-lived daze, I visualized my daddy running out, hugging me, picking me up, and swinging me around in the air, swelling with pride. There wasn't any glory or praise for me in that moment. This man refused to come out the crack house until I left the property. Even high out his mind, he had the wherewithal to not let his daughter see him walking out of a crack house. So, I rode away without looking back, leaning on my faith in God and my belief in my daddy. I had to trust that he would choose me over crack today. He did! My daddy came straight home.

As he was getting ready to head out for work, he turned to me and said, "You are your daddy's child. You handled yourself like a real pro. Baby girl, you always got daddy back. Daddy's lawyer came to the rescue again. Daddy is gonna do right. Daddy gonna make you proud as you make him."

As said in narcotics anonymous, "One day at a time!"

Whenever someone, especially my daddy, talked in third person, it was generally a sign of lies and total bullshit. However, I was all for his bullshit; I wanted to hear him talk about being proud of me. For a long time, I ate my daddy's bullshit off a full plate and asked for seconds. His undying belief and confidence in my abilities led me to an unrealistic belief in his capacity as a drug addict. Many times, he still delivered, fostering a greater false sense in his invisibility. My daddy went to work, paid his drug bill in full, with interest, in a week's time as I'd promised. He lived to fight and get high another day. For a long time, I believed he was paying his crack bill so the drug dealer wouldn't kill him.

However, A dead junkie don't pay no bills.

My daddy was going to pay the drug man first and in full to keep his line of credit with neighborhood drug dealers in good standing, so he could return to get high at his pleasure. In any business, he was an ideal client, especially in the drug game. Word spread quickly. Everyone knew that Keyball paid his debts and was an excellent recurring customer. He's the only crackhead I know that doesn't need cash money to buy crack cocaine. He got high simply on his face card and outstanding repayment history. His street FICO credit score had to be at least eight hundred, if not the max of 850.

As a result of his addiction, my sister and I were always handling one crisis or another for, or with, our daddy. Good, bad, or indifferent, we were always right by his side, learning to navigate challenging life situations. The greatest business lesson we learned was that anything can be negotiated under the right terms. This knowledge gave me a relentlessness that would serve me well throughout my entire life from major purchases to employment to life-and-death situations. There was something about maneuvering life in the ghetto with drug dealers, criminals, the mentally challenged, and people from all walks of life, which made fear obsolete, especially when anything could be negotiated and resolved. Well, except fear of my daddy's untimely death due to crack cocaine.

Life in these streets produced my "everything seasoning" in a pretty, little bottle, which gave me invaluable experience. It gave me insight and discernment in ways unimaginable to "normal" people. I never wanted to be normal. All I ever wanted was to be with my abnormal family. Surviving instability and chaotic experiences with my family—that was extraordinary to me. A structured environment likely would have stifled my growth. To blossom and become who I was supposed to be, I had the perfect parents for me—Linda and Anthony!

Dealing with my family, along with all the interesting and sometimes dangerous people it came with, prepared me to be comfortable in my skin from the classroom to the boardroom. I could navigate and shine my light in any room simply because my parents provided me with love, confidence, and knowledge of people and human behavior through street life experiences. I knew my value at an early age. There was no better training for me than the streets. However, my Clark Atlanta University and University of Georgia education were valuable, respected tools, but coupled with the hard-knock life, I propelled beyond my counterparts at a much faster pace. That was fine for me because I didn't want no typical life. I wanted a better life out of the fucking ghetto. Daughter of a Junkie or not, I was gonna have just that!

CHAPTER 9

"Black Man And A White Woman"

Things were looking up for the Gundy girls. We survived the summer and even snuck something wonderful in our suitcase back to Atlanta: our daddy. He decided moving to Atlanta was best to be close to his girls, and blindly hoped to get his bride back. I was over the moon because the Core Four would be back together. My daddy would finally kick his crack cocaine addiction when he was back with his family. We were adjusting and thriving in Atlanta, and for all intents and purposes, it appeared that my mama had made the right decision moving us to a new environment. No one was bullying me or Mia, our grades were good as usual, and we believed our parents were reconciling.

Our mama told him that he could move in with us if he paid the $1,900 past due rent. She was doing the best she could, but that woman hadn't met a bill that she was fond of or cared to pay. Paying bills and being accountable for the household expenses was newfound territory for her, since she hadn't ever been responsible for our livelihood. Clearly, if she needed that amount of money, she hadn't paid the rent since we moved in. Her inexperience with finances and inability to earn a living wage would lead to even more years of instability and countless evictions, just like with our daddy's crack cocaine addiction. I don't judge my mama or other women for their decisions based on circumstances. Many women and children, especially Black, fall into poverty after divorce. Her behavior guaranteed Mia and I would make damn sure that our kids didn't endure that kind of instability. We both pay our rent, utilities, car note, and any other bills timely; Mia's FICO score—not the street one—leaves me in awe of her financial discipline.

During my divorce, my own children came very close to suffering a fate of poverty as well, but for my juris doctorate. My former husband, a Grammy-winning music producer, and I had a whirlwind, five-year courtship after I graduated from law school. It consisted of gifts, big houses, yachts, speed boats, fast exotic cars, and a hell of a lot of fun that resulted in marriage and divorce—that part, not so fun. The divorce was extremely hard on me, but not for obvious reasons. In a million years, I wouldn't have ever guessed I'd lose my oldest bonus son, Kevin Jr., in the divorce.

At my lowest point, my daddy said, "Terrinee, you've got to pull yourself together. I miss Kevin too, and God knows we all love him, but you've got two other babies in here that need their mama to be okay. And I don't know when or how but believe God will bring him back to you. You feel me?"

After mourning the loss of Kevin Jr. and getting over the scorched-earth type of pain I'd experienced, I did exactly what my daddy told me. I got up out of that bed and refused to be broken yet again. My daddy was right! By the grace of God, my son found his way back to me after his eighteenth birthday and promised to never leave me again, a promise he has thankfully kept. Honestly, I don't think I could bear losing him again or his beautiful, scary-smart two-year-old daughter, Zuri.

Our daddy would preach that we shouldn't get married too young. "I would still be married to your mama if I'd been older; she's the only woman I've ever loved. Love ain't enough when you're young. There's no way I had any business getting married at twenty-two years old. No man or woman is prepared to truly commit before living fully and getting to know themselves and knowing exactly what they want out of life. Promise me that y'all will wait until after thirty to get married."

I listened, adhered and didn't get married until I was thirty-one. Mia got married at twenty-six. We both got married the same year, and we both later got divorced. I loved being married far more than I'd anticipated, but I was married to the wrong person. Don't fret for us. We received God's greatest gifts, our children, in the process— Mia Michelle, Kevin, Terrinee Elle, and Mia Elle. Our children's lives are an enormous distance from the existence we survived. Even further, my kids' lives are better in every quantifying way except for one anomaly, which I refuse to discuss out of love and respect for my children.

Unbeknownst to anyone, specifically my daddy, my mama started a romantic relationship with a Bahamian man while we were gone for the summer causing an irreparable tear in the Core Four. She took my daddy's money and kicked him out of our apartment faster than he could count to $1,900. He hadn't "Keyballed" her to his will. Even worse, she allowed her new Bahamian boyfriend to move in immediately after kicking my daddy out. The resentment and disgust I had toward her for this act of betrayal was at one hundred on a scale from one to ten. Let me get this right, I came back to Atlanta expecting my parents to reconcile but instead got blindsided with a new relationship and a new man in our living quarters.

It wasn't fair for me to blame my mama for her choices. Besides, her boyfriend was overall a good man. Mia and I grew to like him because he was patient with our hostility and anger. He never tried to replace our daddy, he provided financially, and my mama seemed much happier than she'd been in a long time. As a divorced woman, I now understand the importance of feeling whole and loved again. I am eternally grateful for the comfort and companionship he provided for my mama at a time when we weren't able, let alone capable, of comprehending her needs. My only issue with her new boyfriend was that he was in the business of pharmaceutical sales—illegal drugs—the kind of drugs that destroyed my entire life. Plus, he and my mama did a shit ton of powder cocaine together.

Growing up, I despised all drug dealers. Childishly, I blamed them for my daddy's poor decisions. I was neither enamored nor impressed with their so-called wealth and riches. I only saw the devastation done to our families and communities from their unlawful acts. Many drug dealers would try to charm and date me, but my disdain wouldn't allow me to see them as human. Truthfully, drug dealers were attempting to escape the hell of poverty just like me. The only difference between them and me was that my parents instilled unbreakable convictions, steadfast determination, and protective love and support in me: principles and values that would guide me through, above, or below the ghetto's trappings. My loving parents convinced me that my intellect along with my work ethic and natural beauty would serve as the tickets to my dream life. Unfortunately, not everyone would be blessed with my God-given talents nor parents like Linda and Anthony.

Back then, I didn't realize that drug dealers deserved my humanity just as much as the drug user, especially when taking a deep dive into the history and exploitation of the American drug trade. One of my dear friends, John Singleton, who I miss dearly, created the series, Snowfall, inspired by the historical crack cocaine epidemic that plagued our communities. He, Lalanya, who cemented our friendship, and I, had a multitude of heart-to-heart dialogues about the disastrous impacts of crack cocaine. In our conversations, I'd developed a deeper empathy for drug dealers' motivations while he simultaneously gained a better understanding of junkies and the impacts on their families. Like many, John was intrigued with my ability to separate the Junkie from the man.

I explained that I didn't view people, especially my daddy, through the lens of their flaws, but for their efforts. I always viewed my daddy, first and above all else, as my daddy! My perspective was that his addiction was a disease. I learned and desired to love him, flaws and all, exactly as he was. I loved and will always love my Junkie daddy with my whole heart. My love, respect, and appreciation for my daddy fascinated John as it has countless others. He molded a poor, Black girl with his two bare hands into a lawyer and judge. In my opinion, my daddy somehow managed to bring a sense of honor to himself while being a crackhead.

I respected my daddy's ability to show up for me and Mia when it mattered most. After my mama conned him out of his $1,900 and moved in with her Bahamian boo, my daddy was stranded with no place to go. I was frightened and nervous that I was about to lose my daddy again, which would've been even more traumatic because I'd just gotten him back. My daddy found a roommate, a Southeast Asian man, and moved into our same apartment complex just up the hill. The Lord knew I needed my daddy, and He provided him with the foresight and wherewithal to remain in Atlanta for his little girls. The innuendo surrounding my daddy and his state of mind about moving essentially next door to his estranged wife and her new man was judgmental, cruel, and endless.

My daddy calmly explained, "I don't care what Linda is doing or who she's doing it with. I only care about my little girls. It's more important for my little girls to have their daddy with them right now than me to be worried about a mess caused by adults. So, I'm going to stay right here and be here for my little girls until I feel like they're okay."

I was extremely grateful for his sacrifices, unconditional love, and support to stabilize me and my sister's world. The best part was we would just walk up the hill, spend time with him and the night whenever we wanted. He had perfected preparing a T-bone steak with a baked potato for us. It was our one and only menu item. We didn't care one bit because it was delicious to us since it had been prepared with our daddy's hands. We were back in our routine as his tried-and-true sidekicks, hitting up our double features again almost every weekend. We must've seen Eddie Murphy in The Golden Child at least five times. Mia and I preferred action-packed, kickass pictures over chick flicks. Based on our life experiences, I'm sure that was no surprise to anyone.

We still had a fragmented Core Four. My daddy was emphatic about our mama needing our devoted love and support to get her through this tough time, especially during the height of their divorce proceedings. Despite the extreme amount of pain and anguish of witnessing his woman with another man, he never wore it on his sleeve—remember, there are no victims in the Core Four. Additionally, he never whispered one bad word about her to us; when it came to him, she didn't either. But he continued to deal with his pain as he always did—smoking crack cocaine.

My daddy preferred to smoke his crack rock alone. I'm not sure if it was because of pride or he just didn't want to share his dope, or both. My daddy's drug supplier lived and worked in our neighborhood, and

I knew it. Everyone in the apartment complex knew it. Even more, there was a small, logical part of me that appreciated that my daddy didn't have to go far to cop That Rock. We always knew where to find him when he went missing. I should've been upset or embarrassed about my daddy freebasing so close to our environment, but I wasn't in the least bit. No one was going to make me ashamed of my daddy. Eventually, he moved from the apartment complex for two reasons: he didn't like his girls being that close when he was getting high, and he used all of his money smoking crack cocaine instead of paying his bills.

Things being what they were, my daddy was forced to rent a single bedroom from one of his coworkers, "Jersey." The good thing was that Jersey's place was close to ours. My daddy was still in walking distance from us. Plus, the apartment complex had a pool that my sister and I stayed in from sunup to beyond sundown on a regular basis. My daddy joined us when he wasn't working—or freebasing. Jersey had a pastime of auto theft from the then Hartsfield International Airport. He cased the airport's long-term parking lot for expensive cars that he could easily break into. Then, he'd hot-wire the vehicle by inserting a screwdriver into the ignition lock cylinder to start the engine. Note: this method worked primarily on older model cars before the 1990s. I don't know if Jersey's handy-work could start the newer cars of today.

My daddy was spiraling out of control, but he was trying to keep it between the lines for appearances sake. He decided that a windfall of money—involving one of Jersey's stolen cars—would get his life back on track. They devised a scheme for Jersey to steal another car, a Cadillac Eldorado, from the airport for my daddy to sell to one of his Jacksonville "contacts." Per the plan, they were to split the proceeds 60-40, in my daddy's favor because he was taking the greater risk of crossing state lines.

I traveled to Jacksonville with our daddy, and Mia stayed with our mama. My daddy's justification for taking me along for this felonious ride was threefold: 1) I would drive the entire five hours to Jacksonville—which I did, 2) He would've never left me alone with Jersey or anyone else to shirk his weekend visitations with me, and 3) No law enforcement officers would suspect that an adult male would be traveling with his young child in a hot car. My naïveté convinced me that this was going to be a fun, short, and exciting adventure with no harm, no foul. Then again, I was only thirteen. How was I to know this kind of criminal behavior with my daddy brought nothing but trouble and jeopardy?

Off we went to Jacksonville to sell this beautiful, yet stolen, Cadillac with a screwdriver sticking out from the steering wheel like an elephant in a room of ants. Our drive down I-75 south was absolutely perfect. The weather was sunny, golden and clear. There were no police officers in sight. We hummed to Michael Jackson's Bad, giggled about this clandestine trip, and let the breeze of the cool air swirl through our hair and hands hanging out of the windows. It was the ultimate daddy-daughter outing. Despite being in this stolen car, I felt loved, happy, protected, and safe riding shotgun with my daddy.

Upon our arrival in Jacksonville, we visited all our family and friends without them being none the wiser of his nefarious game plan. My daddy told everyone he borrowed the Cadillac from his roommate, which was true. He just omitted the part about Jersey not being the rightful owner. Later that afternoon, we were coming from Atlantic Boulevard after meeting with a man to negotiate a fair price for the Cadillac. The guy was skeptical because the steering wheel was damaged with a screwdriver hanging out. They eventually agreed on $600 cash and for the vehicle to be dropped off that night once the buyer had the cash in hand. Based on that price, my daddy would've gotten $400, and Jersey would've gotten $200.

My daddy was feeling good and optimistic about his pending deal until a police car pulled up to our immediate left while waiting for the red light to change. He swore up and down that we were profiled only because he was driving while Black in a nice automobile. Common sense would say the screwdriver was the dead giveaway. Then again, the policeman's car was in the lane to the left, blocking his view of the screwdriver. Otherwise, he would've pulled us over instantly and drew his gun. So, maybe my daddy was racially profiled. Regardless, we were in a stolen car with a Georgia license plate discreetly breathing heavily with a racing heart.

My daddy quietly mouthed to me as we sat at the stoplight for what seemed like an eternity. "I see him, baby girl. Stay cool, baby girl. Don't look at him. Keep your eyes straight ahead."

Of course, I obeyed.

Right before the light changed green, my daddy whispered, "Just pray he doesn't turn on his siren lights to pull us over right now."

He didn't. Finally, we had a green light. My daddy made an immediate right on Cleveland Road. The white officer turned behind us without turning on the blue light sirens. Initially, my daddy was careful not to exceed the speed limits and followed all street signs to a T. The officer was still following us without the blue lights; presumably he'd radioed to have dispatch check the Georgia tag for a status of the automobile. In the 1980s, these kinds of license plate checks weren't instantaneous, especially for out-of-state tags.

As we were approaching the railroad tracks, my daddy exclaimed, "If he don't turn on his siren lights before we get to Durkeeville, he's in trouble and we're home free! I know this white boy out of his depth. Nobody knows these Durkeeville projects better than me."

We saw him in our rearview mirrors turn on his blue lights right as he was about to come over the tracks. We made a sharp right onto Payne Street, and then a sharp left into the beautiful bosom of Durkeeville. It was a maze to outsiders, so the officer never had a shot of catching us inside the projects. He kept straight across the tracks, got turned around at Myrtle Avenue and passed Durkeeville. We lost him! My daddy pulled over to the side of the road to ensure that no one would think we were frantic or on the run.

As he put the car lever in park using the screwdriver, he ordered me, "Leave everything. There's nothing in here that can identify us. When we get out. Walk normal and follow right behind me."

Before we exited the car, the police helicopter flew back and forth over Durkeeville. How the hell did they get a helicopter to Durkeeville so damn fast? If someone had gotten shot over here, they would've bled out and been dead before the police, ambulance, and for damn sure, a helicopter, showed up.

As my daddy wiped the steering wheel, dashboard, radio, locks, door handles and anything else he thought would've picked up his fingerprint, he reassured me, "We're good, baby girl. There's no way they'll find us in Durkeeville. Trust Daddy. I got this. Let's go."

We casually walked away from the vehicle and about fifty yards to the front door of his old neighbor, Ms. Mamie. A frivolous, yet important and devastating note: I left my all white, brand new white Saucony sneakers behind (only sneaker heads would understand).

Ms. Mamie opened the door looking up at the helicopter flying around in the sky as she said, "Anthony, what's going on? What's wrong? Does this have something to do with you?"

"Ms. Mamie," said my daddy. "This is my daughter, Terrinee. Everything is fine. I was just showing her around Durkeeville where me and mama used to live. And I wanted her to meet you."

He continued, "Do you mind if we come in to use the restroom and rest a bit?"

Ms. Mamie was so happy to see my daddy. My daddy and her son, Big Head Bill, were close childhood friends.

Ms. Mamie offered, "Yes! Come on, baby. Y'all hungry? I just finished supper."

My daddy and I shouted, "We can eat" at the same time.

Then, both of us burst out into laughter. Ms. Mamie's hospitality was right on time! While monitoring the news for updates on our little escapade, we feasted at her small kitchen table over fried pork chops, macaroni and cheese, greens, and cornbread with the best damn homemade lemonade. "Breaking News" flashed across the television set.

The news anchor said, "After a high-speed chase, the police are on the scene searching for a Black man and a white woman seen driving a stolen Cadillac. The vehicle has been recovered, but the suspects remain at-large."

Huh? A Black man and a white woman? My daddy and I looked at each other in bewilderment then burst out into a belly laugh about their misinformation.

I wasn't a white woman—mistaken race identity just like my birth!

My daddy couldn't contain his excitement, "Baby girl, we got away! The cop thought you were a white woman! They're looking for a Black man with a white woman."

After the news story, we were even more relaxed and less concerned about the events of the day. My daddy still wanted to play it smart by keeping a low profile a little while longer. So, we hung out at Ms. Mamie's for a couple more hours until the police towed away the Cadillac. He arranged for one of his friends to give us a lift to the Greyhound bus station. We causally left as we came—with our pockets empty. Silly me, as a new teenager in a high-speed chase with the police after us, I still felt protected simply by virtue of being with my daddy.

Surprisingly, Jersey wasn't mad or upset about the plan falling apart and producing no bread. He was more ecstatic that my daddy wasn't caught, and not in a position to implicate him. I have no idea how much longer Jersey stole cars, but I know my daddy gracefully bowed out of that game. He was a Junkie, not a car thief, and decided to find another way to support his gangster crack cocaine habit. My daddy and I didn't speak of it again. Many years later, I told Mia, but no one else, not even my mama. I recently learned that about ten years later that one of my daddy's friends inquired about the bank that he and a white woman robbed. My daddy got such a big kick out of this street committee rumor.

He kindly evaded, "Man, I wasn't with no white woman. I was with my daughter, and you know damn well I didn't rob no bank with my child."

Again, he omitted the part about his daughter being with him in a stolen Cadillac on a high-speed chase from patrol and aerial police. In fairness, my daddy, nor any other man, woman, or child from the Northside, was likely to hand incriminating evidence on themselves to anyone, including and not excluding "a friend." For all my daddy knew that guy could've been a "snitch," wanting to set him up or entrap him.

Nevertheless, the conversation was quite entertaining and funny to my daddy, even after all that time had passed.

The entire shenanigan could've negatively altered my entire life and possibly hindered me from keeping my path toward the law and success. God had a different plan for me, and the Lord knew I needed my daddy. Under normal circumstances, this self-medicated, crack cocaine addict, would've been arrested, convicted, and sent to prison. Again, my daddy hasn't been convicted of a crime that resulted in prison time in his life. And a couple serious questions—who would I be without my daddy? Where would I be without my daddy? What would I be without my daddy?

Good, bad, or ugly, the truth was that without my daddy, there was no me—and probably no me becoming a lawyer or judge. I needed him just as he came. He built me strong as steel. He never doubted me. He made me self-confident, self-possessed, and self-made. He taught me to depend on myself and my abilities regardless of my age or direness of the situation. He taught me there is always a way out as long as I keep believing in God and my God-given talents. I wholeheartedly needed Linda and Anthony as my parents. Yes, their parental styles were nonconventional. However, so was their unconditional love and unwavering confidence in my ability. Looking through a glass window, they could've been characterized as batshit crazy drug addicts. For Mia and me, they were amazing parents who would do anything in the world for their daughters.

On any grading scale, my parents did a fucking fantastic job of raising their girls. The chaos, in fact, was beneficial for us. It prepared us for anything and everything. It was one of the greatest lessons they taught us: how to deal with unfathomable setbacks. Regardless of background or bank account, life has knocked all of us down in one way or another. Most people haven't had a lot of experiences with tough times and don't manage them well or sometimes don't survive them. My parents gave my sister and I the tools of not only how to survive setbacks, despite our challenges, but also how to thrive.

CHAPTER 10

"I'm Not Moving Again"

There were plenty of setbacks waiting for me after my daddy and I traveled back by bus to Atlanta after the stolen car fiasco. My mama moved us fifteen minutes outside Atlanta to Concepts 21 Apartments on Delk Road in Marietta, Georgia. The apartments were much safer, nicer, and with a community pool. My mama's brother, Fred, lived a couple buildings over from us, another benefit since he kept money in my and Mia's pockets for cataloguing his vast and extensive VHS collection. It was still Marietta, though. To reference rapper Omeretta, Marietta is not Atlanta. I loved Atlanta and Atlanta loved me back time and time again. Little did I know, Atlanta's presence had planted seeds of love that would someday return to me tenfold. The connection I felt with the soul of Atlanta would resonate with me for years to come. Atlanta would play a huge role with a profound impact on my forever love story and life trajectory. Forever I love Atlanta. Yeek!

Living in Marietta meant that I had to change schools again to Marietta Junior High School. I was devastated about leaving Camp Creek Middle School and my first real best friend, Toi. Another unexpected move led to another expected lapse in memories. I don't remember much about that school or anyone attending there. Sure, I probably had some good times with some good people, but I would need to be lying in a psychiatrist chair under hypnosis to jog my noggin. Ah, I do recall singing alto in the chorus. I was terrible! This school was more about inclusivity and participation than talent. I wasn't even qualified to be a shower singer.

I also recall Mia having trouble at her school during this time. Some of her classmates believed that Mia could be teased and intimidated as a newbie without repercussions. It was persistently the same story: Mia beat them up, she denied it, and there were never any witnesses to corroborate the other students' stories. Naturally, my mama sided with Mia when called to a parent-teacher conference. She told the teacher that unless she could prove wrongdoing by Mia, it was harmless squabbles between eight-year-olds. The teacher was wasting her time. She would never persuade them or me that Mia had done anything wrong. Technically, she hadn't. She couldn't be held accountable for throwing them Muhammad Ali hands better than the bullies. Pick on someone else's kid or sister! Wrong, right, or indifferent, my parents stood up for and with us. This gave us an enormous sense of security and confidence. They had our back no matter what, when, where, or how.

After the stolen car fiasco and our move to Marietta, my daddy went down fast and hard. He either quit or was fired from his job for his gangster drug habit. During that time, he was frail and fidgety, almost always. He looked bad and was doing worse. It hurt my heart dearly to see my Superman diminished by his crack cocaine kryptonite to this weak feeble state. I wanted so badly for my daddy to return to his mighty self. After hitting rock bottom, my daddy pretended to try to get some help. He went to a detox recovery center. We had so much faith in his ability to get clean and sober at this time. We still believed that he desired sobriety. I won't call him a liar, but he for damn sure wasn't telling the truth. In reality, my daddy was only buying enough time to recover, reset, and start the merry-go-round all over.

During sobriety, his wits and superior confidence returned, and he was actually physically fit, doing daily sit-ups and push-ups like he was training for a triathlon. Apparently, surviving freebasing required a stellar mental and physical workout regime. When he was temporarily free of crack cocaine no one could tell he was a Junkie. He was clean as the board of health, walking around in tailored suits, fancy shirts, and alligator boots with his silky hair laid to perfection. He cleaned up quite nicely every time he was drug-free. His sober work ethic was unmatched. On those days, my daddy was basically a boy scout. He spent all his free time with his kids when he wasn't working. Back on the merry-go-round we go. After his detox, my daddy was briefly clean and sober, so things were looking up—or so I thought.

Marietta Junior High School deserves credit for one thing: providing me the opportunity as a rising high school freshmen to participate in the Upward Bound Summer Residency Program at Morris Brown College. I was headed to Marietta High School, but first I would be going to college—sort of. I was ecstatic about being chosen for the summer program. I received a whopping $60 weekly stipend. I bought my first pair of Air Jordan 3s at Greenbriar Mall as soon as I got my first check. I was the only one on campus with Jordans. I lived on campus for eight weeks, attended lectures in college classrooms, and starred in a stage adaptation of Lorraine Hansberry's historic A Raisin in the Sun. I played Beneatha and her lines aligned with my dreams so deeply. Although Beneatha was a fictional character, I felt an osmosis to the fact that she had the audacity to want to be somebody.

My favorite line from the play was "And forgive me for ever wanting to be anything at all! Forgive me, forgive me, forgive me!"

The Upward Bound Summer Program was going extremely well and soon I was going to be a freshman at Marietta High School. The anticipation of high school for me was like when most teenagers get a driver's license. I had been driving since I was nine years old, so I wasn't excited about that administrative gnat. My daddy actually bought me a burgundy 1978 Plymouth Volare, affectionately named Snaggletooth Wilma, since her front grill was missing, to drive back and forth to school years before I had a driver's license. According to him, he bought Snaggletooth Wilma because he wanted me safe and sound in a solid car that would hold up in the event of a collision. Snaggletooth Wilma wasn't pretty, but she sure was steady. My daddy was right about her holding up in an accident. In Italian, Volare means to fly, but Snaggletooth Wilma's feet were always planted on solid ground. A pickup truck ran into a parked Snaggletooth Wilma causing a loss to its own bumper! Snaggletooth Wilma didn't have a scratch.

Snaggletooth Wilma did break down on me and Mia driving from Tifton to Jacksonville in the Osceola National Forest just fifty miles from my daddy's house (no, I still didn't have a driver's license). We naively hitchhiked with a trucker to a pay phone to call our daddy. The trucker could've kidnapped, raped, trafficked, or killed us—we thought of all this five minutes into the ride. In our young minds, we would've overpowered him, simply because it was us against him, so we would win. No foul, no harm. Our daddy found us safe and sound at the gas station where the trucker dropped us off.

I was excited and ready to fly into high school. Starting high school meant that I was one step closer to college. I was looking forward to my crowning glory as a freshman. Many girls my age were excited about high school because of dating and partying. I had no strong interest in either of those. I've never been boy crazy. Boys were a dime a dozen and would always be right there waiting. Unfortunately, my mama didn't believe me because most of my friends were guys. Blame it on my daddy, uncles, or male cousins, but my spirit and thought process has always been more aligned with the male species 365 days of the year. My soul is more akin to Black men than any other human in the world, which probably speaks to my obsession with and unique ability to love them wholly and fully, despite their flaws.

My mama constantly worried about me being taking advantage of, being fast, or getting pregnant. For the record, her thoughts were equally or more bananas to me. First and foremost, no one was taking advantage of me—no one! None of my guy friends came close to violating or disrespecting me. On the contrary, they never got fresh or flirted with me. I had more street sense and smarts than all of those boys put together. Not to mention, I was a better fighter than them, and they knew it. Sure, some of them may have been stronger than me, but I was more strategic and faster than all of them. Finally, and most importantly, I'd never been fast in my life and damn sure wasn't getting pregnant. I was just one of the guys, but I couldn't get my mama to understand that to save my life.

It was likely that my mama was hypersensitive because of my older cousin, Tanishia, and her predicament at sixteen years old. Everyone including my mama knew that I idolized Tanishia. It wasn't just for her Barbie doll collection, but for her beauty and brains. We were the Aries girls in the Gundy family, who didn't play the radio with big, lofty dreams of going to college. Tanishia and I spent hours upon hours fantasizing about walking across the stage to receive our college degrees. According to the plan, she would be the first college graduate in our family, then, I would follow, and Mia would be next.

Right before Auntie Robin got clean and sober, Tanishia delivered a devastating blow to our co-life plans.

Tanishia, Ronald, Mia, Mario, Auntie Robin, and I were all at Grandma Marian's playing Dirty Hearts. Auntie Robin in her "rockstar" days decided that Dirty Hearts would be more fun by making it a drinking game. Every time one of us lost, we had to take a shot of gin. Calm down, we were all fine and not in any real danger. Besides, she was right! The game was livelier with shots, shots, shots. Her son, Ronald, wasn't a great player to begin with, but he was eager to lose. Everyone but me ended up losing and drinking at least once. We joked, laughed, and laughed some more at the drinking antics along with the excitement of Auntie Robin sharing an adult game with us. Everything was all games and giggles until Tanishia ran to the bathroom to throw up. Initially, we thought she was sick from the drinking game, but she'd only had one shot. Even as a lightweight, her vomiting shouldn't have been so incessant. She couldn't stop sprinting to the bathroom and puking. By the fourth or fifth time, I followed her into the restroom.

"Please tell me how to help you. I think we should go to the emergency room. There's no way you should be this sick over one shot."

She tried to dismiss me. "No, Terrinee, I promise I'm fine."

"Tanishia, we're going to the hospital. Enough is enough."

"I have to tell you something, but you can't tell anyone. Promise you won't tell anybody."

"Promise," I told her.

"I'm pregnant, Terrinee. It's morning sickness."

The same little girl that stood up to the police, chased a robber, and saved her mama's life sat on the bathroom floor and sobbed. I cried, cried some more, and was more upset than her, as if it was me expecting a baby. We were supposed to escape the hells of the ghetto together. How would we make it now with a baby? I told myself that we couldn't, but I would for me and Mia. Tanishia went on to become a single mother at sixteen years old. Just short of twenty years later, Tanishia realized our lifelong dream for herself and graduated from Edward Waters University with a bachelor's degree in business administration. Quite humorously, Tanishia's firstborn child became Dr. Angela Green Guzman, OB/GYN, while both of my kids, Mia Michelle and Kevin, were barely in elementary school.

Determination, discipline, and work ethic were not exclusive to me. Since I became the first college graduate in my family, many college and advance degree graduates have followed including a doctor, a rehabilitation counselor, a teacher, a nurse, a college professor, and following in my footsteps, two lawyers, Nicole and Yanna! We have some powerful DNA running through our blood. Against all odds and through it all, we weren't just surviving, but we were also changing our family's trajectory for generations to come. We were doing our part to carry on the mantle of hope and change.

Mia and I were still living by the "no whoring, no drinking, and no drugging" motto back in Atlanta. However, I was still kicking it on the playground, mainly with boys. I couldn't blame our mama for being paranoid about teenage pregnancy with what happened with Tanishia. I wish that she could've focused on my brain power and hustle rather than my beauty, but that wasn't what life had taught her.

"When I'm gone, stay in this house and away from them nasty little boys. I'm not playing with you, Terrinee. Mia is going to watch you for me."

I'd never heed her warnings, and Mia would snitch on me every time. Our mama would always be furious, and I was always unbothered. My defiance led our mama to prove to my grown-but-still-a-kid ass that she was in fact "The Chief" and we were the "Indians." Like I said before, things were looking up, or so I thought, until my mama dropped a nuclear bomb on me.

One random day that summer, she announced, "We're moving to Tifton. I've decided that Atlanta is too fast for y'all, so I'm going to raise y'all in the country where things are slow. And my family can help us."

The last time she stunned me like this was that dark, cold night we left my daddy in Jacksonville. Now she had the nerve to ask me to leave my daddy again and leave my beloved Atlanta, the place where, for the first time in my life I knew there were other Black folks who wanted the same things in life as me, where I'd gotten Uncle Linwood's roadmap to becoming a lawyer, and where I finally felt like I belonged. What was wrong with this woman?

"Do you hate me?" I asked. "Why are you trying to destroy my life? I'm not leaving my daddy again! I'm not moving again. I'm not moving to [fucking] Tifton!"

Of course, I didn't curse at my mama, but I was definitely thinking it. I was fighting mad, but not out of my damn mind. This was the same four-foot, eleven-inch bionic woman who snatched a tree out of the ground. I would've never tried that crazy ass woman like that. But Tifton? What the hell? As far as I was concerned, Tifton was hell on Earth or worse, a place out of Alex Haley's Roots.

During my parents' divorce, I attempted to persuade my daddy to let us stay with him instead of my mama. I went as far as to say I would tell the judge in their case that I preferred to stay with him. From my understanding, at thirteen years old, I was able to provide input as to what was in my best interest. So, my best interest was to be with my daddy. Still very much a sap for my mama, my daddy pushed back hard every time.

"I could never hurt your mama like that, and it would kill her to be without y'all. She needs y'all. You can't do that to her."

With this Tifton business, it was imperative that I got him and her to see things my way this time. She was trying to move us to Tifton, Georgia. I was desperate to persuade them that it was in my best interest to remain in Atlanta. Once again, Mia was totally on board with moving again, even to Tifton. I refused to relent so easily. I quickly assessed that throwing a tantrum wouldn't help me. So, I came up with a plan where I would stay with my daddy to finish Upward Bound and attend Marietta High to maintain and continue my excellent academic progress. We would visit them on holidays and some weekends. My mama unexpectedly agreed to my plan, and my daddy fell like a house a cards once she acquiesced!

Soon after, my mama packed up everything, except my personal things, and moved in with her parents in Tifton. I had all my clothes, shoes and personal things on the Morris Brown campus with me already. My summer was amazing, and my future was bright in Atlanta. Together, my daddy and I were going to take Atlanta. Wrong. His sobriety was over before it started. He was a full-blown, homeless Junkie living on the streets by the end of my Upward Bound program. Occasionally, he slept on lawn chairs at our swimming pool, and I would go check to make sure he was alive in the morning. I needed to know what was in front of me either way, whether he was dead or alive. Sometimes, he was in place, safe and sound, and sometimes he wasn't.

No home for my daddy, no Terrinee for my daddy, and no Atlanta for Terrinee! On Grandma Marian's orders, his sisters, Barb and Robin, drove to Atlanta to find their vagrant brother and bring him home to Jacksonville. They tried to cheer me up before leaving for a day of family and fun at Six Flags. I will admit that I had a blast, but in my defense, I always had fun anywhere with my family. Just like that, my daddy was gone. I was in Atlanta with just me, myself, and I. No one had to say a word. I knew that I had to move to Tifton after Upward Bound at the end of the summer. To this day, I'm not sure if my mama agreed to me staying with him because she really believed it would work or because she knew my daddy's drug addiction would ruin it all. Neither here nor there—my disgruntled ass would be going to Tifton.

A couple weeks later, Grandma Marian, a certified nail technician, was in Atlanta for the Bronner Bros. Hair Show. Since she would pass through on her way home, my grandma was dropping me off in Tifton. She was staying at the Marriott Marquis downtown, and I spent the night with her before leaving because I had to move out of the campus dormitory. She had a spacious, luxury blue and tan Chevrolet G20 van with tan leather interior seats. It accommodated her show items and all my belongings with no problem. We loaded up her van the night before to make sure we could hit the road bright and early the next morning. Big mistake. We were robbed that night. We woke up to a busted van window with all our belongings stolen. Grandma Marian's stolen items were work-related, but they took all my things—all my prized possessions. Thank goodness I was wearing my Jordans—losing my Jordans would've been too far!

Like my previous house fires, I headed off to Tifton with absolutely nothing. Starting from the bottom seemed to be the story of my life. Good thing my parents taught me time and time again, that life will knock me down, but I always get up. I was an expert in dealing with setbacks and I'm a better, stronger person for it. So, yeah, I was just fine after losing everything again that night before I begrudgingly moved to Tifton. Material things can be replaced and would be, one way or another. Besides, I had everything I needed—my family. In Tifton, I could wear a paper bag with my Jordans and still fit right in. On the other hand, Grandma Marian felt like she had ripped my heart out and destroyed my thriving teenage life. She promised to make it right. Out of guilt and love, she sent me a box of brand spanking new clothes and shoes every month almost the entire time I was forced to live in Tifton. I was so fresh and so clean every single day that I won best dressed and many other superlatives my senior year in high school. Shit, I had hammer pants before MC Hammer—Can't Touch This!

New clothes, new shoes, new digs at my grandparents' house still didn't change the same old South Georgia. I had no idea that all my prior life experiences were simply training me for the extreme tactical course that awaited me. Turns out Tifton would also prepare me for the world ahead, especially future trials related to my judgeship. Today, I understand and I am eternally grateful for my mama moving us from Jacksonville to Atlanta. There is no question that it changed the trajectory of our lives while providing a road map to success. Tifton, however, is an entirely different story. After it was all said and done, I'm grateful for Tifton too and even more grateful for my mama. I publicly admitted as much at my college graduation party that my mama hosted where she gave me a hunter green 325i BMW, with peanut butter interior, at the Hyatt Hotel in downtown Atlanta. I imagine the same force pushing my mama intuitively to get us out of Jacksonville resurfaced and told her to take us to Tifton.

I told my mama upon my arrival and during my entire ninth grade year in Tifton, "I hate Tifton and I hate you for bringing me here!"

Hate and love come from the same place. I didn't hate my mama. Conversely, I loved her very much and she loved me more. My mama has always been there for me, even when I was at my darkest and lowest points. I haven't had many, but certainly I've had several days where nothing would suffice or soothe me, other than having her there to tell me everything was going to be okay. Mama, I apologize for uttering those awful words despite my immaturity and anger. Please accept an abundance of gratitude for giving Mia and I: faith, hope, and love. Thanks especially for the greatest of them all—love. The only proper apology comes from the words of our Lord:

> *"Love is patient, love is kind. It does not envy, it does not boast, it is not proud. It does not dishonor others, it is not self-seeking, it is not easily angered, it keeps no record of wrongs. Love does not delight in evil but rejoices with the truth. It always protects, always trusts, always hopes, always perseveres."*
>
> —1 Corinthians, 13:4–7 (NIV)

CHAPTER 11

"Henderson On Henderson"

Once I arrived in Tifton, Mia and our mama were already settled at our grandparent's house. My grandparents were happy, but not me. I had a piss-poor attitude from the moment I stepped foot into their small, non-air-conditioned house on what used to be a red clay dirt road. We were all back to cohabitating in one bedroom. The only thing that kept me going at first were the ice cream runs with my granddaddy and my daily letters from Toi. Per usual, the first thing my mama always did once we arrived in a new location was enroll us in school.

This time the first day of school and beyond was a fucking nightmare. First, the ninth grade in Tifton was junior high; I was no longer in high school. Second, my academic records from my eighth-grade year at Marietta Junior High allegedly hadn't arrived at Tift County Junior High. As a result, I was placed in basic, low-level academic classrooms slightly above special education because I was presumed to be a dumb, Black girl. Lastly, a rumor circulated before I could even have lunch; some high school girl threatened to ride the bus from the high school to junior high to beat my ass over her boyfriend.

I hadn't even met him or knew he thought the new, mixed girl (me—and for the eleventh hundred time, I'm not mixed) was pretty. My only comfort was at lunch, where my mama's sister-in-law, Faye, was the cafeteria lady. Aunt Faye provided a familiar, sweet face and fed me very well.

Most of my time in Tifton was a forgetful dash that not only caused a lot of unwarranted and ugly pain but also provided more clarity about human beings and their primal behaviors than anything else I'd experienced. As strange as it may sound, the folks in Tifton, both Black and white, were bewildered and baffled at the sight of a fair-skinned, blue-green-eyed Black girl with reddish blonde hair. They were even more dumbfounded about a Black girl who was articulate and assertive. I stuck out like a blazing California wildfire, and some of the folks with misguided beliefs felt I'd come there to burn it all down. Why in the hell would my mama, with her good sense, believe this was a safe place for me to grow up? There was no such place in a town like Tifton for a smart, self-assured, beautiful, and Black fourteen-year-old girl.

Let's unpack the more insignificant issues and work our way up to the calamities of my ninth-grade year. Believe it or not, the young lady stupidly rode the school bus to my school and approached me about a young man I'd just seen for the first time as he grabbed her mid-step. She screamed obscenities at me with a surrounding mob of instigating students while maintaining a nonthreatening distance to display her silly antics.

I thought, It's a shame I'm going to have to beat her ass over a muthafucker I don't even know—go figure.

I couldn't believe this girl wanted to fight over a boy, a younger boy at that! Boys had very little of my interest and were dime a dozen to me; and for sure as shits, wasn't worth fighting over. My daddy would've never allowed me to fight over some stupid boy. If I had to box over a guy, he clearly wasn't mine. At no time can I remember myself ever being boy crazy. I had two simple rules when it came to guys: I ain't chasing no man, and I liked who liked me. The childish high schooler and I clearly had different rules of engagement related to boys. However, I would defend myself against any threat if necessary. I never said a word in response to her silliness because this scene was awfully ridiculous to me. I stayed focused on attacking her before she could strike me, should this event turn physical. I gave her a chuckle with a smug look of this ain't what you want, baby girl while shaking my head.

I could hear Kilroy's voice in my ear. "Never flight! Always fight!"

Certainly, I couldn't go to my granddaddy's house the first day of school after retreating or losing a fight. In a small town, the news would make it to his ears before I got off the bus. Fortunately, neither came to pass because the silly high schooler backed down without further action. I subsequently made that guy my boyfriend since it was such a big deal for him to like me. Let me give the people what they want—a true reason to dislike me. I quickly learned to be prepared for all junior high foolishness going forward.

It was inevitable that the Muhammad Ali hands would make a comeback, and a prominent one at that. At one point, I was so frustrated with promises of being jumped by girl cliques after school, I confronted each person one by one throughout the school day alone. I followed Mia's example of no witnesses, because under no circumstances could I afford to be expelled from school and hurt my chances of attending college. But certainly, I couldn't risk being stumped during an unfair, outnumbered brawl. It was astonishing how the tables turned for the better with one-on-one matchups. The matters were resolved without a mere scratch on me before the end of school.

I spent most of ninth grade warding off threats of physical violence toward me for simply existing and ignoring falsehoods about me. My entire life I'd heard the most ridiculous rumors—lies—about me. I wasn't a hard worker—lie. I was promiscuous—lie. I was entitled—lie. I was on drugs—lie. I was pregnant—lie. I was given everything—lie. What was even more insulting than the lies was the assumption made that I thought I was better than everyone else! How could I, Terrinee Gundy, possibly think I was better than anyone? I was the Daughter of a Junkie. Those misrepresentations were the furthest thing from the truth. In actuality, the only thing I ever thought about was surviving and keeping my family together!

Although my personal safety was threatened daily, my academic future was at greater risk. I was finally moved to the appropriate core classes after weeks of waiting and debating with the school about correct course tracking, and after my mama was told to sign a liability waiver. I'm pretty sure my science and history teachers were phenomenal, but unfortunately, I can only recall the English and math teachers who would terrorize me for not knowing "my place" based on the color of my skin.

My daddy was still wilding out of control like a savage beast with crack cocaine, but my hands were full securing my academic career. I had no time to focus on his drug shenanigans. I had to compartmentalize, as I'd done often times, and focus on me. As devastating as the effects of being the Daughter of a Junkie were, that impact took a backseat to the overt racism I was subjected to my first year in Tifton. Crack cocaine paled in comparison to the vile racism I encountered, making me hard-pressed to remember anything from that year related to my daddy smoking That Rock.

At fourteen years old, I found myself dealing with racism and difficulties that no child should have to endure, especially in a learning environment with those who were presumed to be the most trusted. I felt trapped in a typical Jim Crow-ish town where there were two sets of rules: one for Black folks and a whole other for white folks. For example, the Black people lived on the South side of the railroad tracks, and the white folks lived on the North. The town was very much still quasi-segregated. Black and white people kept reminding me to respond with "yes, ma'am" or "no, ma'am." I never did because my daddy never allowed it.

"Never let me hear you say, 'ma'am,' 'yes, ma'am,' 'no, ma'am,' or nothing like that to anyone like you're on a plantation. You're not a slave and no one owns my child. A polite 'yes' or 'no' is more than enough respect."

It was the 1980s and I thought that racism had ended in the 1960s. I quickly learned that nothing was further from the truth, especially in Tifton. There was a tension in the air, an unwritten rule, that Black people shall stay in their place and never challenge the status quo of white dominance. The town folks got along under such pretenses. My disdain for the stench of racism I'd endured decisively surpassed the stench of crack cocaine. It reeked and permeated my skin in such a way that, no matter how hard I scrubbed, the stink would never be washed away.

One of my white classmates told me that he was mad at his father for aggressively professing, "I'll hang that nigger bitch from the tree in our front yard."

I have no idea why the son felt the need to repeat his father's sentiments to me. For the record, I'd never met his father or did one unkind thing to his son. His comment was made simply because I existed in a positive manner in his son's brain. Apparently, my existence bothered several other Tifton folks, including two of my teachers. I can't remember the name of my nasty-ass algebra teacher, but as long as I breath air, I'll never forget my English teacher's. It was Ms. Henderson, just like my mama.

As a freshman, a student's initial GPA was set and had a profound effect on college acceptance and merit scholarships. The last thing I needed, like a hole in my head, was for two teachers to be threatening my GPA, or more importantly, my ability to attend college. Yet, that was exactly what those white women were doing to the poor, little Black girl who was presumed to be weak and lazy.

I was so excited to finally be in the right classes and eager to learn on my first day in Algebra I. The school counselor walked me into the classroom and introduced me while explaining that I was a semi-new student that was mistakenly placed in the wrong classes due to my records being delayed from my previous school. The teacher was dismissive of the counselor and my presence while nonchalantly pointing to a desk in the back of the classroom without so much as mumbling a word.

As the counselor turned to leave, unfazed by the lack of welcome, the teacher barked at me, "My class has a test today. You will be required to take it."

"On what? This is my first day in your class. I can't take a test today. I don't even have a book or know the material being covered on the test."

This lady must have been out of her everlasting mind to think I was supposed to take a graded test within two minutes of being in her class with no notice, preparation, or even a textbook. Yep, she was definitely out of her mind because she slammed the test on my desk as if I was the crazy one. I didn't know what to do except try my best and pray to God that I might possibly know some of the material.

She was gracious enough to give me a math textbook the next day. I was an attentive student who wanted to retain as much information as possible during lecture. I didn't talk, play, or pass notes during class. I preferred the front, center-row seat in the classroom. I was focused and wanted to make sure that I understood the material as it was taught. I also engaged in dialogue and asked questions to ensure I comprehended. I raised my hand often in math class; however, this middle-aged teacher never acknowledged me once while attending her class. Most days she simply ignored me, and after a bit, I lowered my hand from fatigue. She occasionally called on another student who was goofing off while deliberately sending a message that she was going to pass over my raised hand yet again. One time, she called on a white student directly in front of me who neither had his hand up nor was paying attention to her in the slightest. "Do you have a question, Mr. Nobody Worth Mentioning?"

As a person who worked hard at being the best student possible, which led to also being the teacher's pet in most instances, our interactions were quite demoralizing and discouraging. I felt even more demoralized the day she returned the graded test to me. Instantly, my face turned red as my eyes became watery and my entire body stiffened like a board. I grasped the paper so tightly that I almost tore it in half. I was in disbelief and angrier than a mama bear looking for her cub.

I heard my mama's voice in my head as I was totally about to lose my shit. "Don't you ever let your enemy see you cry. Don't you ever give them the pleasure of believing they're stronger than you or can break you. You need to cry, then you come home and cry. We will love you, remind you exactly who you are, and tell you what you're capable of every single time you need it. But when you leave this house, you always, and I mean always, put on your best face."

That racist lady knew she'd rattled me and was waiting for me to make a misstep or give her the satisfaction of my tears. My eyes may have been watery, but there wasn't an inkling of me that wanted to cry. Nobody had died. Besides, she didn't deserve my tears. What she saw in my eyes was fury in a girl who wouldn't be denied and who was determined to correct a wrong to right pronto. It was time for me to be my own lawyer!

I recited Psalm 23 silently as Grandma Marian taught me to do in times of distress. "The Lord is my shepherd; I shall not want. He makes me to lie down in green pastures; He leads me beside the still waters. He restores my soul…"

I gathered my bearings, cleared my throat, and made direct eye contact with her smug face before exiting her classroom at the end of the period.

"I've never made a sixty-three in my life. Actually, I've never failed a test in my life. My mama will be contacting the school requesting that I be allowed to retake this test. I will not accept this grade or your unfair treatment of me [bitch]."

Of course, I didn't say it, but I was definitely thinking it.

There was a calm that came over me as I left without waiting for a response, because I'd decided that she wouldn't win. I wouldn't give her the power to destroy me or my future. I was going to college, and I was going to get my family out of the ghetto. God, my parents, and my life experiences had given me everything I needed to succeed; it was already inside of me. Plus, I didn't need her to teach me jack shit. I had a math textbook with all the materials, and I could read and comprehend just as well as anyone, including her.

I couldn't help but think about the suffering and endurance of my ancestors through slavery and the Civil Rights Movement. If they could survive being taken from their land, separated from their families, sold into servitude after the horrid conditions of crossing the Atlantic Ocean, beaten, maimed, or worse, killed; surely, I could tolerate and defeat a racist fool who wrongly refused to teach me and wasn't remotely smarter than me.

Tolerance wasn't enough, though. I had to beat her with my superior intelligence and unmatched work ethic. I had to do it with the delicate combination of Dr. Martin Luther King Jr., Fannie Lou Hamer, Stokely Carmichael, and Malcolm X all wrapped in one. And I had to do it with the ferocious help of my mama. My mama may not have understood quadratic equations, functions, or graphs, but she sure as shit knew how to stand up and fight for her kids!

Whenever I needed a pit bull, my mama showed up without hesitation or very little explanation and asked, "Who am I biting today for fucking with my child?"

The very next day my mama's tiny self stormed into the principal's office defending my stellar academic record and demanding that I be allowed to retake the math test. Her tirade was so fierce and forceful, the office staff and I heard every word while I sat outside of the principal's closed door. She insisted that the three of us trot down to the teacher's classroom to inform her together that I would be retaking the test. She continued that it was the school's job to protect me, a good student; so far, they had failed miserably. She told him not to worry, because she would make sure her daughter wasn't mistreated by any of them. The racist teacher reluctantly agreed to let me retake my math test. But come on, did she really have a choice once my mama and the principal showed up at her classroom door? It was agreed that I would retake the test in a week after school with the principal and my mama present. There was no way I wanted to be in a classroom alone with that evil lady.

I studied the problems in my algebra book nonstop after school, worked equations forward and backward, quizzed myself over and over and then some more. I was determined to do well on the retake, and without the teacher's help. I had to prove myself and represent my family and ancestors with pride and dignity. I had to make sure she didn't thwart my college and scholarship opportunities. This may seem like an intense exaggeration, but as a fourteen-year-old girl, I was serious as death about school, especially this failed math test. The day was finally upon us, and I was confident and ready. I thoroughly worked on the math problems and checked my answers while the three of them sat looking directly at me taking the test. I knew I'd done well and was quite pleased with myself for knowing the material. I finished faster than expected and the teacher was puzzled about me being done so quickly. She jerkily pulled her answer key out to grade my test while me, my mama, and the principal watched on. Then, she graded my math test again. Wait for it—she checked my test a third time.

"She must have cheated. She made a one hundred. There's no way she made a one hundred."

I was far from a perfect person, but on that day I'd been perfect. I made a perfect score. I'd made my ancestors who crossed the Atlantic Ocean, and even those who didn't make it, proud that day. Their sacrifices weren't in vain. I stood still with a gigantic smile on my beautiful, Black face in an aura of being extremely proud of myself.

My mama exclaimed, "How could she have possibly cheated? We were all here watching her. She earned a one hundred and you're going to give her the grade she deserves!"

The principal interjected before the simpleton could comment. "We know she didn't cheat, and I assure you she will be given credit for her grade."

Unfortunately, Black women, including myself, are often underestimated, certainly with extraordinary work. Somehow, it's easier for mainstream society to believe we cheated or took shortcuts. Nothing was further from the truth because shortcuts led only to failure for Black women; we had to do better than the best. We must be prepared for rare instances, anomalies, or any other unforeseeable setbacks in order to succeed. False accusations of cheating and outlandish lies would follow me throughout my life, particularly once I became a judge. I've accepted that people love to hate and hate to love me because they've made asinine assumptions about my life and God's packaging of me. I don't cheat or lie; that was never winning to me. Winning was simply being the best. I do the work with what God gave me!

My mama knew I didn't cheat but she was still in awe of me making a perfect score. She wanted to know how I did it. I explained that I simply taught myself from my math textbook and worked hard to master the math formulas and problems. I further explained that I was actually grateful to that racist lady for not teaching as she was expected to teach me. In fact, she taught me to never depend on anyone but myself when it came to my education. I never raised my hand in her class again. I never asked for help with my lesson from her or any other teachers in that school. I religiously yet solely, dove into my books on all subject matters with great joy. She made me better than I could have ever expected to be despite her wicked efforts to wreck me. She gave me the gift that kept on giving.

Technically, I did raise my hand again a couple months after my math injustice and asked for assistance from my English teacher, Ms. Henderson. Ms. Henderson was a petite, old white woman with gray hair. She didn't completely disregard my presence like my math teacher, but it was evident from the first day in her class that she preferred a hue like her own. Ms. Henderson was kind and engaging with most students. With me, she was stern, downright nasty, and visibly annoyed with any interaction between the two of us. I was unbothered and more determined than ever that no one would detour my success in school, especially after being victorious against the math teacher. This time, I knew exactly what to do: teach myself. I didn't need her help and frankly didn't want it either.

I was in control of my own destiny and academic success, so I kept to myself, buckled down, and did my work on my own. The time I'd fallen ill, I was forced to ask that old bat for help with information about which assignments I'd missed. Sounded easy enough. Well, it wasn't! I repeatedly asked Ms. Henderson for my makeup work after being sick with the flu and missing several days from school. Being absent from school was newfound territory for the Gundy family, since my daddy had perfect attendance from kindergarten through twelfth grade because his mama made him attend school no matter what, even if he was sick. He promised he wouldn't make his children go to school if they were sick, tired, or just not in the mood. Admittedly, I'd taken advantage of some personal days because of my daddy's leniency, but this wasn't one of those times.

Ms. Henderson went on to dismiss or disregard my inquiries for weeks, using the excuse that she'd get to it when she had time. She'd already manually entered zeroes into her grade book for those assignments. After continual efforts to obtain the missing work, I'd grown overly concerned about the effect these zeroes would have on my class grade and overall GPA and decided to try once more during class. I quietly called her name as she walked by my desk to check our individual class work, only to be ignored again. I then quietly raised my hand to get her attention in an attempt not to disturb the class.

When she noticed my hand in the air, once more, she turned to ignore me.

When she paced down my aisle once more, I whispered, "Ms. Henderson..."

Before I could get another word out, she swung her little body back in my direction and slapped me in my face, squeezing both of my high cheekbones and yelled, "What do you want?"

The entire room moved in slow motion. I couldn't believe this woman had slapped me, and in front of the entire class. I was trembling with fear, not fear of her, but fear of what I would do to her. She knew it too; I could see the fear in her eyes. She smelled the fury running through my veins. I wasn't sure if she feared the fire in my eyes or the fear of how bad she'd fucked up by slapping a student, a Black student, or both. My hands were so tight that I dug my nails into my palms. My natural reflex was to bludgeon her face to a pulp. That slap was hot oil doused on a fierce eternal flame igniting a simmering rage. I would've been broken and burst into a ravaging, unconfined eruption by this incident but for my prior experiences. My life had prepared me not to panic, but to endure this racist, violent moment until I could get help.

It took every fiber of my being not to defend myself and drag her all up and through that school. I truly had to call on the ancestors to anchor me while fighting off my African and Viking tribal instincts. But I saw my entire future washed down the drain if I responded in-kind within those quick seconds.

Restraint in a time when I knew I'd been wronged was one of the hardest things ever. I jumped up and ran. I ran like I was running that day from those vile boys trying to violate me. I ran full speed to a pay phone, never once looking back. I needed my mama! She would get some straightening and retribution like when she pounded her sister's assailants with that tree she snatched from the ground.

"Mama, she slapped me! My English teacher slapped me in the middle of class in front of everyone, for nothing. I just asked her for my makeup work!"

"I'm going to kill her! You stay right there! I'm on my way! Don't you move or say a word to anyone until I get there. Terrinee, I'm on the way and I promise you I will handle this!"

We'd moved into a single-wide, white trailer home on the far South side of Tifton. It generally took me about forty-five minutes to get home from school on the bus, including stops for other riders. I didn't know how my mama got from our house to the school so fast, but she got there in seven minutes flat. When she opened the door to the front of the school, it sounded like she tore it off the hinges. She had fire and smoke coming off her body, and I was immediately relieved that my mama had arrived to save me. After hugging me and reassuring me that it was all going to be okay, she bypassed the front office staff and walked directly into the principal's office without knocking or warning. I followed her inside the office because I was staying by her side today to ensure that no one else would put their hands on me.

My mama instructed me to explain what my English teacher had done, but after every couple of words, she went off screaming and cursing about Ms. Henderson slapping me. She'd heard enough. With the upmost love and respect, get out of the way when a Black mama has had enough! My mama was the best kinda crazy, especially when someone was fucking with one of the Core Four. My mama was about to go off in royal fashion, and I was ready to eat up every crumb of her craziness. In an instant, she stormed out of the office walking toward the halls of the school with me, the principal, and his staff following.

"Where the fuck is Ms. Henderson? Come out of the fucking classroom and answer for what you have done to my daughter. Mssssssss. Hendersonnnnnnnnnnn!"

The principal jumped in front of my mama, begging her to stop. He promised that if she went back to the office, he would bring Ms. Henderson there to discuss this matter like adults. Why did he say that? My mama proceeded to curse him out and asked if Ms. Henderson was acting like an adult when she slapped her child. She wanted to know why the police hadn't been called on Ms. Henderson. She told him that he had five minutes to present that woman to her or he would positively call the police on her because she was going to fuck up everything and everyone in sight until someone answered for what happened to her daughter.

It was like a raging bull seeing a matador in red from head to toe when my mama finally saw my teacher in the principal's office. Ms. Henderson was stumbling over her words, fidgeting with her clothes, and nervously squirming in her chair with my mama's eyes piercing her flesh. It was as if Ms. Henderson was on that crack rock.

My mama ripped a hole in that lady's ass in her true monologue style.

"Bitch, let me tell you something! If you ever put your fucking hands on my daughter again, I will kill you! She will be visiting her mama in prison for the rest of her life because I will kill you! And you better be fucking grateful that you hit my child who has been raised right and didn't get up and beat your muthafucking ass! If you had put your hands on any other kid in this school, they would've gotten up and beat your muthafucking ass and right to do so! If it had been me, I would've beat your ass from here to the graveyard! But my daughter was worried because she has a future and isn't going to let your feeble ass rob her of it! That's why she got a mama! Her mama is here to beat your muthafucking ass! Let me tell you this one last thing: my name is Linda Henderson! If you as much as breathe on my daughter again in your life, it's going to be Henderson on Henderson! And I'm going to muthafucking kill you! Do you understand me? Because I don't want no more muthafucking misunderstandings! And you better apologize to my daughter right here, right now and pray she accepts your apology. And you better mean it!"

I sat there just as pleased and proud of my mama while cheering on the inside that she'd annihilated Ms. Henderson. Never underestimate the power of parental advocacy combined with passion and fire on a child's everlasting security and confidence. However, I was astonished that other than my mama giving Ms. Henderson the business, nothing else happened to her. She did as my mama said and emphatically apologized to me, but the police weren't called, and she wasn't suspended or reprimanded. I wasn't even moved out of her class. If I hadn't been me, she could've destroyed me and my future in an instance free of blame or consequences for her actions. This was what Dr. Thompson's wife had done to Grandma Marian all those years ago. If I'd been a little white girl slapped by a Black teacher, all hell would've broken out, and maybe even pointy white hoods with holes for eyes in a town like Tifton. Since I wasn't a white girl, Ms. Henderson was home by supper, enjoying dinner with her family without the threat of punishment for her racist and violent acts.

It would've been easy for me to feel defeated and distressed about my safety based on the school's lack of action or discipline for Ms. Henderson. But I didn't. My mama stood up for me. She fought for me. She threw her David rock at the Goliath of racism. She vindicated me. After all was said and done, I felt supported, loved, and confident that my mama would fight anybody for or with me. Going forward,

Ms. Henderson was sweet as pecan pie with whipped cream on top to me.

Fate would have it that Mia would encounter Ms. Henderson five years later in junior high; of course, she was amazing to Mia. My mama and I handled Mia's light work, and no one wanted the trouble of another fight with a Gundy girl. It was smooth sailing for my sister. Tifton was euphoric for her. She absolutely loved it. After hard living in Duval and Atlanta, Mia welcomed the easygoing lifestyle of Tifton. She regularly referred to it as "Mayberry." Needless to say, we had two very different experiences in Tifton. I'm grateful that I suffered so Mia wouldn't. After all, isn't that what big sisters are for?

Interestingly enough, I ran into Ms. Henderson at Mia's high school graduation ceremony while I was a graduate student at Clark Atlanta University headed to the University of Georgia School of Law. She carefully approached and politely asked to speak with me in private. At first glance, I thought this woman must be crazy. Hesitantly, I stood there staring her in the eyes while awaiting her true reason for interrupting my snack run at the concessions stand.

"Terrinee, I am a Christian and have prayed for forgiveness from the Lord. I also prayed that the Lord would grant me the opportunity to ask for your forgiveness before I left this Earth. I hope you will forgive me—not simply because I was wrong, but because I've learned better. I'm an old white lady who grew up a different time and didn't know any better. I'd never met anyone like you before. I'd never interacted with a Black person that strived so hard to achieve and wanted so much out of life. Of course, that wasn't your fault. It was my own ignorance. I've kept up with you and followed your achievements. I'm proud of you. You made me see Black people differently and you made me see the world differently. So, I hope you will accept my apology, and I also hope you will accept my gratitude."

I was flabbergasted and moved. "Wow, I didn't expect any of this. That was a lot. Yes, I do forgive you. I forgive you because it takes too much to be angry, especially when I can focus my energy on bettering my own life. It also takes a lot for any woman, especially a white woman, to admit when she's wrong. Your actions changed me too. I became stronger and better. After our incident, I knew that no one would break or stop me from achieving my God-given destiny."

"Is it okay if I hug you?" she asked me.

Without hesitation, I leaned in and embraced her, and she grasped me tightly. "Terrinee, I really am sorry for what I did to you."

I whispered as we departed from one another, "I know, Ms. Henderson. I believe you."

As big as my brain was, and as huge as my dreams were, I could've never imagined those words or sentiments would ever come from Ms. Henderson's white lips to my Black ears. But of course, I still had a lot of life to live and more surprises to come.

CHAPTER 12

"Mia Michelle Gundy"

I was right about Tifton being the pits in more than one way, especially since the most devastating news I'd ever receive would come out of there: a life-altering phone call while in graduate school at Clark Atlanta University. Before I answered the phone, I knew in my soul that something bad had happened to Mia. We had an out of this world connection, an intense bond like identical twins, spiritually and divinely bound. If I close my eyes, I can still feel myself stumbling. After gathering my bearings, I hopped into my 325i BMW and sped over one hundred miles per hour the entire way to Tift General Hospital.

My entire family from all over Jacksonville, Atlanta, Philadelphia, and other parts of the country were in the waiting room before Mia was out of her thirteen-hour surgery after hydroplaning on a wet road into a cedar oak tree. Our high-as-a-kite daddy scarily and speedily drove himself from Jacksonville straight from the crack house (where he was found) in just over an hour to get to his baby girl. God only knew how fast he must've actually been going to have arrived safely in

Tifton in record time. My daddy never failed to pull it together when it mattered most and managed to stay clean for a time.

Mia was everyone's favorite, and we were devastated at the thought of losing her at seventeen. However, there was hope because we were at the hospital, unlike the family of her first love, Nakia. His family was unfortunately at the morgue after he'd been decapitated on impact. Nakia's family were thankful that Mia was alive, and after leaving the morgue, they came to support, fight, and pray for Mia's life with us, because that's where Nakia would've wanted them.

Nakia and Mia were hopelessly in love, inseparable and a prime, beautiful example of young, sweet love. Nakia was her Mi Rey. He drove a custom candy-apple red 1984 Chevrolet IROC with black and red crushed velvet seats to our house every morning. Nakia would always be bumping the sweet sounds of Al Green to take Mia to and from school, and anywhere else she needed to go, including her part-time job at Burger King. Mia was a fanatic about wearing seatbelts, except in older model cars, after getting stuck in one and having to be cut out.

That fatal morning, she hopped in Nakia's car without securing her seatbelt. Upon impact with the cedar oak tree, Mia was ejected from the front passenger seat and landed over thirty yards on her left side into a tall, grassy field covering her small frame. Ironically, Mia being thrown out of the car was the only reason she was still alive. The seat belt trapped Nakia and led to his instant, unfortunate demise. Concurrently, as Mia's body was flying out of the vehicle, her foot was chopped off midair, giving an entirely new meaning to taking flight.

I believe Nakia's spirit of love and soul followed Mia throughout the entire day with the permission and blessing of our Lord. Without a doubt, every event surrounding my sister's accident became miracle after miracle after miracle. How many miracles can one person have? The answer is simple: however many the Lord deems. God is God. He wanted her to live, and He knew that I needed my sister. Without her, I would've never reached my full potential. Mia was the reason I woke every day trying to be better than I had been the day before. Without her, I can't imagine what I would've turned out to be. There were so many life-altering or life-threatening events that we'd survived together that could've derailed our future or broken us in every irreparable way. Surely an automobile wouldn't do what the hells and depths of the ghetto couldn't. Mia was tough as steel after thankfully surviving a steep fall and terrible bicycle accident. This time would be no different!

According to the paramedics and the woman who rescued her, Mia was conscious, lucid, and screaming for help when they found her. Mia needed to survive long enough to make it to the hospital, so God sent a retired nurse with a cell phone to find her on the side of the road. The woman ironically happened to be the grandparent of one of her classmates. Steve Jobs and Apple hadn't changed the world of communications quite yet in 1996. At that time, it was miraculous for a person or vehicle to be equipped with a cell phone. While the retired nurse called 911 to get an ambulance, she used makeshift bandages to stop Mia's hemorrhaging from four major arteries, especially her left leg which had been severed completely below her knee. She managed to prevent Mia from bleeding out before the paramedics arrived on the scene.

Coincidentally, my mama, happened to be driving by in a car with my cousin, Rashid. When they drove past the wreckage, she immediately prayed for whoever had been in such a bad accident. Nakia's car had been obliterated into four parts. Without a clue, the ambulance pulled off with her child. A local police deputy recognized Mia's eyes in my mama's face as they slowly drove past, chased the car down, and instructed Rashid to drive my mama directly to the hospital without disclosing Mia's predicament. By the time Mia reached the hospital, she was so unidentifiably pale from losing so much blood that the staff identified her as a white child. My family sadly joked about that being the reason she received such thorough and urgent care upon arrival.

Mia refused to go into surgery without first seeing our mama. In an effort to accommodate Mia's adamant request, the hospital staff began prepping her for surgery, including inserting a catheter. The staff was praying for our mama to hurry up and get there because Mia needed to be operated on immediately in hopes of saving her life. Our mama finally arrived by police escort and was brought directly to Mia; it took everything inside of her not to break down sobbing while seeing her daughter in that condition. She actually saw Mia's leg severed with her foot gone and her left arm hanging by the tendons and ligaments away from her tiny, bloodied body. She saw Mia in the most unimaginable state. With only the grace of God and love for her child, she managed to keep it together.

The first thing she did with a dry eye was bend down and whisper in Mia's ear, "I love you."

A delirious Mia said, "You don't love me."

My mama repeated, "I do love you."

Next, Mia told my mama she had to use the bathroom. My mama tried explaining to Mia that she had a catheter inserted so she could just urinate without making a mess of herself. Mia disregarded my mama and started shouting at a nurse walking by that she had to use the restroom. The nurse finally took Mia's hand and started gently rubbing it in efforts to appease her while informing her that she had a catheter.

Mia snatched her hand from the nurse's gentle embrace and screamed, "Bitch, I said I have to use the bathroom."

Embarrassed and in disbelief of Mia's rudeness and profanity, our mama snapped, insisting that Mia apologize at once to the nurse. She explained to the nurse that Mia had never behaved like that before and that it was very much out of her character. Mia doesn't have a sailor's mouth like me. I actually can't recall ever hearing her curse. The nurse explained to my mama that it wasn't Mia's fault. She was in shock, and she needed to promptly get to surgery. However, our stubborn, sweet mama wouldn't let them move Mia until she apologized for her bad language to the nurse; a Black mama always gonna "mama" no matter what.

She walked alongside the stretcher as Mia got wheeled into the surgical room without knowing if she would see her child alive again. Mia went into surgery with an older white doctor, roughly in his late sixties, Dr. Mack Freeman. The staff assured my mama that Mia was in the most capable hands. Dr. Freeman had been practicing medicine almost five decades. Several times during her surgeries, other doctors offered to relieve him or at least give him a break from standing on his feet for such a long time, but he adamantly refused to leave Mia. She could've bled out from either of her four major injuries including her crushed pelvis, smashed left shoulder, arm and hand, or her jagged-meat left leg. Truer words couldn't have been spoken about Dr. Freeman. After saving my sister's life, we can even put a ruler to Mia's scars. They're very straight with precision.

Walking out of the operating room and attempting to lighten the mood by expressing how famished he was, Dr. Freeman said, "First and foremost, she's alive and doing well. However, she's still in critical condition and has a long road ahead of her. You should know that I've been practicing medicine almost fifty years and I've never seen a man, woman, or child as strong as her. She fought to live the entire time. She had four major surgeries, so I had to bring her back and re-sedate her each time. I had the hardest time keeping her under anesthesia; each time, she fought to stay awake and not go under again. She never cried or screamed once in thirteen hours of what was excruciating pain for her."

Like an idiot, I frantically inquired, as if we were in an alternate futuristic universe. "Can I give her my leg?"

Dr. Freeman replied with a smirk and slight chuckle. "No, ma'am! It doesn't work that way."

I have no idea why, but I kept blurting out quasi-dumb questions while standing with our mama and daddy. "Why did you stay with her the entire time? Weren't you tired or sleepy?"

"I was never weary. God's presence was in the room, guiding my hands as I stitched her wounds, and her skin felt like silk. She never grew tired of fighting for her life, so I decided that I wouldn't leave her. We were going on this journey together today. I knew she was one of God's chosen ones; and I knew He was going to help me save her life today [yes, a doctor said all of this]."

Once he mentioned God, it led me to ask, "Will she still be able to have kids?"

He calmly responded, "Yes, I believe so, but because of her pelvis damage, she won't be able to have a vaginal birth. Let's just focus on getting her out of the woods. And she keeps asking about the driver. Let's not tell her about him or losing her leg until she's stabilized. Now, I'm going to grab a sandwich."

Dr. Freeman was correct. Mia was persistently asking about Nakia when we went into the surgery recovery room. Dismissive of her condition, she grabbed my hand with a tight grip and squeezed as she told me to find him. It never crossed her mind that he was harmed. I brushed her request off and started explaining her medical state to her. However, once she was moved to her ICU room, I couldn't delay any further. Now, she was borderline hysterical about Nakia and wanting to know why her leg felt weird. I couldn't distract her any longer and was forced to inform the doctor.

"Dr. Freeman, I've never lied to my sister or kept secrets from her, and I'm not about to start. You said she has to remain calm, but I know her, and us not telling her the truth is only going to further incite her. So, I'm about to tell her everything, and I'm just asking that the staff be ready for what comes next."

Dr. Freeman and my parents agreed with my decision because Mia was visibly upset about not knowing where Nakia was. A doctor's duty to deliver bad news over and over must be a true burden and today that weight shifted to me. The piercing release of high-pitched pain with delayed puncturing of the ears couldn't come close to describing the bellowing agony that tormented my sister's beating heart after hearing the news that would shatter her world. We are two sisters with one heart. Her pain was my pain. The transference of the throbbing heartache felt unbearable, and there was nothing I could do to make it better, except be there to share the burden.

Once she composed herself, Mia asked, "And what's wrong with my leg?"

Thinking this would further upset her, I slowly explained, "You lost a part of your leg in the accident and the doctor explained to us that you would feel phantom pains like your leg is still there, but it isn't. It was severed below your knee."

"Really?"

Mia never complained about losing her leg. She would've given her other leg to save Nakia's life. Dr. Freeman informed us that he had to remove some more of her leg above the knee because an infection set in Mia's leg. Dr. Freeman wanted to speak with Mia privately to gently let her know about another amputation surgery. He asked us to step into the hallway while he spoke with Mia. We obliged and left the room.

As the doctor exited the room after speaking with my sister, our mama asked, "What did she say about losing more of her leg?"

"She told me that I better cut all that's needed because this was the last time. She's not going to keep going to surgery letting me cut on her," said Dr. Freeman. "She'll be just fine. I know it. I've never come across anyone with the strength and determination to live like hers."

Silly me pleaded again as the doctor ignored. "Please take my leg and give it to Mia. Please, doctor! I should be the one without a leg, not her."

Mia insisted that I not worry about her leg because it was her burden to carry. Before it was all said and done, Mia would've had at least another half dozen life-threatening surgeries. She never made a fuss about the pain since she was granted unlimited access to an intravenous morphine drip. None of us thought this would lead to an addiction since this was extenuating medical circumstances. However, we didn't realize Mia was not in fact using the morphine for pain, but instead to mask her suffering related to Nakia's untimely death.

Mia was still fearless as ever. One night in the hospital, with a metal brace attached to her pelvis that raised three feet in the air, she insisted on driving a car. Although she wasn't driving Nakia's car the day of the accident, Mia wanted to face that demon head on. Strangely, Mia and I both have Nakia's tag number forever imprinted in our brains. In her mind, she needed to immediately conquer the fear of automobiles. Without hesitation or consultation, I wheeled her from the hospital bed with the brace still attached and suspended in air to my 325i BMW in the hospital parking lot. Driving was the easy part but dealing with the sudden death of the love of her life, would haunt her far pass physical healing.

Dr. Freeman ordered Mia not to attend the funeral held five days after the horrific accident. It didn't go over so well. The Gundy girls have a way of getting our way! Dr. Freeman decided to let her attend only in an ambulance with paramedics because she was still fighting for her own life. Dr. Freeman wanted to give her closure, but not at the expense of her own health. There was one condition: we would have to pay the $500 cost of the ambulance. For the record, that was a lot of money for us.

"No problem! We got it."

We had a joint savings account at C & S Bank from where Grandma Vera retired after working over thirty years. We were prepared to clear it out for my sister to attend Nakia's funeral. The paramedics rolled Mia to the front of the sanctuary in a standing room only funeral, reclined on the stretcher with her IVs and metal brace still attached, along with me and my family following behind. Nakia's mom, Cherry, and his brother, Darius, came to hug and kiss her. Presently, Mia still has a relationship with his family. Nakia's home-going services were beautiful, and Mia held up unbelievably well the entire afternoon until Al Green's version of "Amazing Grace" was played. She had an outburst belting, hollering, and screaming far worse than the night we told her he'd passed away. It caused everyone to weep even more. Unfortunately, Mia's vital signs elevated, and the paramedics removed her just before the end of the funeral.

We tried paying the paramedics when we returned to the hospital, however they refused and insisted that there was no way they could charge Mia. Those two gracious white male medics assured us that they would handle any fallout related to waiving our fee. Candidly, Mia had blessings and favor in abundance throughout the entire ordeal. Dr. Freeman also refused to apply charges for his services. He told us that it would be ungodly for him to profit off Mia. Additionally, the blessings kept coming. Mia's JROTC teacher, Sergeant Purvis, applied and succeeded in getting her admitted for extended care and rehabilitation at the Shriner's Hospital in Tampa, Florida after being discharged from Tift General Hospital.

Mia still had quite the fight ahead of her to survive the aftermath of such life-threatening injuries. There was a small glimpse of hope during this time; shortly after arriving at the Shriner's Hospital, we were informed that Mia was pregnant with Nakia's child. Of course, Mia and Nakia's family were over-the-moon happy that a piece of him would still be on Earth. After my initial shock, I was ecstatic that God decided to give Mia a life while taking a cherished one. We talked and planned nonstop that Mia would still go to college, but we would live and raise the baby together.

Ironically, I predicated that Mia would lose her virginity to Nakia months earlier while she lived with me that summer in Atlanta. We were sitting in a McDonald's drive-thru waiting on Filet-O-Fish sandwiches. My sister had the look of submission in her eyes, and I supposed telling her I knew gave her permission. The decision was hers, but I wanted to reassure her that I wouldn't be upset and that I would be there for her from beginning to end. The crazy part was that Mia and Nakia used protection and she still got pregnant. Heed the warnings: condoms are only 98 percent effective.

Considering all that I'd been through, my sister's accident was the event that devastated me unlike anything I'd ever experienced. Mia almost died, and that was still extremely difficult for me to process. The most painful parts of Mia's accident are still excruciatingly tough for me, and as real for me as it was at that time. I still see her in the recovery room, ICU, and at the Shriner's Hospital along with the accompanying smells of the sick and injured. A little too much for me to bear and relive. At the wonderful suggestion and sage advice of two of my besties, Dr. Jackie and Iman, I decided to stray from the script a tad bit by requesting, without direction, that my sister finish the story of her accident in her own words. Besides, she has always been the strongest of the two of us.

Firsthand Recollection
By
Mia Michelle Gundy

On or around November 1, 1996, I was transported on a stretcher from Tift General Hospital to the Shriners Hospital for Children in Tampa, Florida for physical therapy and a prosthetic fitting. Before then, two Shriners showed up unannounced in my hospital room with me and my daddy at Tift General. My dad and I were wondering who these white men were that appeared out of nowhere to talk to me; at the time, I had no idea that my JROTC teacher, Sergeant Purvis, had referred me to them.

One of the men explained to my dad that they could help me with physical therapy and a prosthesis without any associated costs. My dad and I were a bit skeptical about what they were saying, and we didn't take it for face value. It just sounded too good to be true. When things sound too good to be true, that was usually the case.

The two Shriners continued to inform us about their children's hospitals and how they helped kids with disabilities. They spoke about how they could help me. But I would need to go before I turned eighteen in December because they could only assist me at no cost while I was a minor. They said they would transport me at no cost to Shriners Children's in Tampa. My dad, still in disbelief, said we'd discuss it and get back to them.

My mind was all over the place. I thought they were trying to take advantage of me in a predator-type way. We just hadn't heard about the Shriners and their generosity was a lot to process. Once we asked around about them and realized that it was all true, my family and I were excited that I'd been selected for this remarkable organization and opportunity.

A couple of days after I arrived at Shriners Children's Hospital, I found out that I was pregnant, which I couldn't believe. My mom was present when they told me, and we both questioned if they were sure about the results. Then, we immediately requested they test me again. We were told that they tested it three times to be sure, and all three had the same positive result.

I was totally astonished and ecstatic at the same time. This pregnancy was a blessing for me. I felt that I was given the greatest gift from God to remember Nakia, who I called "Tater." It was the good news that I needed to hear to mentally get on track. I was happy, and I wanted to give my baby a chance to live.

Up until hearing the news, I hadn't been eating. I ate a couple of spoons of food here and there during mealtimes. I had no appetite or will to eat. I was seriously depressed about Tater passing away. We had plans. My senior year in high school was not supposed to be like this.

Unbelievably, when I arrived at Shriners, I was in no physical pain at all. To everyone, it was a miracle for me not to have any physical pain with all my touch and go injuries only a month after my accident. However, I was constantly in extreme mental and emotional pain and agony. I didn't want to accept life without Tater, and I was avoiding it with the pain meds. The pain meds were putting me to sleep and out of my new nightmare of life. In my mind, I was hoping that I could at least see Tater in my dreams.

I was upset that my doctor at Shriners wouldn't give me the machine with the morphine shots that I'd been using to escape my pain of living without Tater. The staff tried to give me pain pills, but I told them that I didn't take pills, only shots. When my nurse told the doctor what I said, he paid a personal visit to inform me that I wasn't even going to get pain pills after my comment. Even though he never said it, I'm sure I sounded like an addict to him, and I knew it too. So, I didn't get combative. Actually, he probably saved my life. I know all about addiction and I was headed to a place I'd never imagined.

The nurses got worried about me because I was quiet and I kept to myself too much. I didn't want to live without Tater, but I wasn't suicidal. However, if someone didn't personally know me, it might've been easy to assume I would hurt myself because I could be very quiet. This was just a part of my personality since I can be a person of few words. I've never been suicidal in my life and the events of the accident never changed that for me. There's a difference in not wanting to be present versus harming myself.

In my defense, I was almost eighteen years old; in a month and a half later, I would be an adult by law. I was one of the oldest patients at Shriners. Frankly, I had more in common with the staff than the other patients. I saw them as kids, and I didn't want to be there away from my family and friends. Taking away the medication and finding out that I was pregnant essentially got me in the right head space for healing. I was open to anything that would get me a prosthesis and out of there.

Shriners Children's Hospital was a godsend, and I realized that I needed this opportunity for me and my family. I was assigned an occupational therapist, physical therapist, counselor, schoolteacher, OB/GYN, psychologist, psychiatrist, and a prosthetic team to get me through my rehabilitation. I used the mental health sessions as a platform to talk about my late boyfriend, which always made me happy. My counselor told me to journal, so I did that to talk to God and Tater.

At Shriners, I prayed constantly to keep my mind positive. The psychiatrist prescribed me an antidepressant, Paxil, and I was surprised when it helped. I had weekly checkups with a male obstetrician coming to monitor me and my baby. The doctor warned me that it was a fifty-fifty chance that my baby would survive through the first trimester after all the trauma and pain meds my body sustained.

Optimistically, I believed my baby would be fine. I was up to doing everything that I needed to better myself for me and my baby. My sister wasn't happy about the baby and questioned if I was having it. I had no doubt that I was having my baby, and I wanted my baby. Mentally, I was in a better place. I wanted to live.

My evening life counselor, my sister, and I talked for hours each night that I was at Shriners when she wasn't visiting. The long-distance calls were astronomically expensive. We didn't care; my dad would be the one to pay. Besides, it was an exceptionally good cause. Both of us needed those conversations, Terrinee needed to know I was okay, and I needed to know she was okay. This was another reason that I wouldn't ever harm myself. I couldn't ever knowingly leave my sister behind. I knew she wouldn't make it without me.

I thrived at physical and occupational therapy. For about a month, I was only allowed to stand up during physical therapy because I still had an external fixator screwed into my pelvis, since I couldn't risk falling on it for obvious reasons. I stood up for hours on a walker, and they couldn't believe how long I stood up on one leg. I had outstanding balance. Also, I always did my leg exercises to keep as much strength in my residual limb as possible. I knew all of this would prepare me to walk out of Shriners.

My occupational therapist assisted me with learning how to dress myself more efficiently and to get as much function as I could from the injured left arm with permanent nerve damage. I was always very independent, but putting on something as simple as a bra became difficult for me. I was accustomed to using two hands to put on a bra and buckling the back strap. But she demonstrated how I could fasten and strap my bra and then pull it over my head like a shirt.

Later, when I was fitted with a prosthesis, I always took off my leg to use the bathroom, which was a big ordeal for me. There was a strap that went from my pelvic area to around my waist to keep the prosthesis attached. The occupational therapist explained that I could leave it on to use the bathroom. I didn't know these things until I knew.

Schoolwork was the only thing that I couldn't focus on. I just couldn't focus on something as trivial as schoolwork at that time. I had too much going on in my mind to deal with during my rehabilitation. I took a few classes by phone with my Shriners' teacher. I always attended the telephone classes, but I wasn't mentally there either. The Shriner's teacher brought my work to me from Tift County High School. I just looked at it, then my mind would wander on other things like my therapy and things that would get me back home.

Don't get me wrong. Shriners Children's Hospital was a very generous place, and it was the best rehab that money could buy. They were always very giving regarding health care and activities. We played various wheelchair games and had field trips to restaurants like Olive Garden, the movie theater, and Busch Gardens. One day, a couple of players from the Tampa Bay Buccaneers visited and gave us autographed footballs. Also, there was one Black nurse in the infant unit who braided my hair to make sure it was nice, neat, and presentable. All around good people were at Shriners. But, still, I wanted to be home.

I enjoyed the visits with my family the most. One of my favorite visits was when my sister and Xaver surprised me on my eighteenth birthday. Before that, Shriners let me visit home once, and that was a real boost for my morale. I was crowned Tift County High School Homecoming Queen and I had the honor of Sergeant Purvis wheeling me out onto the field. The school made a point to let everyone know voting occurred before my accident, so I won without pity and sympathy for my condition, which was nice.

The most impactful time for me was when Terrinee came for Christmas, and I was allowed to stay with her at the hotel. It was just the two of us; and for the first time, I felt safe and centered again. It was literally the first night I'd slept since kicking the pain meds. I had no ill experiences at Shriners except for when I suffered my miscarriage. I believe I'd made it to about two and half months. One night, I had the urge to use the bathroom. I wheeled myself to the bathroom and got on the toilet. After I started urinating, I saw more than urine fill into the toilet. I saw this clear formation of what appeared to be my tiny baby. I instantly knew it was a fetus and that I had just miscarried. I pulled the emergency lever to call the nurse as I cried out in grief for my baby.

After losing my baby, I was depressed for a couple of days. Shriners sent me to Tampa General for a D&C to make sure nothing was left behind from the baby. Initially, I was upset while blaming everything, including myself, for the loss of my baby. I blamed myself for taking all the unnecessary pain medicines and believed that I starved my baby by not eating. I was upset and blamed Tift General for never giving me a pregnancy test the entire month that I was a patient there.

This pity party lasted only a few days before I got myself together mentally. I had already been praying constantly, so I prayed on this matter too and I realized that God terminated this pregnancy because it simply wasn't meant to be. I was still dealing with losing Tater and I wasn't meant to be a teenaged mother on top of everything else. In my head, I decided that God didn't want me to go through the problems of having an unhealthy baby or a baby with many disabilities. This was just another blessing in my favor. I thanked God and I moved passed that ordeal quickly into a good place.

I put my focus back on rehab. Initially, I couldn't feel any part of my left arm or move it. Really, I was just glad it was still attached. I knew it was barely hanging on after my accident. However, due to occupational therapy, I began to regain slight feeling in my left elbow and above.

I was able to move it and increase my range of motion.

When it was time for my external fixator to be removed, I didn't want my doctor at Shriners to remove it. I was still being very stubborn with him every chance I got. So, I called and spoke to Dr. Freeman. I trusted him when it came to surgery, so I wanted him to remove the external fixator. He assured me that he could and would do it, but any orthopedic doctor could since it was a simple procedure.

Unfortunately, my doctor at Shriners wouldn't approve of transporting me back to Tift General for Dr. Freeman to complete it. I was stuck with my doctor at Shriners. I can't believe I don't remember my doctor's name, but I don't. I do remember he loved M&M's and kept a jar of some in his office, which he always offered to me. As a bona fide candy lover, I indulged.

After my fixator was removed, I was finally ready to begin getting fitted for my prosthesis. Fred was the lead prosthetist and Tammy was the other prosthetist; she may have been a resident at the time. I loved both of them and we always had a good time during the fitting. At that time, things were very slow when it came to getting fitted for a prosthetic leg. It took around six weeks for me to get fitted for an above the knee prosthesis. And I hated the way it looked; nevertheless, it was my ticket to freedom. My socket had a mechanical knee and a chocolate brown foot because I was Black. Back then, prosthetic feet only came in two colors. I made the comment that they should've given me a white foot since that would've been closer to my complexion.

They always told me that when I could walk, I could go home. Soon as I put on the prosthesis, I was walking like I had been my entire life. I was upset though, because they had a gait belt on me for support. I felt like I didn't need the support. But I was walking again, and it was just like riding a bike for me. All I was thinking about was finally going home. In physical therapy after I was fitted, the therapists wanted to show me the best way to fall and how to get off the ground after falling. I was still being stubborn, so I refused to fall on purpose. It was too unnatural for me to practice falling. I said, "I'll figure out how to get up if I fall, but I don't plan on falling." And I didn't. Before I left the hospital, I went outside to see if I could run, and I ran on the first try without falling once. My sister was so happy and proud to see me run.

About two weeks before my prothesis was completed, I found my focus to complete my schoolwork. My tele-teacher couldn't believe it. She said I told her that I would complete my work and not to worry. I did just that! She was in further disbelief that I completed all of it in just two weeks. She thought it would be impossible for me to complete my makeup work before leaving Tampa. I completed almost four months of work in two weeks.

I had one more stubborn episode with my doctor before I left Shriners. I'm sure I gave him gray hair because I unfairly took most of my hostility out on him. I loved my prosthesis, but I hated the fact that the first socket was so oversized. I looked strange in my clothes, like I had a pillow in my jeans, but it was my leg socket. He assured me that it was temporary until I came back for my follow-up appointment in a month, since I probably would need a new socket due to my limb shrinking from wearing the prosthesis daily and being active. I told him that I hated that leg and I wasn't going to wear it. The socket was just too big. This doctor had a specialty in me, and he knew exactly how to deal with me. He sent me home with my custom wheelchair that Shriners made for me when I arrived. However, he ordered for me to return my custom wheelchair when I returned for my one-month checkup.

This chair was designed for me and my specification, so it was very unlikely that it could be used for anyone else. Cunningly, the doctor basically told me that I was walking no matter what because he wouldn't allow me to use the crutch of a wheelchair. I never used that wheelchair. Not once. I made a promise to God that if he got me out of that wheelchair that I'd never sit in another one. Needless to say, I brought that wheelchair back, and I was even happier to inform my doctor that I never used it once when I left the hospital.

I wouldn't be who I am if I didn't try to scare as many people as I could with my leg when I got home. I started a habit of leaving my leg fully dressed in jeans and a shoe in the bathroom every night. I heard scream after scream when someone went to the bathroom at night and flipped the switch while half asleep. Trust me, that leg woke them up every time and it never got old or stopped being hilarious to me.

Finally, I was home. Since my sister was back in Atlanta, I spent most of my time with my best friends, TK, Tressa, Nikki, Jenny, and Jason. TK was always with me before the accident, even when I was with Tater. She sat with me all day and night at Tift General. Naturally, she returned to always being with me when I returned to Tifton from Shriners. I truly appreciated her being there for me and my family.

I went on to graduate from high school on time with honors and attended Clark Atlanta University the same year that my sister started law school at the University of Georgia. I was always going to the same school Terrinee attended, and I knew the campus well because I was always with her during holidays and spring and summer breaks on campus. The Gundy girls were always going to be one mind. Terrinee took an extra step to ensure our joint destiny because she sent in my college applications; she intentionally only mailed the one to Clark Atlanta University. Everything happens for a reason, and as it should. My sister and I are forever and a day two girls with one heart. If her heart stopped, so would mine. And vice versa, she is my forever soulmate, and I am hers.

CHAPTER 13

"As Smart As You Are Pretty"

I finally made it to high school. I wasn't happy to still be in Tifton, but I was ecstatic about being one step closer to college. Tift County High School had a few bumps and bruises, but things were primarily going well for me academically, socially, and extracurricular activities. Since I was the boys' basketball statistician, most of my friends were still guys and mainly basketball players. This time my mama wouldn't say much since Cousin Xaver was with me almost always. She had no choice but to accept the fact that I was seen as one of the boys, a real guys' girl.

Most of my teachers saw my potential and fostered my growth and development. Mr. Sumner (geometry) and Coach O'Brien (honors government) were amazing men and instructors. Both of them left instructions for the substitute teachers to take roll and let me teach the class as a student. Their trust and confidence in my abilities propelled me into a better exemplar. Mr. Bussey (AP English) truly expanded my love of writing and insisted on me being on the debate team. After my disastrous learning experiences with two white women from junior high, I was pleasantly surprised to be fully supported, encouraged, and believed in by three white men in South Georgia.

I finally learned where the hell my blue eyes came from in Biology. Everyone has two DNA genes for eye color: dominant brown and recessive blue traits. Apparently, both of my parents must have one dominant and one recessive trait since their eyes are brown. I inherited one recessive blue-eyed trait from each of them. Neither of my kids were born with blue eyes; however, they both have inherited the blue-eyed trait from me. I might have some blue-eyed grandchildren one day. This time no one should be surprised.

I was participating in many clubs and organizations while working two jobs: National Honor's Society (NHS), Future Business Leaders of America (FBLA), McKnight Achievers, 4-H Club, debate team, student government, wrestling (mat girl), Boys' Basketball (statistician), Girl's State, Girl's Nations, Homecoming Court, Spanish spelling bee, swim team, tennis team, JROTC, and Miss Black Tiftarea. I was Winn Dixie's head cashier and a science research assistant for a Black male scientist from Abraham Baldwin Agriculture College (ABAC), whose name I regrettably can't remember, but admired and respected very much.

I prided myself on being promoted to head cashier who supervised workers and prepared the daily bank deposits based on the cash collected from the safe. My daddy told me to be the best. Even if I was sweeping floors, be the best floor sweeper because excellence in everything breeds winners. I was never late or called out to work. I stood sideways, using both my hands to simultaneously pull and wave grocery items across the scanner like I was saving lives. I had self-satisfaction in being dependable, reliable, and competitive by scanning the groceries faster than my coworkers.

My mama, however, wanted me to have a little more pride in my room cleanliness and closet organization. We lived in a ranch-style house with a snake-filled pond out front in Vanceville, about five miles outside of Tifton. It was an older house, but light-years from the projects with crying rats that sounded like they were having babies. The snakes greedily ate any rats for lunch that dared come onto the property. Interestingly enough, I wasn't fearful of snakes but terrified of rats. The only downfall was that we didn't have a car and my mama's pride and ego prevented her from asking for rides to town. We had to regularly and often walk for miles despite Kilroy constantly volunteering to pick us up. The Taurus' bullhead within her picked the damnedest times to show up. She and Mia were so chipper and happy-go-lucky walking down the highway, and I was religiously a quarter of a mile behind, slowly pacing and sulking.

Ms. "Taurus the Bull" appeared out of nowhere. She was in full "I'm the Chief, and y'all the Indians, repeat after me" mode. I was going to school, doing extracurricular activities, and working doubles to pay off a loan shark, Big Billy, for jewelry I was buying for her birthday and Mother's Day. I was busy. Yeah, my clothes were all over the room and my closet had the remnants of a tornado combined with a blizzard. But, come on. I was doing everything right except for having extra time and energy to organize after twelve-to-fifteen-hour days. That woman made me stay home to clean my room and closet causing my only work blemish. I was pissed, but I'll admit it was probably for the best. Even though she was the least organized person I knew, she knew her child and what I needed. It was necessary for me to remove the clutter to sustain being at my best. She also wanted me to take a breather and reset because I'd been hitting it so hard. She was providing me with the wherewithal of balancing work, school, and home. Like my daddy preached, I had to be excellent in all things, including cleaning up my room.

More importantly, I had to excel at improving my chances of getting into college with a scholarship. I knew getting into college wasn't enough since my parents couldn't afford to live and pay for college. I needed a scholarship. So, let's talk about the Miss Black Tiftarea Scholarship Pageant or should I say, the mean, nasty contestants from the pageant. It was a scholarship pageant for young Black women, a competition including an interview, opening dance number, swimsuit, talent, and evening gown segments from the age of sixteen to twenty or so. Traditionally, the winner was either a high school senior or college freshmen; it was welcome assistance for college tuition and fees. As a rising high school junior at sixteen, I decided to enter the pageant to prepare and practice with hopes of winning during my senior year in high school.

With all my years of modeling and pageantry, I could walk with the best of them and of course would crush the interview portion using my big brain. My mama's inherited Coke bottle shape made swimsuits and gowns fit gloriously. I couldn't dance for shit, and everyone knew it. Thus, these petty ass girls decided not to teach me the opening dance number since no sixteen-year-old had ever won, and it was assumed that I wouldn't be the exception.

Big mistake! Never tell me what I can't do because I will spend every moment proving that shit wrong. After hearing about my mistreatment at pageant practice, my mama declared that I wouldn't only win the Ms. Black Tiftarea title but every single category. There was a difference between winning and not losing that some people may not understand. For clarity, I didn't just want to win. More than anything, I refused to lose. In the beginning, I was doing the pageant for fun and the experience, but now I was determined to decimate all of them for underestimating me.

First, it was those white teachers from junior high, and now these Black teenage contestants who were unfairly mistreating me. Seriously, what had I ever done to any of them that warranted being treated like the bottom of their cheap ass shoes, other than being born? I couldn't call this racism, but I certainly felt a prejudice from my own race. I was a child, a teenager, but still a child that didn't deserve to be bullied and knocked around. I wouldn't get mad—I would beat all of them! I would make history and win the whole damn thing at sixteen.

Since I couldn't dance or sing to save my life, I needed to figure out my performance for the talent section. "Mama, I need someone to help with my talent. I won't win the talent section, but I still need to get a decent score. Everything else I got on lock!"

"You are going to win it all, including talent. So, you need to do a monologue. You will be great, and I've got the perfect person to help you—Ms. Cummings. She's an acting coach and her daughter, Marsha, was Ms. Black Tiftarea 1988."

It was on! Ms. Cummings and I hit it off like peanut butter and jelly from our initial meeting. She had the perfect monologue for me to perform, "Bobo the Clown." It was about a clown aspiring to have his name in lights more than anything, including being present during the sickness and death of his father. The piece required a dramatic, emotional oration that encompassed hope, love, despair, anger, passion and loss.

Ms. Cummings explained, "Those other girls are simply jealous of you because you're so good looking. I can help you win because you have everything it takes to win, but I can't want it more than you. I won't waste my time if you won't do the work."

I assured her. "I promise you that no one will work harder than me. No one! I will do exactly what you tell me because I'm going to win. I want it more than you and my mama want it for me. I want it for myself."

I was Keyball's daughter and had been working since I was five years old. No one would outwork me. I committed to practicing every day that summer until the pageant in August. I practiced my poise and grace daily, modeling in the high heels that I would wear on the big night, then, Ms. Cummings would edit or critique my recitation of "Bobo the Clown." I didn't miss a session all summer. By the time the pageant was upon us, she told me that I had taken her direction and suggestions very well. I'd perfected my monologue. Bobo and I had become one.

During the pageant, I hit my dance steps perfectly, marveling in my lavender one-piece swimsuit. I was so excited that I almost walked off the stage, literally, onto the judge's table. I stopped myself mid-step, in possibly the biggest disaster of my pageant life, but I never lost my composure and caught myself before walking into thin air. My mama assured me backstage that it didn't matter because it was more important that I never stopped smiling or lost my shit. She insisted that I focused on what was in front of me and still in my control, not what was behind me. Once again, I had to tap into my superpower of bending reality my way.

It was time for my talent, and I was slated to perform first since my contestant number was one. My mama's old profession as a seamstress sure helped; she sewed a true clown costume with matching oversized clown shoes from the thrift store; a giant curly, rainbow, afro wig; and a painted face like a professional clown. When I walked onto the dark stage with only a spotlight, I was totally unrecognizable; she'd morphed me into Bobo the Clown. I owned the stage, utilizing every inch and hitting every mark. In practice, I could never actually cry because tears were reserved for the dead in my head (and it depended on who died), but that night Bobo cried real tears at the end of the monologue. As I dropped to my knees to belch out Bobo's closing tearful lines, the entire auditorium jumped to its feet, cheering and clapping with a standing ovation.

Now it was time to get all that clown paint off my face and transform into a graceful beauty for the evening gown segment. As usual, Auntie Robin, Auntie Barb, and Grandma Marian made sure that it was another $1,000 pageant gown. My mama cleaned me up in a split second, pinned my hair up to display her full creation, and left the rest for me to conquer as I glided elegantly onstage. In pageants, gowns can make a winner just like speeches can do for politicians. My gown was so breathtakingly gorgeous that my mama insisted that I not show it to any of the contestants nor the pageant organizers as traditionally required. She believed it would cause the other girls to reevaluate and change their dress decisions. Of course, I obeyed my mama and thank goodness. My gown was by far the most stunning of them all. It sparkled like a frosty blue icicle in the dead of the night.

It was time for the moment I had been preparing for months. The queen was about to be announced. First, the category winners would be revealed: Miss Congeniality (I voted for myself because I knew no one else would), best interview, best swimsuit, best talent, and best gown. I didn't win Miss Friendly and honestly don't remember or care who won. She wasn't nice to me.

The MC announced, "The winner for best interview is contestant number one, Terrinee Gundy."

Next, he yelled out on the microphone, "Best swimsuit goes to contestant number one, Terrinee Gundy."

The crowd was going crazy, screaming and yelling "number one, number one, number one."

When the announcer said, "The best talent of the night is contestant number one, Terrinee Gundy," the auditorium went wild.

The announcer screamed over the crowd, "Our last award before announcing the queen is best evening gown, and yes, it goes to contestant number one again, Terrinee Gundy."

Most of my family from Tifton and Jacksonville, along with my high ass daddy, were in half of the audience jumping up and down, roaring so loud that it was hard to hear my name when I was crowned Miss Black Tiftarea 1990. There was no shortage of vision between me and my mama. Both of us brought our creativity, style, and talents to getting me that crown. As always, my hard work paid off!

I may have been beautiful and graceful, but I came from a scrappy family. I can't quite remember all the Henderson brawls because they were so often and regular. My mama and her siblings were in one club fight after another. She was even "knocked the fuck out" once by some random man while fighting with her brothers. Her oldest brother hog-tied a man to the back of his monster truck, affectionately known as "Big Foot," for some personal offense that I wasn't privy to. My beloved cousin, Baraka, whopped this kid's ass for offering me a hit from a joint. None of that compared to the colossal mistake of two guys. One guy made the mistake of owing Uncle Jerome some money, and the other fucked with his little sister—Pete—was what he called my mama.

My uncle was one of the most generous, loving, and kind men that I've had the pleasure of being acquainted, yet violent and batshit crazy, from which we blamed his service during the Vietnam War. He went there one way and came home an entirely different way, but I loved him all the same. He was the best, always so loving and caring toward me. Honestly, all my family poured so much into me. It would've been a travesty if I hadn't done something positive with my life. Uncle Jerome's sweet gestures were clearly reserved for family because I thought he was going to legitimately kill his debtor and my mama's second husband.

On a random sunny day in Tifton, Uncle Jerome's red and gold Camaro casually pulled up to Mia and me at the Pennywise Corner Store. Uncle Jerome was his normal, upbeat, and pleasant self, all while holding an unidentified man gagged and bound sitting in the passenger seat, presumably against his will.

"How was school today? Y'all had a good day?"

Mia and I hesitantly responded. "Yeah, we're good."

Uncle Jerome saw the distraught on our faces and assured us, "Don't worry about this guy. He owes me some money and he's going to learn not to play with my money. Speak to my nieces."

We nodded in affirmation but didn't mum a word. We dared not tell Uncle Jerome that the man wasn't able to speak since he was bound and gagged—a small detail.

"All right. I have to go, but I'll check on y'all later," Uncle Jerome said. "Here's some money for y'all to go get something out of the store."

Uncle Jerome rode all around town with this man in his front seat for at least two days, releasing him only after Kilroy's insistence, but not before beating him for almost two weeks while being held against his will. To my knowledge, not the police, my family, the guy's family, or anyone else challenged or interfered with Uncle Jerome's cynical retribution plan until his daddy showed up. Oddly enough, we never had another discussion about it. It was just another day in the neighborhood. It probably wasn't healthy to be so detached and unmoved, however, it was what it was—that was the reality we survived time and time again. Ultimately, everyone got the message not to fuck with Uncle Jerome a.k.a. lil Vietnam. Well, everyone except my mama's silly ass second husband.

After being with the nice Bahamian man, my mama went on a roller-coaster ride of romantic relationships with several men between Atlanta and Tifton. Allegedly, she found a man who wanted to marry her, provide financial stability, security in a good neighborhood and help with her girls. Times had been hard, so I understood my mama's desire for love and a helping hand. She shouldn't have left my daddy for all his flaws, in my humble opinion. Our lives were inconsistent, but better off with him.

Time after time growing up, I'd hear women say, "Better the devil you know than the devil you don't."

My mama didn't know jack shit about that second husband of hers, and to this day, I wished she'd listened to me and Mia in that Tift General Hospital parking lot. Back then, a blood test was required to get married to ensure neither party had a venereal disease, sickle cell trait, or getting hitched to their cousin. Times have changed due to medical advancements and stricter privacy laws. Presumably, my mama and her man had none of those hinderances to marry. Our mama informed us as she walked in to get the blood test, that she would be getting remarried. My sister and I literally were on our hands and knees, in the parking lot, begging and pleading with her not to marry this pretender. Child or not, I knew in my soul this guy was not good for her or us, no matter the airs he put on. Our desperate warnings were no match for her hope for love, optimism for our future, and her Achilles heel to see the good in everyone.

Mi Rey often told me, "You have so many superpowers, but one of them for sure is your ability to see around corners."

As many times before with my God-given sight, my intuition and gut were spot on; unfortunately, they were rarely wrong. Her new husband was what we predicted and much more—the devil we didn't know. He was a womanizer. I saw him out frolicking with other women, and he saw that I saw him. I decided not to tell my mama because it wouldn't have made a difference. She wasn't leaving him, so there was no need for me to be the bearer of bad news and break her heart again. Those were his burdens and misdeeds to bear, not mine.

Financial stability and security my ass! With him, we were back to the same bullshit of having the utilities disconnected, and presumably, he wasn't a Junkie. So, what was his excuse for being a sorry ass provider? One time he had the audacity to sit by and watch her call my daddy for money to reconnect the electricity in "his" house. I begged my daddy not to give them a dime. Let them sit in that dark and cold house alone and figure it out for themselves. I told him we could go stay with our grandparents. I preferred for them to simmer and suffer in their mess.

My daddy insisted, "Terrinee, what kind of man would I be to let my kids stay in a house with no lights? One day you'll understand, but it's no way I can do that. I have to send your mama the money."

He immediately wired her the money and we had lights again. He was right. Later in life, I understood what he was saying, especially after going through my own divorce. However, I still didn't like him sending that money, and probably never will. I do appreciate that both of my parents loved us more than hating each other. Their work showed up in me and Mia. We may have had other issues, but none that I can remember relating to an unhealthy relationship between the two of them after their divorce.

Besides being a whore and broke, there were signs of physical and mental abuse inflicted on my mama. Like most battered women, she protected him. I called the police on him for abusing her because he wouldn't let us in the room to confirm that she was okay. When the police showed up, she covered for him and even let him call me a "little lying bitch" in front of them. I may have been little, but I was neither a liar nor a bitch. I just wanted to protect my mama. Prior to that, she would've slapped the taste out his mouth in front of the police for calling me out of my name. His behavior was hurtful, but her response or lack thereof was downright disappointing and excruciatingly agonizing. My mama had been replaced with a clone and a shell of herself. What happened to my "Shero" who fought anyone for or with me? Where was the woman who cursed out those two racist white teachers? Why would she protect a man that was so wrong for her and us? Where was her always fight, never flight attitude with this sorry muthafucka?

Later at Clark Atlanta University, her behavior was the impetus of my senior thesis project on why Black women don't report abuse at the same rate as women of other races, regardless of their socioeconomic status. Our mama and Mia were proudly observing when I presented for my professors, but I wasn't sure if my mama knew it was truly all about my love for her and heartache for her situation. I presented that my data, research, and subject interviews concluded that Black women primarily feared Black men being incarcerated or killed by the police more than their own safety and survival.

Failure to report or any other reasoning wouldn't save her husband from Uncle Jerome's wrath. When Uncle Jerome found out that he'd abused my mama, he came over to burn him alive inside their house. Uncle Jerome made our mama, Mia, and I come outside while he barricaded the exits and paced and circled the house while dousing gasoline all over it.

She was a frantic mess, crying and hollering. "Jerome, please don't do this. Please don't kill my husband."

Just as laid back as he was when that man was hog-tied in his car, he quietly replied, "Pete, it's above you, now. Sorry, I'm going to kill him today. I gave him a warning and promised him this would happen if he ever touched you again."

Mia and I sat on the street curb cool as cucumbers watching the entire scene play out. All that was missing was the popcorn. Wished I could say we were worried, upset, scared, or bothered, but we weren't the least bit concerned. In the moment, I didn't want Uncle Jerome to kill the man, but if he had, I surely wouldn't miss him abusing my mama. It was another day in the neighborhood except this time it was a white neighborhood on the prestigious side of town. Guessing that was why Grandma Vera crossed the tracks so fast to stop her son. But Uncle Jerome ignored her and kept dousing as if he was in a faraway land, thinking of his time in Vietnam.

Seconds before he was about to fling a lit match on the house, Grandma Vera lay her petite, round body in the middle of the street screaming and crying, "Jerome, if you love me at all, please don't do this. I'm begging you to stop this. Son, please, do it for me, please!"

Before that day or since, I hadn't seen my grandma so emotional and vulnerable about anything; the woman was tough as steel. She was fighting for the lives of her children. Uncle Jerome's actions would've destroyed both his and my mama's life, and possibly ours too if we lost her to the justice system. A mother's love indeed conquers all. Finally, his mama's voice and tears penetrated the black hole that he'd found himself in. Uncle Jerome slowly backed away from the house, gently blew the match out, and drove off in his Camaro without a word to any of us.

As far as I knew, my mama's foolish husband never put another hand on her from that point forward. The greater damage was unfortunately already done. He still had control of her mind. Every single relationship in our household was frail and held on by a thin thread, except for mine and Mia's. The worse things got, the more determined I was to protect and provide for Mia. We were under the same roof as them, however, Mia and I confined ourselves to one side of the house, using our own entry. We didn't congregate with them, eat with them nor cohabitate with them in any traditional way. I worked two jobs and used my pageant winnings to provide our food and clothing.

Hostility had grown so high and became so unbearable, that I decided I wouldn't leave for college. Rather, I would stay with Mia in Tifton and attend the local college, Abraham Baldwin Agriculture College. We would leave together after Mia's high school graduation. What good was a dream realized if it would simultaneously leave my sister permanently wrecked and damaged in ways that couldn't be repaired? We were getting out together or staying trapped together! She was my North Star, center of my Earth, the gravity that kept me grounded and the oxygen I breathed; Mia was the reason I existed. As much as I desired to be a college graduate, I loved my sister infinitely more. For me, it wasn't even a second thought. My young soul and determined spirit were at peace with my decision. Besides, it would be fun for Mia and me to be college roommates in five years after her high school graduation.

Cool as a sea breeze, my daddy said, "Terrinee, we respect how you feel and understand your belief that you must protect Mia. We will respect your decision no matter what, but I want you to think about one thing before you make your final decision. Don't do this for me, don't do this for your mama, and although you may want to, don't even do this for Mia. If you do this, only do this because you want to do it for yourself. Do it for Terrinee and only Terrinee. You hear me? If you do this for me, or your mama, or Mia, one day you will wake up filled with regret. If you do this only for you, and it doesn't work out, it won't be a regret. It'll just be a learning experience. Daddy want you to have a life full of great learning experiences. Not regrets. Live a life for Terrinee with no regrets. You feel me?"

Those words of making decisions for me, and only me, struck a chord for me well beyond that day. Just as my daddy instructed throughout the ups and downs, I must say that I've had a full life with no regrets, including the day I doubled down on my decision.

"Let me say this as slowly, clearly, and as respectfully as possible. I'm—not—leaving—my—sister—in—that—house. I've made my decision. That's that!"

My parents could see the sincerity and resolve in my fierce eyes, and worried that their adult decisions and bullshit had derailed my entire life plan. Wisely, neither of them attempted to change my mind. Instead, they worked to come up with a safe and secure solution for Mia. My parents knew that was the only way to reverse my course of action.

"Even a broken clock is right twice a day."

Those broken, damaged parents of mine never failed to show up amid the chaos when it was all on the line. For them, the line was too close and uncomfortable because my future was in doubt for the first time. Dysfunctional as they were, my parents were still sharp on their feet with endless possibilities of creativity to clean up their mess, an acquired skill for most Junkies. We all agreed that Mia would go and live with our daddy in Jacksonville when I headed off to college. And nope, he wasn't close to sober. He was still pretending to be a functioning addict, whatever that means. There is no such thing to me or him! However, I appreciated the nobility of him making the effort to get clean and avoid derailing my college plans.

During her short-lived time in Jacksonville, Mia would experience another calamity at the ripe age of fourteen. One of her closest friends was gunned down outside their house and killed by another teenaged boy who lived across the street. He was found not guilty based on his "stand-your-ground" defense. I knew Mia was upset, but I don't remember her crying or showing outward emotions during or after the tragic event. Unfortunately, normalizing trauma, loss and death was ingrained and interwoven in our existence.

Our mama showed such courage and sacrifice for bearing the pain of losing her girls at the same time. She knew she was damaging us with the instability of her predicament and refused to drag us any further through that dreaded ordeal. Our relationship with our mama, had been forever changed. It was so tough and heartbreaking to see her meek, subdued, and kowtowing to that man. I couldn't process how a woman so strong, resilient, and kickass acquiesced to a nimble, unworthy fool. Even more unreal was the way she allowed him to mistreat us with his dismissive, and sometimes derogatory words as well as actions without her muttering so much as a whisper. It was almost too much to bare when he turned her against us. It felt like she chose him over us.

Mama felt as though we punished and judged her harder than our daddy for his flaws and shortcomings. Maybe we did. She didn't understand why we never believed he chose crack cocaine over us. There was no wrong or right answer that I could give her. Maybe our daddy's insistence on not smoking crack cocaine in front of us worked in his favor. All I knew was that I didn't feel slighted or overlooked by crack cocaine, versus the complete opposite, with her undesirable love affair. Even as a kid, I saw addiction as a disease. My daddy remained himself around us while being a Junkie, but she temporarily lost herself in a man. The ill-feeling of our mama's marriage was front, center, and overwhelmingly in our faces. I believed marrying and staying committed to the wrong guy was her choice. Despite all the trauma I'd seen and survived, this was the first time in my life that I'd actually felt unsafe; there was an intruder mercilessly penetrating the Core Four.

It would take many years for me to fully understand that my mama wasn't choosing him or anything else for that matter; she wasn't capable in her circumstance. Unhealthy and abusive relationships have the tendency to make the victim feel powerless with no choices at all. She wasn't weak. She was trying to survive as a Black woman who was making personal sacrifices of dignity and self-worth for what she thought was right for herself and her daughters. A home in the right neighborhood with a husband for an intact family was the life and example she wanted for us. Unfortunately, she made a bad judgment call with that particular man, and we all paid the price. The harm was unintentional because her heart was always in the right place.

My mama's heart was also in the right place when I got her best advice about one of my test grades from math class. This time I didn't fail, but I scored a ninety-nine, a far cry from the sixty-three in the ninth grade. Nevertheless, I was fighting mad. My mama was perplexed and quickly grew tiresome of the anal attitude I brought home from school. Carrying on like a spoiled brat, I was throwing things, raising my voice, and scowling at anyone looking into my fiery, blue-green eyes. My eyes change colors, especially when I'm upset.

When she couldn't stand my tantrum another minute, my mama tried giving me the benefit of the doubt as she asked, "What the hell is wrong with you today? Did something happen at school? Are you okay? Did someone hurt you?"

I snapped back. "No, none of that, I'm fine, and you wouldn't understand."

"Try me. Because I'm not going to take this little attitude of yours much longer without an explanation. Any time you say, 'I'm fine,' you're not fine."

It was a waste of time to explain my test grade because she was an average academic high school student. She required that Mia and I only get all A's because she knew what we were capable of. She wouldn't accept anything from us less than our best, but she wouldn't care about a ninety-nine because it was still an A.

"I'm upset because I got a ninety-nine on my test instead of a one hundred. Please let me explain before you say a word. I would have rather failed because I didn't know or understand the material, but to get a ninety-nine means that I made a mistake. Clearly, I knew the material, so I should've gotten a one hundred and not a stupid ninety-nine. I made a stupid mistake that cost me my perfect score. For me, that stings."

There were no words that existed to adequately explain the befuddlement on my mama's face. She didn't say the words, but her facial expression screamed her child was absolutely, fucking bananas. This was the most ridiculous shit she'd heard in all her days on Earth. Her nonverbal communication was the exact reason for my hesitation about telling her in the first place.

After a long pause, she said, "There's no difference in a ninety-nine and a one hundred because they both say you're smart as hell. Terrinee, I hope you hear me and hear me good. You are the smartest person I know, but you'll never be as smart as you are pretty. In order to become everything you want in life, you need to learn how to use all God has given you. I know you and your daddy focus on smarts, and I'm glad he has given you confidence in your God-given abilities. But take it from your mama, you are going to have to stop ignoring your equally exceptional, God-given beauty. Embrace it all and use it all. As a Black woman, I promise you will need it all! Listen to your mama. You already have everything you need: beauty and brains! God gave you that pretty face and big brain for a reason, and I expect for you to use both for good. Use both to help people. And for goodness sake, be a little nicer to yourself because you're way too hard on yourself."

My mama's monologue hit differently that day! Sadly, I was condescending toward my mama for being just a "pretty girl" and I wanted no part of that stigma. In the ghetto, pretty girls were as common as colds, but pretty girls who were smart and hard-working were far and few between. My mama insisted on me not selling myself short while championing it all. She gave me permission to shine magnificently at full wattage. She was absolutely correct that I had to embrace the gift of my beauty too. I had to face the facts of this reality, just as I had done with being the Daughter of a Junkie.

CHAPTER 14

"You Are The Light"

My daddy was Keyballing his way back on his feet. The comeback kid was backtracking to retail clothing. This time he pitched an open tent with a carpet floor on a vacant dirt lot where a house once stood at the intersection of Myrtle Avenue and Eight Street. Voilà, we had "The Corner." He sustained The Corner in one form or another for over thirty years. The neighborhood declared him the "King of Knockoffs." He was teaching himself how to have a business outdoors, literally. He was convinced that his old business model of brick and mortar was dated, costly, and unsustainable; he had this premonition prior to the internet boom. Candidly, he couldn't afford a building with rent, maintenance, insurance, utilities in addition to employees. He only had enough of borrowed money from Grandma Marian for a bare minimum amount of merchandise, which no one could tell because of his high spirit, eager showmanship with customers, and meticulous maintenance of the grounds. He insisted on the tent being kept immaculate with all the inventory perfectly folded, organized, and stacked. He ran The Corner like Publix and The Gap had a baby.

My daddy also began a side hustle of referring clients to a bondsman for a 10 percent referral fee. For over twenty-five years, he partnered with the bondsman in getting people out of jail. The folks in the neighborhood respected him for this deed and appreciated that they could call day or night. My daddy would allow anyone who was recently released to come get a new outfit and $100 in cash once, if they had served at least a year and one day. He essentially implemented his own prison reentry program.

When Mia and I asked why he did it, he said, "People need to look good to feel good, and nothing does that like a new outfit. After they've paid their debt to society, they deserve that at least. And I know what it feels like to be dead broke. It's a terrible, desperate feeling. People need some money in their pocket. Money gives people hope and hope changes lives. I just want people to know I'm doing more than rooting for them. I'm jump-starting them with a chance to be better because I've had so many chances myself."

Pretty sure he isn't aware that I implemented a hybrid of his reentry program while growing up. I started giving a little pocket change minus the outfit to those I knew returning to society from incarceration. And for that, they have my daddy to thank! Both of my parents and grandparents instilled service to others in me and Mia. Grandma Marian has been hosting a Dr. Martin Luther King Jr. breakfast to feed others for as long as I can remember. She also became a breast cancer crusader by selling decorated bras for cancer and copies of Dr. Jackie's Perfect Imperfections, which I am featured in to increase awareness.

Following my family's example, I combined my entrepreneurial and service skillset to one day become the CEO and co-founder of a 501(c)(3) nonprofit, the Collective Renaissance Guild (CRG). My co-founder, Christine, and I literally sat on my living room floor with a group of like-minded women: Ericka S., Tiffany, Angela, Davida, Kamille, Staci, Deshanna, Jessica, Kamal, Adrienne, Nicole, and Erica B. to develop civic and cultural leaders while integrating arts, philanthropy, and social change. We couldn't have done it without the undying support from our initial supporters, especially Beni, Tara, Cecilia, Carolyn, Andrea, Jerry T., Deanna, Danita, Chaka, Eugene, Sam, Linkston, Mike, and Jerry C.

CRG hosted youth conferences, women's leadership brunches, and men's leadership forums attended by the likes of Ambassador Andrew Young; Senator Raphael Warnock; General Colin Powell; Congressman Kwanza Hall; EPA administrator, Daniel Blackman; and Mayor Kasim Reed, along with many other local leaders. We had the pleasure of honoring so many great, impactful people such as Xernona Clayton, Evelyn and Joseph Lowery, Jamie Foxx, Ludacris, Wynton Marsalis, Toni Braxton, Keshia Knight Pulliam, Andre 3000, Cornell West, Nicole Ari Parker, Will Packer, Rob Hardy, Phaedra Parks, Kenny Burns, and many more.

During this time, I had the great fortune of being invited to the White House for the annual holiday party hosted by President Barack Obama with First Lady Michelle Obama. It was a grand affair filled with dazzling lights, festive decorations, and exquisite delicatessens. My sister was my plus-one to witness this joyous and historic occasion. While standing in the West Wing, directly in front of President John F. Kennedy's portrait sipping hot tea, Mia and I burst into infectious giggles.

"Mia, we did it! From the crack house to the White House. Only in America! I fucking love this country!"

I have multiple photos with the Obamas, and even got my mama and sister a President Obama photo. My daughter, Mia Michelle, had a cameo in the Becoming documentary after I took her and my sister to see the first lady. In one hundred years, I'm sure my descendants won't truly appreciate the significance of this part of our family history, but at the very least, I hope they're proud enough to think that this was the stock I came from. If all of this wasn't to bend the trajectory of our familial line for the better, what was it for?

Becoming a judge from the slums of Duval against the odds was nothing short of miraculous. Under all normal circumstances, I wouldn't have made it to the judiciary. I had an intestinal fortitude to force outcomes, especially adversity, my way. I was taught to bend reality. I'd bent addiction, poverty, racism, sexism, and anything that stood against me because I refused to succumb to guaranteed obstacles and useless excuses. I didn't have the luxury of excuses when we were abandoned at Publix, resuscitated my mama back from the dead, negotiated my daddy's life and freedom with drug dealers, or endured unexpected racism from my teachers. So, I wouldn't use my daddy's latest disappearing act as an excuse to cancel Christmas. I had to bend reality yet again.

I never realized the prevalent theme Christmas played in my childhood. Now, I see it clear as day. After we moved to Tifton, Mia and I spent every holiday and school break, big or small, with our daddy in Jacksonville. This Christmas break, my daddy was Casper the Friendly Ghost, nowhere to be found. Allegedly, he was in West Palm Beach with one of his childhood friends, Brother Carl, looking to Allah for sobriety. No luck. His ass was missing like the Holy Quran in a Southern Baptist church. No one had heard from him in weeks. We had no idea if he was dead or alive. He wasn't in Jacksonville, so we weren't able to look around or check his usual debauchery locations.

My daddy had us on the ropes several times before that Christmas, and, as expected, many times afterward. His last job before The Corner was as an assistant manager of a large grocery store chain. He loved the grocery business, but his drug habit was raging out of control by this time. He'd taken that job only to discreetly rob those people and feed the yearning crack cocaine beast inside of him. He had keys to the safe and was responsible for the daily count. He would withdraw from $500 to $1,000 daily, depending on the gross receipts. The night Hurricane Hugo hit Jacksonville, the electricity went out, so the store was operating solely on generators. My daddy was in Crack Cocaine Candy Land! He took $6,000 from the safe in one swipe.

He would take between $75,000 to $100,000 out of that safe within a nine-month period. That was a lot of Rock 'n' Rolling! He voluntarily decided to go to a full-fledged drug rehabilitation center on the store's dime to get in front of that nine-month hijack. When the time came to explain, he blatantly lied. He said he was an alcoholic to avoid the terrible stigma directed at crackheads. The store is still none the wiser about his addiction or theft. Thank goodness for the statute of limitations.

My daddy had me on the ropes yet another time when he bought me a used convertible, white Cadillac Eldorado. I loved that damn car because it fit me so well. Too bad, I'd only get to drive it once. Yes, I said the Junkie bought me a car. Actually, he has purchased four cars to date, for me. He persuaded me to let him run a quick errand before I took full possession and like a damn dummy, I let him. Don't blame me for loving my daddy and always wanting to believe and see the best in him. But I knew better. I never saw that convertible Cadillac again. Buying a car for me was daddy behavior; taking the car to the drug man was absolutely Junkie behavior.

My daddy is either solely abusing crack cocaine or solely working his ass off; he never mixes the two. He prefers to freebase alone and not trick. Very few people knew he got high because he stayed out of sight during his drug marathons. My daddy has an undeniable charm, charisma, hustle, and a magic about him that is honorable for the most part, which makes people trust and believe in him. Crackhead or not, my daddy is a force, a freak of nature. It's hard to believe that a full-fledge, bona fide Junkie could pull the wool over so many people's eyes for such a long period of time. He prides himself on never doing people wrong or playing with their money. He even pays his drug dealers back, religiously and timely. With all of that, please don't believe that he was a functioning addict.

"I am a nonfunctioning addict. I got a gangster drug habit. I can't do anything when I'm getting high except get high! It debilitates my body and changes my physical appearance. I can't work, eat, or have sex when I'm freebasing. I am a stone-cold abuser of crack cocaine. I can only concentrate on my next high."

This time he had an innocent woman on the ropes, but she was none the wiser. That year, Christmas fell on a Saturday. UPS's last cash-on-demand inventory delivery would be on Friday. We needed $11,000 worth of inventory off the UPS truck, and we didn't have the money! Yet! My daddy went to Mrs. Lee, a Korean convenience store owner, across the street from The Corner. He Keyballed her into loaning him, the Junkie, $11,000 worth of money orders for twenty-four hours. Mrs. Lee gave him $11,000 worth of money orders while telling him that she trusted him, the Junkie, to pay her back. We raked in $22,700 on that unusually bitter, cold Saturday. We were so busy that I ran the entire time waiting on customers; I didn't have a moment to walk or stand still. I can still feel all of that money sliding through my frigid, tiny hands. My daddy kept his word! He paid Mrs. Lee back the entire $11,000, leaving us with a whopping profit of $11,700. Mrs. Lee continued to loan him money time after time again, for years. He was never late paying her back. Not once! Shockingly, Mrs. Lee had no idea my daddy was a Junkie for the twenty years she remained working in his neighborhood because he'd carried himself with integrity whenever at work. As far as I know, she still doesn't know he's a Junkie!

By the time I was seventeen years old, The Corner was jumping and making bags of money, as long as my daddy was there to wheel and deal with the neighborhood customers. When he was missing, Grandma Marian set it up for him, but she was never as profitable. He belched out $12 for one or two for $20, versus his mother's flat announcement of $12. Never mind the fact that the prices were the same. With no idea of her son's whereabouts in West Palm Beach, Grandma Marian planned for Mia and me to continue to come for Christmas break that year. She needed us, along with our brother, Mario, to help with the busiest time of the year at The Corner. Daddy or not, we needed that money!

We went to work for a couple of days, unpacking, repacking and setting up the tent nice and neat. Even for me, the "master packer," the process went too quickly. Our inventory was sparse. We had no daddy, thus no one to order more merchandise to save Christmas. Wrong. We had everything we needed—me! My daddy had been preparing me for this day since Pistol Pete's. All those years ago, he saw himself in me and gave me the best parts of him. I was my daddy's child in every good way through and through. I gathered, organized, and analyzed his old invoices to determine what was selling or not selling based on his reorders. I got on Grandma Marian's landline and placed orders to vendors across the country planning for inventory boxes to arrive every day up until the day before Christmas via UPS with cash on demand. Then, I hired my daddy's consistent security person, Billy, to watch our backs since we were two little girls, a small boy, and an old lady.

My daddy had been robbed a couple times, one time with Mia there. Although, the stickup was over before she realized what was going on. Getting robbed in our hood was a matter of when, not if, so we needed Billy. He was a diagnosed schizophrenic, a heavyset man who walked the neighborhood having robust outbursts with himself while looking like a killer. Never mind that he was the nicest of us all and wouldn't hurt a fly. I know there is a "Billy" in every ghetto. Billy loved me and Mia more than anything. Although he didn't have a gun, he would've taken a bullet before letting harm come our way. I gave Billy the same instructions as my daddy—stand directly in front of the tent with his hands in both pockets like he was holding two guns, without cracking a smile.

Mia, Mario, Grandma Marian, Billy, and I were going to run the three-card monte with a dab of robbing Peter to pay Paul and a little bit of Unusual Suspects. Call us Houdini, our magic trick worked! The boxes started arriving one after another. Initially, we were barely making enough to pay the UPS driver to get our packages. However, barely was more than enough to keep us afloat until we sold enough to get ahead. When we were short on cash, the driver doubled back at the end of his route in admiration of how hard we were hustling on The Corner. Best believe we'd made the money needed to get our boxes when he returned.

We had an uncommon break in our busy schedule one afternoon. With a little downtime, we decided to talk to Grandma Marian about random subjects while Mario slept in the car. As kids often do, I began asking a bunch of questions out of temporary boredom while waiting for the next customer rush. Surprisingly, she never once appeared agitated by my adolescent harassment.

My "too smart for my own damn good" ass thought I got her now with my next inquisition. "Grandma, you're always preaching to us not to be fast and become teenaged mothers, but I just did the math. You were fourteen when you had your first baby. To me, that sounds like you were the one being fast."

With no inflection in her voice or change in her demeanor, she responded in an octave just above a whisper. "I wasn't fast. I was raped."

Reach over and close me and Mia's mouth while removing the ton of bricks that fell on our heads and sunk us into the quicksand of disbelief and shock. Then, remove the mountain of wax out of our ears. Her first child was my daddy's oldest sister, and her father was my grandma's first husband, Tody. Did my grandma marry her rapist?

"Grandma, let me get this right. You're saying that at fourteen you were raped and had our auntie as a result?"

"Yes, that is right."

"Wait, wait, wait a minute. Grandma, you're saying Tody raped you?"

She replied just as nonchalantly as before. "Yes, that is right."

My head was spinning out of control, and I could not process the words coming out her mouth, but I continued anyway. "Grandma, if he raped you then why in the world would you marry him?"

"Well, he raped me outside underneath an open tree with onlookers from the neighborhood. Even though I was screaming and crying, not a soul offered to help or rescue me. Once he was done, I went home and cleaned myself up. I didn't tell anyone including mother. She found out I was pregnant but didn't know I was raped. In only a way mother could, she marched over to his house telling Tody's mama about him getting me pregnant and I wouldn't have the disgrace of being a single mother, so he would have to marry me. His mama agreed and sent him over to marry me. That's what happened."

Mia and I mumbled in unison. "Huh?"

"So, you never told anyone that you were raped—by your husband?"

"No one ever asked. So, no, I didn't tell anyone before right now."

She could've slapped the taste out of my mouth, but I couldn't resist further inquiring. "Grandma, why did you have to marry your rapist? I know we don't believe in abortion in our family, but you were raped and a child yourself. Why couldn't you just get an abortion and not marry a man I now know you must have hated?"

"You have to understand. It didn't work like that when I was growing up. We didn't have abortions, not the kind that might not also kill you with the baby anyway, or birth control. And mother would've never let me do that. Back then, you got pregnant and you had a baby, simple as that. Yeah, I was a child, but not for much longer. I was a wife and a mother now. So, it was no need to be crying over spoiled milk."

I was still stuck on "nobody asked" as her explanation for failing to tell any of her family that she was raped—by her husband—before he was her husband. What the entire fuck? Observing and internalizing Grandma Marian's disposition, lack of emotion, and concern made me further appreciate my fucked-up life. No victim should have to make a commitment before God or anyone else to their assailant. The most asinine concept if there had ever been one. I never cared for Tody since he called us names and was never present until he was sick, blind, and stinking of cigarettes. He was the actual cockroach, not me and Mia.

It's hard to be a Black mama, and harder to be a Black grandmama because they must balance the weight to carry us all. They make it look so easy, especially considering all that has been tolerated. Grandma Marian deserved to be free of this lifelong burden; she has carried it long enough. More importantly, generational curses must be dealt with by confronting them head on, lest I want to make sure no one in our family believes that these burdens are theirs to bear alone. Our family must address generational evils at full throttle to break the damaging cycles that have plagued us. I passionately refused to let anyone humiliate my sister or I about our daddy being a crackhead. I'm just as adamant about making sure my grandma doesn't feel the shame of being raped. Even the strongest of us are worthy of unconditional love and support, no matter what or who the circumstances involved. This reveal was not to hurt anyone or besmirch the name of a deceased man. It was to show my unconditional love and support for all Grandma Marian had endured.

I also loved and supported my daddy unconditionally which was why I was so determined to save Christmas and his business! I was going to make damn sure he had something to come back to while making him proud by doing everything he taught me. I knew Grandma Marian was nervous about relying on kids, but she believed in our ability to hustle. She knew that if anyone could pull this off, it was going to be her son's kids. Her insecurities and concerns faded more and more until they'd disappeared by Christmas Eve. I was the dealmaker, just like my daddy. We hustled all day, working our tails off keeping up with the nonstop demand of customers. We were so busy that I'd forgotten about my daddy's absence. When it was all said and done on Christmas Eve, we'd made over $10,000.

It was Christmas Day, and Mia and I were excited to go to work after having such a profitable night; we let our little brother stay home and fully enjoy the holiday since he hated working on The Corner. Customers were steady all day and we were anticipating closing down around four-ish to make it home for a good holiday meal. With no customers in sight, we sat there with our feet kicked backed, basking in the glory of our success when suddenly an unknown van pulled up. We received a special delivery on Christmas Day with none other than our daddy in the passenger seat. He hitched a ride home from West Palm Beach to be with us on Christmas. His first stop was The Corner. We popped up out of our seats and took off running like Flo-Jo. He ran equally as hard toward us. Seconds before we reached him, he planted his feet, squatted down, and opened his arms as wide as the ocean. We jumped into a bear hug and screamed as loud as we could!

"Daddy, daddy! You made it!"

Full of glee he said, "Y'all knew that Daddy would never miss Christmas with his girls. Never! I love y'all so much."

We immediately bombarded him with details of what had transpired during his absence. We intentionally saved how much money we'd made for the end of the story. Finally, we burst out with the figure. He was filled with pride and respect for the daughters he'd raised and molded into formidable businesswomen. We kept the business going, and my daddy was home alive and well. It was a Merry Christmas after all, except my daddy didn't expect my next move. I decided it was time for me to break my business decision to him when we returned home to enjoy the festivities and the fruits of our labor.

While sitting on the sofa next to him with my plate on a TV tray, I turned to him. "Daddy, once we pay all our expenses, we will have close to $6,000. You need to understand that you won't be getting any of that money. I know you need money right now, but we can't help you. We saved Christmas, not you. We earned that money, not you. I hope you're not mad, but I've made my decision."

My daddy replied with water in his eyes. "I've never been prouder of y'all. I've done my job, baby girl. Y'all going to make it. That's all daddy ever wanted for y'all to be better than me, and to make it in life. I could never be mad about my kids doing exactly what I taught them to do. That's how I know you're ready for whatever the world will throw at you. I'm so proud of you and your sister, and I'm proud that Mario finally stepped up too. He did good watching y'all back."

Don't weep for the Junkie! I gave him $1,000 because he needed to know I was more than rooting for him. As his child and protégé, I was always going to give my daddy another chance, then another one and another one, until he and I lost count, because I never counted him out. He was my daddy!

CHAPTER 15

"Let's Go Home"

During my senior year at Tift County High School, things were relatively going according to the plan. I'd been accepted to the University of Georgia (UGA) and offered a scholarship. I also received an additional half dozen smaller scholarships I'd use for living expenses while away at college. I used my Winn Dixie wages to plan and buy enough supplies to set myself up for my entire freshman year at UGA, known as the Harvard of the South. If it worked for all the Georgia governors, surely it would work for me, especially since I also planned on attending UGA's law school.

A couple of months before my graduation, a young woman named Courtney, who was from Tifton and attended Clark Atlanta University (CAU), recruited several students to attend a scholarship weekend retreat. Basically, CAU was awarded federal dollars to produce Black students with math and science PhDs. Since I was determined to major in political science for my future law career, it was a hard pass for me. Courtney insisted that I at least agree to visit for the weekend and hear out the scholarship group. Of course, I wouldn't pass up a weekend in Atlanta versus being stuck in Tifton.

Those three days were the most fulfilling and exhilarating days of my life. I stayed on campus, audited college courses, including one by the professor who would become my favorite teacher, Ms. Morgan. She was my honors English college professor who demanded perfection of me and pushed me to become a better writer. For my first assignment, Ms. Morgan gave me a B when I felt as though I'd clearly earned an A. Determined to get my proper grade, I challenged her on the less than expected mark after class.

"Ms. Gundy, that may have been A work for another student, however, not from you. You will not receive an A in my class until you have given me your best. I'm looking forward to your future assignments with your 100 percent effort."

During my visit, I also met Dr. Thomas Cole, president of Clark Atlanta University, and his first lady, Judge Brenda Cole. They were a brilliant and graceful couple if I'd ever seen one. Mia and I loved them both dearly and cherished our identical graduation photo when Dr. Cole presented our undergraduate degrees to us both, five years apart. Additionally, I attended Student Government Association meetings, an Inspirational Voices of Faith Gospel Concert, an AKA event, a fashion show, a step show, and hung out on the yard admiring the bustling and thriving confidence of the flyest as well as most attractive men and women. I'd never felt this comfortable and at home in my skin outside of the Core Four. With every fiber of my being, I knew I belonged at Clark Atlanta University.

I bombed the scholarship interview because I refused to commit to getting a PhD. No one, and I mean no one, was changing my mind about political science. Yes, I was aware that law school accepted all majors, however, I wasn't reinventing the wheel. I did end up minoring in mathematics based on the persistent nudging of my differential equations professor, Mr. Ahmed Flournoy. Go figure, I volunteered to take advanced math classes for all my electives while other students took art or physical education. I loved math, and it was easier for me than running laps.

I informed my parents as soon as I returned home of my decision to attend C, but the new dilemma of how to pay for tuition was ever-present at my high school graduation. Despite that, graduation day was still a marvel for me. As class president, I had the distinct honor of speaking during the ceremony. Any other day, I would've been mulling over that fact, trying to understand how that was possible, but I let myself enjoy the moment. My daddy's family chartered a bus from Jacksonville. I had over one hundred proud people screaming for me during this ceremony and at my undergraduate and law school graduations. I loved that both sides of my family showed up whenever something positive was going on. They showed up when it was fucked-up too!

As many times as my mama showed up for me, the one time she didn't was the one I remember most. By sheer determination and will, I was headed to the illustrious Clark Atlanta University. My daddy declared he would figure out how to pay the $4,000 owed for my first year's tuition after my ancillary scholarships were applied. I promised if I didn't get a scholarship by my second year, I would transfer to a more affordable school. He kept his end of the bargain, and so did I. Dr. Jenkins, Honors Program Director, awarded me a full scholarship after earning a 4.0 GPA in my first year. I begged every single day for money to stay at my beloved Clark Atlanta University, and proudly maintained that 4.0 GPA in my sophomore year.

None of this compared to the begging I did the morning my mama decided not to come with us to take me to college for the first time. The Core Four had worked and planned so hard for the day when I would attend college. Now that day was upon us, my mama let her husband interfere with our precious, hard-earned day because he didn't want her riding in the car with my daddy. He refused to drive her to Atlanta or let her drive her own big, grown self. She just acquiesced. How could she let him spoil and ruin our day? How could I go off to college without my mama? I was utterly devastated and heartbroken beyond measure; it wasn't supposed to happen like this.

Mi Rey would ask me on the hard days, "What do you do when you don't know what to do?"

There was nothing to do but keep going because I had come too far; it was truly a bittersweet day for me. The Core Four, minus my mama, drove to Atlanta in almost silence the entire trip. I gazed out of the window, counting markers, hoping it would ease the weight crushing my heart at the thought of her not being in the car with us. Riding in that car, sappy and sentimental, I realized three very important things about myself that I would forever hold near and dear throughout life. The first was that I could rise and push through life's toughest moments even when they seemed too hard to bear. Another was how I refused to let disappointment, despair, or even damage, distract or destroy me. Lastly, I couldn't take everyone with me, even if that was my heart's desire, not even my own mama. Some journeys were mine and mine alone. Besides, I was ready and have always been ready; everything I truly needed was God-given and already inside of me.

No, I didn't need her, but she was my mama! I wanted my mama! I wanted her to reassure me, to validate me, and be proud of what she'd created. It was as much her day as any of ours. She deserved to be a part of our family milestone that would lead to crushing generational curses of poverty and trauma. As soon as we drove onto campus, I felt the spirit and the blood of my ancestors that walked on those same holy grounds carrying me through the day and reassuring me, mama or not, that I was right where I belonged.

As my daddy unloaded my things into Ware Hall Dormitory, he scanned the scene outside and called over two spry young fellas. "Hey, young men! Can you give me a hand with the chest? What's y'all names?"

The tall guy answered, "I'm Rick and this is Jamal, sir. We got it. Where do you want us to take it?"

After my daddy let Rick and Jamal do all of the work, unloading and carrying my things up two flights of stairs, he turned to them while pointing at me. "This is my daughter, Terrinee, and I love her very much. I'm asking y'all man-to-man, please take care of her. Look out for her, please."

Rick responded, "Yes, sir. We got you and we got her."

Rick and Jamal took my daddy's charge to heart and are men of great character and dignity. From that day to this one, they have been right there covering my front and my back, no matter what. My AKA big sisters and line-sisters, 21 Pearls of Perfection, stepped up as well. Freshman week on any college campus was chaotic, noisy, and rumbustious. But for me, everything was still and tranquil. I didn't see the well-to-do parents with their perfectly dressed kids or the confident upperclassmen orientation guides or the scholarly professors or the music-filled cafeteria with the sounds of Atlanta's world-famous Super Friends: DJ Mars, DJ Trauma, DJ Drama, DJ Sense, and Tai Boogie.

All I saw was my future and a better life for me and Mia! As far as I was concerned, we'd made it because Mia and I were one, inseparable. She spent all her holidays and summers with me in the campus dorms. She did what I did, went where I went, worked when

I worked. She did it all with me at fourteen years old. She also went to Tupac Shakur's hotel room with me the night he was accused of shooting an off-duty policeman. We weren't there for any fornication or sex tropes. I was working as Tupac's homecoming student handler. Jamal, my now good friend, was the SGA president and heavily involved in the entertainment aspect for Clark Atlanta University's homecoming concert. With the help of Tupac's cousin, and my now good friend, Chaka Zulu, Jamal secured the rapper to perform during homecoming. Tupac was and will forever be the greatest rapper/poet to me and Mia. Of course, I had to ensure she was on the scene with me to meet our favorite rapper.

Since Mia and I were so enthralled with our family, we'd never been star-struck but Tupac Shakur had our full attention. The university and administrators were not happy for a litany of reasons. Tupac was three hours late, rolling and smoking weed on stage and profusely cursing throughout his short performance. Mia and I had a giggly good time gazing talking to him all night, and even went to the after party. We weren't in the vehicle with him, but in the caravan following him to his hotel. We stuck out like lions, bears, and tigers in the middle of a living room with our baby faces wearing tomboyish Champion sweatshirts and Girbaud jeans as opposed to the tight, short, and skimpy dressed women. Shortly after Tupac complimented our shell-toe Adidas and questioned our ages—seemingly out of care for our well-being, the police showed up and arrested him for an alleged shooting incident. Mia and I looked on in shock as they handcuffed and escorted him to the hotel lobby. I'd seen enough to know when a person was rattled. Tupac was the opposite that night. He was actually endearing, kind, accommodating, and a true gentleman the entire night. We were thinking, When the fuck did he have time to shoot anyone?

Then again, who were we to judge his reactions after remembering all the near-death experiences we'd survived with zero emotions. His personal trauma and ours were similar and related in many ways. It was no shocker that his and our ability to keep it moving would be any different. Like us, that night was just another bad thing in a bad day in a string full of bad fucking days that he'd move pass. The chaos and despair of the ghetto produced him, and us, which simply didn't leave room for the luxury of being flustered or shaken. We all had to go and be the best version of ourselves in the best way we knew how, with the tools our parents had given us.

By this time, I'd mastered the art of leaving the past behind while focusing on my future. I'd made it to the promised land as far as I was concerned once my feet landed on Clark Atlanta's soil. Certainly, I'd made some bad decisions in life, but by the grace of God, I'd made enough good ones to be standing in my destiny. The road ahead would be a cake walk compared to what I had endured and survived. I'd survived when those boys tried to violate me and my eyes were straight ahead, never looking back; when I rode off from that drug dealer's crack house on my bicycle after finding my daddy there, never looking back; and when we walked away from the stolen car during the high-speed police chase, never looking back. If I hadn't, I wouldn't have made it this far for damn sure. The love had gotten me through it all—my sister's love, my mama's love, my daddy's love, and the love of my entire family. My daddy may have been a Junkie, but he was my Junkie and he sure as hell loved me a lot. Love conquers all; always.

I was at Clark Atlanta University to succeed, to thrive, to defy all odds, and to "find a way or make one"—never looking back. There are few days that rival the pride and joy inside of me while standing on Clark Atlanta's campus: graduating from college with a huge party thrown by my mama; law school graduation with Mia's $2,000 gift along with her and my college best friends, LaKesha, Courtney and Sidney, taking me on a trip to Puerto Rico; or being the only person in my student group to pass the bar exam on the first attempt. I'd say my sister surviving her accident and giving birth to my two children (eighteen months apart) were my greatest days.

As long as I'm six feet above ground, I'll bask in the day my daughter, Mia Michelle, and son, Kevin, came into this world. Motherhood defined the reason I was born. As an avid breastfeeder, it was the closest I've felt to God. The first time I held Mia Michelle, I proclaimed that she looked just like me. I'd planned to be a working outside of the home mama, especially since I'd worked up to the day I delivered at full term. Instantly, I knew I wouldn't, couldn't leave my baby when I looked into Mia Michelle's eyes. Just like my daddy couldn't leave me more than thirty years before to ship out to the army. Like daddy, like daughter. My daily routine changed overnight. I breastfed, pumped, made my own baby food, washed, ironed, and obsessed over my babies with an occasional Target outing. I loved every single minute of it and would do it all over the exact same!

My daughter is her mommy's child in every way; she wanted nothing more than to please me. At her birth, the world stood still for this tiny, gorgeous force of a human. Mia Michelle was the favorite of all who knew her, especially my mama and Grandma Marian, who both were present during her delivery. She nursed for forty-five minutes every feeding, talked before her time, potty trained before her time, counted and read before her time, and with the strength of Wonder Woman, jumped her bed rails like she was running from the police to avoid sleep time. She was the most independent and creative child I'd met. Clearly, she'd been here before or was marinating in my body, soaking up all the good in me then came out taking both the world and me by storm.

On her very first day of school, she stopped me at the door and insisted that I let her walk in by herself. Devastated, but willingly, I complied, since I didn't want to stunt her lightning speed growth and maturity. Mia Michelle went on displaying this same sophistication beyond her years while working as a styling assistant for Iman Ramadan at The Fresh Hotel in the eighth grade. At only fourteen years old, she assisted on a Stacey Abrams cover shoot for two major publications. Everyone presumes Mia Michelle is much older because she is extremely levelheaded, quick-witted, and carries herself with such grace, especially while working hard.

Stacey Abrams joshed with Mia Michelle. "You're only in middle school? That's impressive! You are the youngest twenty-eight-year-old I've ever seen."

Kevin, on the other hand, was in no hurry to grow up and wanted to be my baby forever. He fell out kicking, screaming, and crying as soon as the car pulled up to school on his first day. Unashamedly, I absolutely loved his hysterics; he was utterly obsessed with me. As long as I was in his periphery, he was joyfully blissful. If he couldn't see me, he would fall the fuck out. If any grown man looked in the direction of me, Mia or his grandma, Kevin would sincerely threaten them, including family except for my daddy and his older brother. He'd drop down and do push-ups as he gave them dirty looks. As a baby, my daddy was Kevin's best friend. He pushed him and Mia Michelle on daily walks to the park in their double stroller. Mia Michelle's first word was "mama," but Kevin's first word was "granddaddy."

Kevin was a savage breastfeeder who was in and out in ten minutes flat. He slept as long as I allowed and threw a fit at the slightest indication of having to do anything for himself. Kevin didn't talk until he was two years old yet did so in full sentences once he finally graced us with verbal communications. He refused to sit down to complete his daily homeschool assignments. I was forced to teach him during diaper changes, meals, and bath time. He tricked his first teacher into believing he couldn't read, count, or write his name to have recess the entire day. This went on for months until I uncovered his shenanigans. No student had pulled the wool over her eyes in her ten-year career, except for Kevin.

Kevin's creativity came in a different form than Mia Michelle's. Nevertheless, it was in him too. I also love Kevin's headstrong ways. No one, absolutely no man or woman, could persuade him to do something he doesn't want to do or isn't interested in doing, which meant he was always going to be the leader. Mia Michelle looks just like me, but Kevin acts just like. My pregnancy with Kevin showed his mama was headstrong too. I was about seven months pregnant and having excruciating chest pains causing my heart rate to skyrocket. Dr. Jackie informed me that she was going to have a nurse administer morphine to alleviate my pain and eliminate the danger to my and the baby's life. My chest pain paled in comparison to the thought of giving my unborn child morphine who would be the grandson of a Junkie.

"Jackie, you know me, and you know what I come from. Neither my baby nor I can take morphine. Our DNA is prone to addiction. I can't give my baby drugs. I can't."

"Terrinee, I love you and I know you think you're a doctor, but you're not. As your doctor, it's my job to keep you and your baby well and alive. I have to get your heart rate down in order to keep the both of you safe. Unfortunately, I have to give you pain meds to do so."

"I will get it down. Just give me a minute. It's mind over matter for me. I will tell my brain the pain is gone, and it will disappear. Trust me, I will get it down."

"Uhm, no! It doesn't work that way. I will give you ten minutes because I don't want to make you even more upset and cause your heart rate to further increase. In ten minutes, if there's no change, I will be back to give you the morphine myself!"

No two brains are the same, but my mind was and has always been a powerful thing. When Dr. Jackie returned, my heart rate had significantly decreased. No one in the room could believe that I really convinced myself that I was no longer in pain. Never doubt the strength of and the lengths a Black mama will go to protect her babies, especially this Black mama.

In September 2021, Mayor Kasim Reed introduced me to receive a Woman of the Year Award where he perfectly articulated my love for my children: "Her proudest accomplishment and most meaningful achievement above all, is her family, her wonderful son, Kevin, and her daughter, Mia Michelle. They are the center of her existence and the reason she does what she does. And in my judgment, the reason she is an exemplar for us all."

Mayor Reed was absolutely correct in every word he uttered. I couldn't have asked for more perfect children than the two of them and I'm eternally grateful to them for defining my life. I have an abundance of pride and gratitude for Mia Michelle and Kevin demonstrating their values, insight, and strength on one of my darkest professional days as a judge. Most days, I let the lies, slander, and false rumors about me personally and professionally roll off my back because I know the truth of how hard I've worked to be a good person and a good judge. However, on this particular day, I was filled with anger about my mistreatment, sorrow for my children, disbelief of the situation, drowning frustration regarding the unfair and wrongly motivated political attacks against me.

While holding me tightly, caressing, comforting, and reassuring me in unison, my preteen children proclaimed, "Mommy, you don't have to be mad or upset because it had to be you. No one else is strong enough to get through this. No one else is strong enough to make it right. God got you, and we got you. Don't worry about us because you are our mommy. We will be okay. You just have to keep fighting for what's fair because you have to make sure that no one else is treated like this again. We are proud of you, and we love you so much."

Amid this career nightmare, my children had been forged into resilient, formidable forces that absorbed all of the life lessons I mistakenly thought they'd ignored. It happened without generational trauma. Just like me, they had everything they needed inside of them already, even the ability to uplift and strengthen their mommy in her darkest days. If I do nothing else in life, I've done what I was sent to do on this Earth—be Mia Michelle and Kevin's mama. There's no comparison to the birth and gift of my children. However, the day I was sworn in as an Atlanta Municipal Court judge was one of the best days of my life.

I was sitting in Judge Dixon's office during my shift as a magistrate judge when she informed me about the judicial vacancy announcement in the newspaper. I was hesitant to apply, but with some nudging I decided to throw my name in the hat. It was a tedious, months-long process. Ambassador Andrew Young nominated me to the judicial nominating committee for the vacancy. Then, I completed my application in detail. Before the interview with the committee, I practiced like I'd practiced for the Miss Black Tiftarea Pageant, nonstop and relentlessly, every single day with mock interviews. I attended and observed the different municipal court sessions at least once and spoke with several current judges.

By the day of my interview, I was ready. I confidently walked in the room wearing a navy skirt suit with a cream cami top with matching pearl earrings and necklace. I was the only interviewee waiting without notes, briefcase, or anything. I didn't need anything because it was all in my head. I'd been preparing for this day my entire life since I was five years old when my daddy told me I had to work on Christmas Eve. All of it had been for this moment. The interview panel threw questions at me left and right with curve balls all over the place. I crushed my interview, even quoting my daddy during one of my responses about hard work and experience.

It all matters!

I made the short list of three to be interviewed on a Saturday morning by Mayor Kasim Reed. This time, I wore a blue pinstripe skirt suit and cream top with my same matching pearl earrings and necklace. During my interview, his chief of staff asked most of the questions. She looked astonished at my thoughtful, thorough responses. This was my shot, and I wouldn't be rushed while laying out my vision for my future and the court. Mayor Reed finally chimed in at the end with one question that I could tell he thought would stump my smooth sailing interview.

"The other two candidates have more litigation experience than you. Both of them have been prosecutors and would argue that this is a disadvantage for you. With that said, explain why you are more qualified to be chosen as the next judge for municipal court."

"Mayor Reed, the answer is simple. I am the only candidate that is a judge right now. As you know, I am a Fulton County Magistrate Court judge. Thus, I am the only person on the short list with judicial experience. Respectfully, sir, that would make me the most experienced person for the judgeship."

Got him! I stumped the mayor, which didn't happen often. After my stellar interview, I was confident, but still very anxious about finding out if I'd be appointed. On Monday morning, I received a phone call from Mayor Reed. It had to be good news because the top guy never delivers the bad news, right?

"Good morning, this is Mayor Kasim Reed. It's my birthday and I decided that as a gift to myself, I would appoint a judge to the municipal court today. Terrinee Lynette Gundy would you do me the pleasure of accepting my appointment to the Municipal Court of Atlanta?"

I screamed my ass off like I had won the Georgia lottery!

Being the statesman he was, he laughed and continued, "I believe that's a yes, but I'm going to need to hear the words."

I blurted out, "Yes! Thank you so much for appointing me, and I promise I will not let you down! This is the job I've wanted since I was nine years old. This is my dream job! Thank you for making my dreams come true!"

Mayor Reed concluded, "Congratulations, Judge Gundy. You are the newest member of the Municipal Court of Atlanta. It gives me great pleasure to make your dreams come true on my birthday."

"Judge Gundy."

Wow, I liked the sound of that but couldn't bask in it quite yet. The fat lady was humming, but not singing. Now that I'd secured the appointment, it wouldn't be official until I took my oath and was sworn in by Mayor Reed. The mayor was heading out of the country and wouldn't be back until the following week at his annual scholarship golf tournament. Due to The Corner and my upbringing, I was old-school with handling all business expeditiously; time was of the essence. My swearing in would have to be the same day as the golf tournament despite the objections of his senior advisor and scheduling team. I immediately sent out invitations, confirmed program participants, printed programs, returned my employment paperwork and planned a reception in seven days. I was moving with the love and essence of God.

The mayor's senior advisor was totally baffled when he asked for a change to my investiture program, and I responded that my programs were printed already.

"You were just appointed yesterday. How is that possible?"

"True. You think I've planned all of this in a day? I've been planning for this moment since I was nine years old; this has been in the making for thirty years."

"Understood, judge. See you next Tuesday."

I went back to planning and preparing for my day. I was happy that my daddy's first cousin, Pastor Reginald Gundy, was going to be able to make it from Jacksonville to do my invocation. It was important to me that my family was on the program in some capacity. My mama, now a caterer, planned a lavish, beautiful reception in the Old City Council Chambers. Standing room only, my kids and I arrived dressed to the nines at my investiture in the City Council Chambers, same room used at the end of Black Panther. Upon the encouragement of Judge Dixon, I went out and bought my first St. John suit. Apparently, it was a signature move into the judge's club. Everyone was there, of course, except for Mayor Reed.

Finally, Mayor Reed walked onto the rostrum to sit next to me, and I whispered, "You're late!"

Mayor Reed responded, "A mayor is never late, only delayed."

As I put on my fake smile and slightly rolled my eyes inside my head without the motion of doing so, Mayor Reed joshed, "I think I've changed my mind. I'm going to get up and tell everyone that I'm going to appoint someone else."

I was forever and a day straight from Duval. It will take more than a silly joke to rattle me, so I leaned to the edge of my seat, looked squarely in Mayor Reed's eyes and declared, "There will be a ceremony today. So, you can get up and swear me in or I'm going to get up and tell everyone we're getting married. There will be an announcement today. Makes no difference to me, so you decide."

With the entire room standing still as we sparred with words, Mayor Reed burst into uncontrollable laughter from the pit of his stomach. I got him again, just as I had done in the interview, I was always quick on my feet. Needless to say, I was sworn in as a Municipal Court of Atlanta judge in front of my family, colleagues, and friends. The culmination of my swearing in summed up everything to that point: the great days, the good days, and even the bad ones. Not too bad for the Daughter of a Junkie, if I say so myself. And I must. Where else on Earth can a poor Black girl climb out of the bottom of the ghetto and ascend to the judiciary? Only in America! My life has been intertwined with unconditional love and so many love stories woven into the fabric of me. I am a mommy of two amazing children, a sister, an aunt, a friend, a lawyer, a judge, and forever, always and proudly, the Daughter of a Junkie. This is my story—the American dream powered by true love. In the process, the new silver lining was that I found eternal, infinite love with Mi Rey, El Uno—My King, The One.

Ponder this, was there an existence in this lifetime for a Duval girl like me to have it all—smart, beautiful children, dream job, and a loving, divine soul mate? There has never been a question about how much I loved my daddy. Other than him, Mi Rey was the first and only man I've loved unconditionally, with all his beautiful flaws, unmatched strength, and sweet tenderness. He and I have a divine love and connection where the vibrations can be felt in every corner of a room within our presence. I love Mi Rey and I will always love him until the last beat of my pounding heart.

Love is supposed to conquer all but would it with Mi Rey? Could it conquer unforeseen life circumstances, egos, pride, duty, obligations, and responsibilities? Our love and bond was a once-in-a-century type that pierces the soul and every fiber of the being while making the hairs on the back of the neck stand at attention with stomach flutters and deep passionate elongated breathes. It was the kind of love that sent empires and men to war with Trojan horses, but was it enough to survive all that was in front of us? Guess, we shall see. Better yet, how could we not?

After my swearing in, after my reception, after all my guests left the mayor's suite, Mi Rey turned to me in his office. "Let's go home, Judge Gundy. I love you!"

TO BE CONTINUED

Acknowledgements

Mia Michelle & Kevin III
Anthony Gundy & Linda Henderson Alaydi
Mia Michelle Gundy, Terrinee Elle & Mia Elle
Grandma, Brothers, Sisters, Aunts, Uncles, Cousins & Friends
M. Kasim Reed, ESQ, 59th Mayor of Atlanta
Precious Anderson, ESQ
Gabe Banks, ESQ
Angela Rogers, ESQ
Iman Ramadan
Lalanya Abner
Ambrose King
Duwon Robinson
Robert Ector
Denishia Nix Horton, Najah Hofman & Sheldon G. Horton
Dr. Jackie Walters
Dr. Marcus Green
Freddie Figgers
Oronde Garrett
Balewa Muhammad & Sonic Hotel Studios
Kevin Briggs, Jr.
Anthony Bell
Benjamin Garrett

DJ Toomp
Clay Evans
Lil Duval
Medina Islam
Taiyo Obafemi
Burchel Anthony Villieres
Tanesha Blacks
Bobsled Jimmy
Jen Drake & Keinon Johnson
Whittley Agency, Dora Whittley, Mike Whittley, Aiyisha Obafemi & Deanna Hamilton
The HBUC, Caleb Seales, Travis Cochran & Don Julio Jr.
Braynard Stevenson
Angela Watts
Disturbing Tha Peace, Chaka Zulu & Jeff Dixon
DigiHouse Studio
Book Reviewers: Judge Myra Dixon, Courtney Graves, Robin Gundy, Chris Hicks, Jihad Ramadan, Terry Ross, Jahmel Terrell, Jessica Washington, Deshanna Wiggins & Chasity Williams

www.ingramcontent.com/pod-product-compliance
Lightning Source LLC
Chambersburg PA
CBHW020338010526
44119CB00035B/450/J